U-Tube list
to Eric Coen ♡ W9-BAN-128
God's Love thaws the
hardness in us.

Search for goodness
in myself + others leads to
More good health

Mystical Love accepts
with PEACE + is not on a
hunt to things to criticize
I understand how
kids get into gangs +
drugs. His dad threw them
out on the streets- at 9
went to tell his dad
he forgave him

AVID

READER

PRESS

Also by Gregory Boyle

Barking to the Choir:
The Power of Radical Kinship

Tattoos on the Heart:
The Power of Boundless Compassion

The

Power

of

Extravagant

Tenderness

The
Whole
Language

Gregory Boyle

AVID READER PRESS

New York London Toronto Sydney New Delhi

Avid Reader Press
An Imprint of Simon & Schuster, Inc.
1230 Avenue of the Americas
New York, NY 10020

First Avid Reader Press hardcover edition October 2021

AVID READER PRESS and colophon are
trademarks of Simon & Schuster, Inc.

For information about special discounts for bulk purchases,
please contact Simon & Schuster Special Sales at 1-866-506-1949
or business@simonandschuster.com.

The Simon & Schuster Speakers Bureau can bring authors to
your live event. For more information or to book an event
contact the Simon & Schuster Speakers Bureau at 1-866-248-3049
or visit our website at www.simonspeakers.com.

Interior design by Lewelin Polanco

Manufactured in the United States of America

5   7   9   10   8   6

Library of Congress Cataloging-in-Publication Data is available.

ISBN 978-1-9821-2832-6
ISBN 978-1-9821-2834-0 (ebook)

For Doug Christie,

Paul Lipscomb,

and the Tuesday Night Gang

Contents

Introduction

M ost of this book I've written during the first nine months of our viral awakenings: COVID-19 and the deepened reckoning of our country's systemic racism, America's searing and formative pathology. The pandemic has widened the health and economic divide and has pulled back the curtain, revealing the need for radical changes in the social contract. It's true enough that we were all caught in the same coronavirus storm, but we soon saw that some were weathering it in ocean liners and some in inner tubes. Some, even, clinging barely to a piece of driftwood. We are in different-size vessels, facing the same storm.

The fault lines have been revealed. We've come to see that inequality is not a defect in the system. It is the system. We saw the white, rich curve flatten while the darker, poorer curve was on the rise. (I've buried many who succumbed to the virus, which includes three double funerals.) We are all trying not just to make the present bearable but the future possible. We want a different world.

Eight-year-old Dorothy Day was in San Francisco when the 1906 earthquake struck. What she remembered most was the unifying and generous response of everyone in this time of crisis. She asked herself, *Why can't we live this way all the time?*

It's a good question that we've posed to ourselves during these months. Clearly, 2020 has been our collective "annus horribilis." And yet, maybe we have also been given a new way of seeing more clearly, seeing that scarcity is a myth and abundance our newfound truth. 2020 vision. They say that when we have more than we need, instead of constructing a higher wall, we build a longer table.

Surely our nation was ailing long before the virus arrived. The pandemic didn't create our disparity, but it did exacerbate it. It's become hackneyed to say we don't want to return to "normal." We want to put a stick in the spokes of normal. With both systemic racism and poor communities of color disproportionately suffering from the virus, we all would like an invitation to a new paradigm, please. Our current times have reinforced the notion that we don't change people by arguing with them. The invitation should not enfeeble with guilt but rather enable folks to high purpose. Once we abandon "winning the argument," we can begin to make the argument with our lives.

Masked and at a distance, I participated in two marches during this period. The experiences for me seemed to obliterate long-held narratives that undergird the lie and denial that hold up a racist system. White folks, I think, felt an epiphany of our complicity in four hundred years of systemic racism, awakening in us a new language and a resolve to grow more and more antiracist. We needed to see each other with the eyes of belonging. Now we must choose to be allies as never before.

-⚬│⚬-

For every one of us, the pandemic didn't just alter plans, it also torpedoed identity. Who am I, after all, if how I am relational gets toppled? Giving talks, presiding at mass in detention facilities, or kicking it in my office with gang members. It all stops and there is grieving to be done. So, you lean into the grief. You allow yourself to be curious about it. This curiosity will always lead to savoring. It will blossom into what Saint Ignatius calls "relishing." Before you know it, next stop: joy. If we're lucky, grief never leaves us where it found us.

Kurt Vonnegut wrote toward the end of his life: "If a person survives an ordinary span of sixty years or more, there is every chance that his or her life as a shapely story has ended, and all that remains to be experienced is epilogue. Life is not over, but the story is."

Epilogue. It's okay, really. Once you're a geezer, I'm not sure how "shapely" the story gets. I was interviewed on a podcast recently and the woman asked what I wanted my legacy to be, "you know, now that you're sliding into home plate?" I said that I didn't "do legacies" and that I mainly felt I was still at bat. But surrender is the order of the day, and you relinquish things all the time. Eventually, life itself.

While I write this above paragraph, I am interrupted by a call from an LAPD officer, telling me about a guy in the psych ward at White Memorial Hospital Medical Center who says the voices in his head are telling him to "kill Father Boyle." I've never met him. Apparently, he's never even been to Homeboy Industries. The officer asks if I'm "scared," meaning, I think, do I feel threatened? and if I am, he will need to pursue this. I ask him to tell the gentleman to "take a number and get in line." Not sure the cop fully appreciated my humor.

We know that the kinds of stories Jesus told were parables. A man, after a weeklong series of talks I gave at the Chautauqua Institution, told me, "I'm Irish, so don't tell me what to do; instead, tell me a story." Okay. I'm Irish, too. And besides, people hope for our attention, not our opinions. Arguments don't change minds, stories do. Jesus seemed to understand this. Parables don't tell you what to do and they have no didactic endings. After all, what's the conclusion of the Prodigal Son? The "moral of that story" is what we put on it . . . our response to it. Parables were how Jesus tricked people into things. This book will also have parables.

Years ago, I was in the office, all alone, at 7:30 a.m., and I answered the phone.

The voice on the line said, "Hey, G. Are you there?"

I just repeated the question back to the homie on the other end. "Are . . . you . . . there?" The homie quickly recognized it as a less-than-stellar question and tried to repair things. "When I said, 'Are you there,' I meant, 'Are you ALL there?' Like, you know, right in the head?"

"Good recovery," I told him.

I suppose this book is about being all there.

It's not every day I get called to testify in a deportation hearing at the Federal Building. The hearing was about a kid I know named Peter, who after ten years in prison now faced being shipped back to Uzbekistan. He came to this country with his mother when he was seven years old and settled in a part of Lincoln Heights where, once he hit his teenage years, he found himself incorporated into a Latino gang. I knew him only from detention facilities. I was happy to help him not get deported.

Throughout the brief proceedings, Peter would try and jog my memory. He was seated behind a table with his lawyer. I was in the witness stand. He'd blurt out, "I was your altar server at Camp Miller." Or another time, he said quite loudly, "I made my first community with you at Central." Finally, the judge admonished him enough and threatened to cancel the entire hearing. (Months later they allowed him to stay in the country, and upon his release he worked at Homeboy. Some on the staff took him once to eat sushi. I asked him how he liked it. "I'm doin' things I never done before, G. I never ate sushi. I still never been to Six Flags, and I never even been to a strip club." Well, at least . . . cross sushi off your bucket list!)

After testifying that day, I returned to the office and ran into Mario. I knew he and Peter were from the same gang, so I asked about him. "That's my dog right there. Yeah . . . we call him Russian Boy." Mario continued, with a degree of excitement, to reconnect to the memory of "his dawg." "Watcha . . . we were locked up together in County. Cellies. And he'd go out every night and talk to his mom on the pay phone. He talked . . . Russian . . . with her." Then Mario gathers the energy a bit. "Damn, G . . . he spoke . . . the WHOLE language."

Mario meant fluency when he said the "whole language." I wish to suggest the same here. We are on the lookout for a fuller expression and a wider frame within which to view things. Allow the extravagant tenderness of God to wash over us. Permit the lavishing of such love to surround and fill us, then go into the world and speak the "whole language." This is the fluency of the mystic, who chooses to live in the soul, inhabiting the tender fragrance of love. The longing of the mystic is to be at home with yourself and then put the welcome mat out so that others find a home in you. In this, we want to be "all there." The Magi hear in a dream: "Depart by a different route." In this book, I hope to whisper the same invitation. The whole language sees us departing by a different route.

If we're honest, the world kind of yawns at "religion," but snaps to attention when offered the authenticity and authority of the fluent, mystical, nondualist view. We want to both hear and speak this whole language, because, mostly, we only know the half of it. We get stuck in a partial view.

This mystical kinship, this speaking the whole language, is the exact opposite of the age in which we currently live: tribal, divisive, suspicious, anchored in the illusion of separation—unhealthy, sad, fearful, other-izing, and demonizing. Mystics replace fear with love, vindictiveness with openhearted kindness, envy with supportive affection, withering judgment with extravagant tenderness. Now is the time, as author Brian Doyle suggests, to embrace "something other than combat."

A mystic wants to imagine a world without prisons, for example, then set out to create that world. Prisons, after all, are where we practice exclusion. As Pope Francis says, "the only future worth building includes everyone." At Homeboy Industries, we long to see deeply—to see homies in their soul fullness. We want to see beyond rap sheets and past behavior; beyond tattoos and trauma. We aspire to see the mystical wholeness of the other. God sees this way. Jesus sees this way. We want to see this way.

The poet Rumi writes: "Where am I going on this glorious journey? To your house, of course." This house we create will be filled with acceptance, nonjudgment, and peace. Refining how we will love in this "house" will always be a good use of our time. A homie, working alongside his enemy in the Homeboy Bakery, told me, "I found an ease with him already." The ease is brought to you by tenderness. We are mindful that the power of the tender heart needs to be activated always. A homie Sergio told me once, "We need to fan the flames of tenderness in each other." Once we are reached by tenderness, we become tenderness.

This book is the last of my three Power books. *Tattoos on the Heart: The Power of Boundless Compassion*; *Barking to the Choir: The Power of Radical Kinship*. Now this one. Like these previous works, the stories, parables, and lessons learned in this book are gleaned from my thirty-seven-year involvement with gang members and Homeboy Industries, the largest gang intervention, rehab, and reentry program on the planet. Like my other books, there is some theological tree climbing here, with some occasionally half-baked musings.

I find that I write like I talk. When I am speaking to a group, I give some content and ideas until I sense that eyes are starting to glaze over. Then I'll shift to a story. My talks can be scattershot and move from something funny to a moment that is moving. Laugh, cry, and change your mind on something. These are always my goals in a keynote address, and they are the same here. I am not the proud owner of an attention span, so that gets reflected as well. I personally like to change things up, so my assumption is that others feel the same. I could be wrong. But I write jumping from story to concept to quote to homie wisdom. I ask your indulgence and permission to explore these notions together and in this way.

Homeboy Industries, along with providing concrete help and a culture of healing and transformation to gang members, also wants to be what the world is ultimately called to become: a community of kinship and a sangha of beloved belonging. Homeboy doesn't want to simply point something out. We want to point the way. Not just a solution, but a sign. It points the way to the power of transformation; the holiness of second chances; a commitment to demonize no one; and the power and possibility of redemption. If Homeboy were a volume, you'd have to cover your ears. Homeboy Industries reminds us that we belong to one another. There is no "Us" and "Them." Surely, we stand with those left behind, but we also ask, what keeps them behind? Our organization wants to be the front porch of the house we all long to live in. Especially in these polarizing, tribal, and divisive times, Homeboy Industries modestly embodies a world of interconnection and relational wholeness. As the homies who now run the place often say, "We are saved by the relationship."

I use the word "extravagant" here because our tenderness needs to be generous. The word means to "wander outside." It originally meant "unusual" and "outside the norm." It meant this until the 1700s, when it started to mean "spend too much money." When someone lavishes us with an extravagant gift, we say, "You shouldn't have." The extravagant gesture doesn't hold back nor show restraint. It has "wandered outside," beyond our expectations . . . outside of anything we know. It hobbles us a bit as we feel unworthy in the face of such largesse. Because tenderness begets tenderness, we insist on extravagance, which liberates our hearts. The view is wider and the container more spacious. Saint Francis writes, "No obstacles in my heart—everything a frail-boned kindness." We find rest in this.

In this book, I will draw upon my beloved Sufi poets, the gospel, a wide variety of mystics, and the spirituality of Saint Ignatius of Loyola, the founder of the Society of Jesus—the Jesuits—of which I am a humble son.

The homies, generally speaking, don't know what a Jesuit is, though anywhere from two to four of us Jesuits accompany the ministry at Homeboy Industries at any given time. One day, Arturo is giving a tour to a fairly large group. Formerly a lifer, he's starting to discover comfort at Homeboy and in the world. He is robust in his sense of liveliness and I admire this in him. He also has what the homies would call "a loud-ass voice." He parks his tour group in front of my glass-enclosed office. It is the observe-our-founder-in-his-natural-habitat moment. I'm in a meeting. I wave faintly. Arturo bellows: "THIS IS FATHER GREG . . . THE FOUNDER OF HOMEBOY INDUSTRIES. HE . . . IS A JUJITSU PRIEST." From behind my desk, I display some of my best karate moves.

The usual disclaimers apply to this book as to the previous ones. I don't mention the names of gangs and I change the names of gang members in the telling of these stories, parables, and snapshots from the barrio. Everything is true and remembered as best as I have been able to recall. I will admit to some telescoping of details in the interest of economy, and the merging of moments to be expeditious. I make references to my years as pastor of Dolores Mission Church, as chaplain at Folsom State Prison, and to my numerous moments in countless detention facilities.

The Whole Language acknowledges that we are all born into the world wanting the same things, and we are all naked under our clothes. We start from this place, then, of our own unshakable goodness, so we jettison blame and embrace understanding. We see God's light in everything and thereby choose mysticism over morality. We choose connection, not perfection. We explore the things that help us feel beloved rather than on probation. We want to know the God of love, which is more than knowing the love of God. We long to see the wholeness of things and find our wholeness in Christ.

I travel here through essays and prolonged homilies on our notion of God, the immeasurable goodness present in every human being, and the need to re-sacralize things. I look at death; the church; the methodology of Homeboy's therapeutic mysticism; tenderness; and a sangha of beloved belonging, among other themes.

It's probably been ten years since funders and others have asked about some "succession plan." At Homeboy Industries (HBI) we are a sangha, which is to say, a community of practitioners. A homie told me that he "was Homeboy Industries raised," and so, he now "practices" the culture of it in how he sees and operates. We are all called to be practitioners. Otherwise . . . we're audience.

At the Chautauqua Institution, four homeboys and four homegirls were leading a brown-bag discussion at lunchtime. I snuck into the back of the very packed room and no one knew I was there. During the Q and A, an ancient woman stood, grabbing the back of the chair in front of her for support, and said with an emphatic and overly loud voice, "FATHER GREG IS GOING TO DIE." (I startled immediately, thinking she was privy to some information I didn't have.) "SO, WHAT ARE YOU GOING TO DO WHEN HE'S GONE?" The panelists knew it was a question about a succession plan. José stood and gestured to the other panelists and said simply, "All of us . . . have keys to the place." The cramped room was filled with deafening applause. Frail-boned kindness. Practitioners, all.

A Southwest Airlines flight attendant, after finishing her takeoff instructions, signed off, "Now sit back and relax and enjoy the flight . . . OR . . . sit up and be tense all the way . . . Up to you." It is up to us.

Let's all depart by a different route.

But where are we going?

"To your house, of course."

The
Whole
Language

Chapter One

You're Here

Nothing is more consequential in our lives than the notion of God we hold. Not God. The notion of God. This is what steers the ship. Our idea of God will always call the shots. Meister Eckhart, the mystic and theologian who died in 1328, said, "It is a lie, any talk of God that doesn't comfort you." This was his notion. Granted, our conceptions may change and evolve, but when we "hold" them, they direct our course. What matters, in the end, is what kind of God we believe in. "All concepts of God," Teresa of Ávila writes, "are like a jar we break."

A few years ago, I buried my ninety-two-year-old mother. She died as we would all want to: in her own bed, in her own home, surrounded (off and on) by her eight kids and many grandchildren. I had buried my father some twenty-two years earlier. My mom was sharp till the last moment. In fact, in the last year of her life, she watched so much MSNBC, she was becoming Rachel Maddow. And she was not a lick afraid of dying. Some three weeks before she died, she said to me, giddy and exhilarated, "I've never DONE this before." It was something you'd say just before skydiving.

In fact, the day before she died, I was alone with her, the rarest of things, and she was asleep. When her eyes opened and she saw me there, she scowled. "Oh, for cryin' out loud." And she closed her eyes. She was pissed . . . that she wasn't dead yet. (Sorry.) But the next day my sisters went out to retrieve lunch and I was alone with her again, sitting at the foot of the bed. At exactly noon, she opened her eyes, lifted her head some, let out a glorious, wondrous gasp (skydiving), and she left us. And no one in earshot of the sound would ever fear death again. *like my dad*

During those last weeks, one or two or six of her kids would be keeping vigil around her bed, and she'd be in and out of consciousness. When she came to, she'd lock onto one of us and say with breathless delight, "You're here. You're here."

After we buried her, I recalled this and grew convinced that this may well be the singular agenda item of our God. To look at us with breathless delight and say, "You're here. You're here."

We have this image of Jesus spending forty days and forty nights in the wilderness, the precursor of our forty days of Lent. It supplies us with Polaroids like "dark night of the soul," grumbling stomach, wild wilderness animals, plague of self-doubt, anguish, and torment . . . Jesus wondering if he should have given up BOTH scotch AND chocolate for Lent. Yet I suspect it was all mainly God saying tenderly, "You're here!" and Jesus not really knowing what to say in response, but, "YOU'RE here." God meets our intensity of longing with intensity of longing. Turns out, the Tender One whom we long for, longs for us.

Maybe the desert is really a time to notice the notice of God. We hear and receive the tender glance of God, and, like Jesus, we acquiesce to the tenderness. The mysticism of Jesus, that succumbs to this tenderness, is anchored in love. This is the fundamental architecture of his heart. Above all, this mysticism is available to us. We realize that heaven was not a goal for Jesus, but loving was. We come to see that to follow Jesus is to change our understanding of God. Then we leave the wilderness, ready to extend this tender, loving glance in the world. The goal of our extraordinarily humble God is less union with God, but union among us (which is, of course, unitive with God). Then we can rest in the stillness of love and go forward, to love in the stillness of God. Then we are the river winding its way to the sea: union with God and "neighbor." We're all just trying to get to the sea.

Two part-timers are just "kickin' it" in my office. Their shift is over and they'd rather stay here than go home. I "notice" them. I will admit that this doesn't always happen. I'm filled when it does.

"How'd you guys turn out so good?" I ask them.

"It's what God wanted for us," says one.

"That's right," adds the other, "not just us, but for everybody." Notice the notice of God, and with any luck, we start to notice each other.

A homie says to me: "I see now that I never made it easy for my parents to love me, and yet, they never stopped loving me." The God who never stops. So, God, in this same way, has a limited vocabulary. God never knows what we're talking about when we judge our own worthiness or let ourselves get fixated on God's "deep disappointment." Often when we think God is silent, this Tender One is just nearly speechless. God is monosyllabic. Love. I'm afraid that's it. Never stopping. It is, as the Hindu poet Meera writes, a "love so strong a force it broke the cage."

If we're honest, this cage has held us back. During Lent at Dolores Mission, the women would sing a dirge at mass or penance services. Part of the lyrics were sung to God: *"No estes eternamente enojado."* Don't be angry forever.

How could we have gotten this so wrong? There is no moment when God gets pissed off. WE do (*eternamente*), but God never does. God is never toxic, but quite often our version of God, to which we cling, can be. We need to lose patience with such a puny god. I always tell homies when they begin work with us: "Just imagine that we are a big old net ready to catch you if you fall." We often use the concept of being "held" at Homeboy, reflective of the God who will not drop us. Hafiz, a twelfth-century Muslim mystic, puts it this way: "Pulling out the chair beneath your mind and watching you fall upon God. There is nothing else to do that is any fun in the world."

At one time or another, we all had a version of God that was rigid. But the depth of our own experience tells us that our idea of God wants to be fluid and evolving. As we grow, we learn to steer clear of the wrong God. We "break the jar" and it radically challenges our way of seeing reality. Consequently, a change in our conception of God can transform the character of our culture. The judge in the Boston Marathon bombing case, at sentencing, quoted from Verdi's *Otello*: "I believe in a cruel God." Consequential. The Tender One has no need to judge, because this God understands.

If our God makes us feel unworthy and in debt, wrong God. If God frightens us, wrong God. If God is endlessly disappointed in us, wrong God. A man I knew, after being fired from his job, said, "It's a good thing I believe in God, who says, 'Vengeance will be mine.'" Uh-oh. Wrong God.

A homie sends me a cell photo of his car . . . completely totaled. But there is not a scratch on him or his wife and kids. Then he writes: "God is unbelievable." And indeed, God is. But if his kids had died in that accident, what would we be forced to say about God? The Tender One is unbelievable in lots of ways that don't occur to us. God roots for us more than calls shots. With tenderness as the scaffolding, we cease trying to change God's mind, and allow God to marinate ours. This God says, "You got this" more than "Do that."

Erick's tattoos were an announcement that he must have spent the last many years behind bars with idle time on his hands. On his start date, we were getting to know each other.

"Actually," he said, "we've met." I certainly didn't recognize him. "Yeah," he continued, "I was like fourteen and locked in the SHU at Juvenile Hall and you visited me." We didn't call it the SHU (Security Housing Unit); that's more of a prison designation. But it was a place reserved to "keep away" the most surly and misbehaving minors. I often went there to visit kids I knew from the projects. Perhaps a staff member had asked me to speak with Erick. I don't remember.

"And I'll never forget . . . till the day I die . . . what you said to me that day." I leaned in. I was curious. "You looked at me and said, 'God . . . has a plan for you.' I'll never forget it."

Now, all of us know our own lexicons. "God has a plan for you" is not in my toolbox. I know I didn't say it, because I don't believe it. God no more has a plan than holds a grudge. There is, of course, a short hop between "God has a plan for me to become an orthopedic surgeon" to "My four-year-old son just died of a brain tumor." Short hop. You can't have this both ways. If God "plans" you getting your medical license, God also has orchestrated your son's demise. I don't believe it, so I wouldn't have said it.

But this is what Erick remembers. I suspect he translated how he felt after the visit into some advice. I hope he felt seen, cared for, and listened to, and then he put all that dough in the pasta maker and it came out "God's plan" fettucini. We are all meant to be in the world who God is: loving, compassionate, and kind. Our grown-up notion of God finds us sustained by the Tender One to be this in the world, but not to expect blueprints, paths, or plans along the way. God just hopes we choose love.

We ask ourselves, what can move the dial on God's love for us? Nothing. It is always at its highest setting. After all, God's love for me is zero dependent on my love for God. But our notion of God can atrophy and get stuck in our own arrested development. And it can be hard to shake the transactional god who puts us in debt. The I-love-you, now-love-me-back god. Yet our God is utterly reliable in this unconditional love that does not waver. It has pleased God not to be God without us. God never has second thoughts about loving us. Never.

Beto and Eddie hop in the backseat. Riding shotgun is my pal Nickie, a regular visitor to Homeboy from London, where she works at the home office and is something of an expert on knife crime in the United Kingdom. She has been a partner in our Global Homeboy Network for the past few years. We are all heading to a fancy hotel in Hollywood, where I will deliver a keynote at a conference. They are all coming along for the ride.

"Introduce yourselves to Nickie; she's from London." They shake hands from the backseat. Eddie chimes in, "London? That's where they eat snails." Nickie graciously suggests that maybe he's thinking of France.

"Hey, you guys," I say, "tell Nick how long you've been at Homeboy."

Eddie is always quick on the draw. "Four months."

Beto quietly offers, "Three weeks . . . today." Then Beto looks out the window, and in a whisper, almost to himself, adds, "Best three weeks of my life." We allow these words to rest in the reverent silence.

I say at the beginning of the talk, "The day won't ever come when I have more courage, am more noble, or am closer to God than Beto and Eddie." I point to them in the front row and the room filled with a thousand school superintendents serenades them with applause. Later, in the body of the talk, I point to the two of them again and say, "You are exactly what God had in mind when God made you." It is as if some electrical current is connected to their chairs. The both of them, in unison, are jolted upright, their entire beings pledging allegiance to the words.

Afterward, we all have lunch in the hotel and then make our way to the elevator connecting us to the underground parking structure. Beto and Nickie stroll together some distance behind Eddie and me. Eddie is tiny and looks like he's twelve though he's nineteen. We get to the elevator before the other two and we await its arrival. Eddie places his hand on my left shoulder and rests his head on my arm. He's not tired; he's tender. We stare at the closed elevator door and he says, "Hey, G . . . you know what I love the most about Homeboy?"

"No. What, son?"

"That you're not embarrassed by us." The words now move through me, with some bright energy, and my eyes glisten with a start.

The God we've settled for is red in the face and pretends he doesn't know us at parties. But the God we actually have is never embarrassed by us.

When a homie's infant son died of SIDS, a police chaplain showed up before the coroner arrived and told the young couple, as they finally removed the baby, their only child, from the house, "God took your son." Apart from the ministerial malpractice this represents, we begin to recognize that some of our versions of God need to be replaced, in a hurry.

Spooky, a sixteen-year-old homie, walks into my office and asks, "Ya want me to do nuthin'?" I thank him and say I have plenty of people doing that already. He shifts to small talk and asks me, "Hey, G . . . you ever win the Nobel Peace Prize?" I laugh and tell him no. He scrunches his face and says sympathetically, "Haven't did enough?" I tell him that I'm sure that's it. And, yes, the god who thinks "we haven't did enough" is the wrong god. Too small.

My friend Mirabai Starr, a mystic, who writes about mystics, says, "Once you know the God of Love, you fire all the other gods." It is always hard for us to believe in the nonjudgmental, loving, and merciful God, and yet, that is the God we *actually* have.

Joel, a man who did considerable time in prison, told me, "When my toes hit the floor in the morning, I'm on the lookout."

"On the lookout for what?" I asked him.

"For God," he said. "God is always leaving me hints. He's dropping me anonymous tips all the time." This is the God of love trying to break through. This God will not be outdone in extravagant tenderness. Leaving hints as "deep as the nether world or high as the sky," as the prophet Isaiah reminds us. We get to choose: the god who judges and is embarrassed, or the One who notices and delights in us.

Anthony is in his midthirties and in his tenth month as a trainee at Homeboy Industries. He and his wife have three very young daughters. He was mainly missing in action for the birth of his first two. When the third is born, he holds her in his arms and tells me later, "Damn, G . . . I looked at her face and I thought, 'She looks exactly like her mother—angry.'" We laugh.

Half of Anthony's life had been spent in jails and detention facilities. Before coming to us, a meth addiction crippled him surely as much as his earlier gang allegiance did. We're speaking in my office one day and he tells me that he and his twin brother, at nine years old, were taken from their parents and a house filled with violence and abuse and sent to live with their grandmother. "She was the meanest human being I've ever known," Anthony says. Every day after school, every weekend, and all summer long, for the entire year Anthony and his twin lived with her (until they ran away), they were forced to strip down to their *chonies*, sit in this lonely hallway "Indian style," and not move. "She would put duct tape over our mouths . . . cuz . . . she said, 'I hate the sound of your voices.'" Then Anthony quakes as the emotion of this memory reverberates. "This is why," he says, holding a finger to his mouth, "I never shush my girls." He pauses and restores what he needs to continue. "I love the sound . . . of their voices. In fact, when the oldest one grabs a crayon and draws wildly on the living room wall and my wife says, 'DO something! Aren't ya gonna TELL her something?' I crouch down, put my arm around my daughter, and the two of us stare at the wall, my cheek resting on hers, and I point and say, 'Now, *that's* the most magnificent work of art . . . I have ever seen.'"

Here is the Good News: The God we most deeply want IS the God we actually have, and the god we fear is, in fact, the partial god we've settled for. God looks at us and is ecstatic. This God loves the sound of our voices and thinks that all of us are a magnificent work of art. "You're here." God's cheek resting on ours. God's singular agenda item.

God is only interested in lavishing us with extravagant tenderness, and yet we are convinced that god is thinking we all could just do a better job. How do we get beyond the idea of us being "sinners in the hands of an angry god" (or even lummoxes who haven't "did" enough) and find, instead, this Upside-Down God?

Images are all we really have to find the Upside-Down God, the counterprogrammed one.

Gloria's bumper sticker on her car, I suppose, was a window to how she saw herself. It read: "You say I'm a bitch like it's a bad thing." A tough cookie of a homegirl, Gloria navigated more abuse, violence, and sheer abandonment in her lifetime than most. The first person she met at Homeboy was one of our senior staff, Mary Ellen Burton. Gloria marveled at her kindness: "She welcomed me like she was waiting for me."

Gloria's periodic bouts with addiction would visit her like some very unwelcome relative. Once she walked into my office so "smoked out" it took my breath away, and she deflected it with, "I've lost so much weight; I look like a wet food stamp." It was during this period, when the darkness was hugely enveloping, that she stood by herself, peered over a bridge overpass, and indeed contemplated seeing her body sprawled at the bottom.

Just as this seemed feasible, a car passed and a guy on the passenger side leaned out the window and yelled, "JUST JUMP ALREADY."

Gloria turned with a quickness and a fury—"FUCK YOU, MOTHERFUCKER!"—and the whole moment jolted her into what she later told me was "a useful anger." Then she howled with laughter on the bridge, as we both would later in my office at the telling of it.

Part of Gloria's return to self came with an admission and a revelation. "When I walked through those doors, I didn't have a heart," she told me. "I had a rock. I wanted to cover my pain instead of feel it. Now, I can feel pain. And it's a beautiful thing." Once, when she was working at Homeboy and close to the near wholeness of herself, she shared a dream she'd had the night before. She told me in her dream, she's dancing with God and folks, "more important . . . more valuable people, keep trying to cut in . . . and God won't let them." She said this, and our eyes met like never before and they moistened. We sat in silence at an image of God so perfect.

If it's true that only the false self is offended by anything, maybe only the false god is offended? The King-on-his-throne-god says, "My subjects, you have offended me," or "His Majesty is pleased with you." But, frankly, both are human projections. God as the divine version of me has proven to be a dangerous projection. Even Thomas Merton thought God had mood swings. God is not fickle, we are. It feels more accurate to know the God who loves us into things. The Tender One who is not so much offended that we've separated children from their parents at the border, but who insists on "loving us into" not doing it.

There is a character in the novel *A Passage to India* who worries that there won't be "enough God to go around." The God who loves us into loving is plentiful and abundant and is not in scarce supply.

It may now be safe to say that our God does not need to be calmed down, nor is ever irate nor filled with wrath. All the mystics have come to see this. Julian of Norwich knows that she's been told constantly of this angry Divine One but just can't "find this God" in her experience. We still can't shake the narrative of the God who seeks our measuring up and demands some high level of performance. We don't measure up to this God; we just show up. We allow this Tender One to fill us extravagantly, then we go into the world and speak the whole language of it, unrestricted, openhearted, and loyally dedicated to its entirety. Tender glance meets tender glance. Behold the One beholding you and smiling.

For the Tender One, it's simply never about worthiness. But, I'm afraid for us, it's ONLY about worthiness. The centurion wants Jesus to cure his servant and humbly tells him: "Say but the word . . ." "I am not worthy that you should enter under my roof . . ." The centurion feels unworthy. But Jesus just wants to notice and connect to him. He pays attention to him. We stare at the cure and the faith of the guy, but Jesus wants us to look at how false our sense of unworthiness is. In the face of this tender glance, we find a God quite speechless—too in love with us to chitchat.

"A jar we break." It is our exhilarating task to cause constant breakage. We, simply put, are the objects of God's longing and we return the longing, in walking toward the utter fullness of this spacious God, who never has a second thought about loving us. This God won't let "more important" people cut in on the dance. Both cage and jar . . . broken.

It's a fool's errand to assert the existence of God, when God just hopes we'll act on God's behalf. God's hope as well is that we won't continually project onto God how we would run things if we were in charge. Somebody told me once, "God's love is unconditional—as long as you're obeying Christ." Well . . . so much for your "unconditional." On a freeway overpass, painted

on king-size bedsheets and hung for the whole world to see, are the words: TRUST IN GOD or BURN IN HELL (and I'm thinking, *These are my only options?*). I saw a sign on a truck once: NO . . . HIS NAME IS NOT THE MAN UPSTAIRS, IT'S JESUS! The "God of love" is not losing any sleep here. Zorba the Greek said, "I think of God as being exactly like me . . . only bigger, stronger, crazier." God in our own image. Surely, the God of requirements was born exactly from our projection. Someone told me once that we needed "to follow the demands of God." I wasn't aware that God took hostages. What are these "demands," anyway?

The homie Mouser was complaining about the religious fanaticism of his mother-in-law. She apparently felt that God commanded her to ALWAYS be in church. I asked him, "What kind of God would ask you to be in church all day, every day?" He was steady. "I don't know. Their God is different. He's, like, from Argentina." Well, that explains it.

God doesn't require anything of us except to receive this love that will change everything. This will guide what we do, not be a list of requirements. Then the Ten Commandments become a placeholder as we move from the "outside in" God to the radiance of the "inside out" God.

It is our lifelong task, then, to refine our view of God. We won't be able to speak the whole language until we know the wholeness of God. We search always to find the deeper current that can finally change our innermost way of seeing. We want to return to some depth of interiority, beyond our saying prayers, trapped in our dualistic thinking. Find the wellspring. This task will only end when we locate a really good parking spot . . . in the graveyard.

God doesn't want us to be good. We already are. God only longs for us to be joyful. God has little interest in our behavior, only in our abundant happiness. I always need to move beyond

my spiritual sleepwalking so I can recognize God as the Tender One. Our brilliant therapists at Homeboy don't so much try to alter the behavior of our trainees. Their controlling statement invites to joy: "You know, you might feel better if . . . " Equally, for God, it's simply not about "Good or Evil" or "Right or Wrong." It's about Sorrow or Joy.

I took Hector, Stevie, and José with me to give a series of talks in Belfast. They are among the wisest human beings I know. Their wisdom is born of a depth of suffering and deprivation that has finally connected them to their deeper current, to this abundant wellspring. Prior to our Belfast arrival, we spent some days in Dublin, sightseeing, walking endlessly, and eating gloriously. I noticed that, at every restaurant, I'd order by saying, "I'll have the lamb" or "Give me the stew." But the homies would always order the same way: "I'll have the roasted lamb rump, with the chili, cumin rub, and honey-roasted heritage carrots, pomegranate seeds, carrot and brown-butter puree, pea tendrils, and red wine jus." They'd never say, "I'll have the lamb." I never corrected them. Though it was a bit of "fish out of water," I found it to be oddly magical—it contained a delight that invited me to my own wellspring. It was as though, if you didn't say the entirety of it, you wouldn't get it all. Ordering food as the whole language.

Homies in their recovery are constantly trying to shift the energy field. They want to move from a sense of scarcity that there isn't enough to go around (so I will delineate every ingredient and piece of this roasted lamb dish) to a pervasive sense of abundance. Pretty soon, they take up residence in the house of plenty. They locate their inner abundance. They move from the impasse of some previous scarcity to the doorway of "enough for everybody." The truly abundant person as the already whole one. Then they find themselves preferring playfulness over judgment. They don't identify with narrow categories anymore but only in their abundance. "They shall eat," it says in the Second Book of Kings, "and have some left over." It looks like this when we realize we are the object of God's longing. Then God's dream come true is this soul abundance and relational connection with each other.

In whatever form our contemplative practice takes, we are being offered the God of abundance. At every turn, this God wants to restore, not be retributive or punish. So, we surrender to this and allow it to wash over us like a fresh waterfall, never needing replenishment. Then we practice this abundance in our lives, in the likeness of God.

Junior is telling me about putting his three-year-old son to bed at night. "He has to feel my skin, otherwise he won't go to sleep." Jesus, in his own contemplative practice, was able to rest in God. It is from this anchored self that he is able to move in the world. He feels God's skin, then he can see, feel, think, and touch as God does. He's at home and at rest in this self. Such a self doesn't ever find a home in scarcity. Though visiting scarcity is inevitable, we choose not to live there.

At Starbucks, they never say, "May I help you?" but rather, "What can I get started for you?" God asks the same. We want to be curious about our distress rather than terrified. We want an awakened heart. We want more than happiness, but nothing short of the vitality of joy. We play hide-and-seek from our true selves and Jesus waves us over to the wedding feast . . . none of that fasting stuff or grim duty. Take your shoes off and dance till the cows come home. This has always been what God wants to get started for us.

Scrappy invokes a song made popular when I was in the seventh grade and Nixon wasn't president yet. "God is like that Cream song, 'Sunshine of Your Love.' It says, 'I've been waiting so long to be where I am going . . . in the sunshine of your love.' That's how I see God these days." It is about basking in the sustainable energy of this God. And so, the God of requirements has left the room.

"Come let us adore Him," we sing at Christmastime. As we evolve in our consciousness, we see with clarity that God holds little interest in such adoration. We, on the other hand, would love it if we were on the receiving end of unbridled adulation. This is how we know it is our projection onto God, and we can get stuck there. Acquiring a Christ consciousness, or embracing the marrow of the gospel, or taking seriously what Jesus took seriously, or dedicating ourselves to the creation of tender kinship with each other—now, that's praise God can get behind. Now we're talkin'.

I take two brothers to eat after a talk we gave. It's a burger place but more upscale than McDonald's, with waiters and menus. Sammy and Joey are both gang members and did their stints in prison. Sammy is ten years older than Joey, and at the time of our meal they both had been in our eighteen-month training program for nearly a year. They order their burgers and Joey is quick to ask the waiter, "There's no mayonnaise on the burger, is there?" The waiter tells him that it will be left out if he wishes. Sammy chimes in, "Yeah . . . there can't be mayonnaise." The confused waiter nods and leaves, and I ask the brothers, "You're BOTH allergic to mayonnaise?" "Nah," Sammy says, "we're not allergic. We're traumatized."

"Yeah," Joey clarifies, "*me da asco* [it makes me sick]." I'm afraid I'm going to need more enlightenment here.

They proceed to tell me that when they were kids their grandmother raised them. No father in the picture and their mom trapped in her addiction. What they remember most was the constant hunger they felt. "Sometimes all we had in the house," Sammy says, "was a big-ass sack of flour and a huge tub of mayonnaise." The grandmother would make these hockey-puck biscuits with only those two ingredients. This was all they might eat for weeks on end. "*Me dio asco,*" Joey adds.

Then Joey brightens and turns to Sammy. "The silver cans . . . remember those?" Apparently, once a week these two little guys would go to the local Catholic church, where there was some Tuesday food pantry, and they'd traipse home with a big box of canned goods. "It was shit nobody wanted," Sammy says. "You know . . . lima beans and crap. And it was some stuff we didn't even know what was it."

Then Joey adds, "But there were the silver cans."

The two brothers would go through the box, hoisted up on the counter, and five-year-old Joey would stand at the counter's edge, on a chair, while his older brother would seize the can opener. They'd place the silver one, whose label had fallen off, right in front of them. "Then," Sammy says, "we'd say the Silver Can Prayer. We'd fold our hands . . . close our eyes . . . bow our heads and pray: 'Please be pineapple. Please be pineapple.'" Then they'd open the can. "And it would be crap," Sammy says, "lima beans . . . stuff you didn't know what was it."

Joey intervenes here to remind us that it's not always bad news. "But remember that one time?"

Sammy nods and picks up the story. "We had the silver can in front of us. We bowed our heads, folded our hands, closed our eyes, and said the Silver Can Prayer: 'Please . . . be pineapple.' We opened the can." Sammy pauses for emphasis and says, "And the gates of heaven were opened. Tears rolled down our cheeks. We looked at each other . . . crying. APPLESAUCE . . . APPLE . . . SAUCE!!"

Come . . . let us adore him.

The Hebrew word for praise is *tehilla*, which primarily means "to radiate" or "to reflect." God's invitation, then, is to be radiant in reflecting God's own tenderness in the world. It's never about telling God how great he is. We enter as fully as we can into the open-handed thrill of God's abundance. Because of our hardwiring, this idea of God will always feel too good to be true. But it is as true and satisfying as an unexpected can of applesauce to a couple of hungry brothers. God as warm, gentle sun and not interrogation lamp. An inmate at Folsom told me, "Grand is the smile of God."

-◇◆◇-

We need not ever hide our fragility from the Tender One. The God we actually have is never enfeebled by anything. So, we want to give ourselves to the love that gives itself to us. We try to find our way to give God permission to reach us. Denise Levertov writes: "With what radiant joy he turns to you, and raises you to your feet, and strokes your disheveled hair, and holds you, holds you, holds you close and tenderly—before he vanishes."

The homie Garry says, "God is the intake of breath and we are the exhaling of it. So . . . we need to take every breath personally." Prayer is as sustaining as a breath and not a plea to God to keep us safe from dangers and temptations or begging for favors. For example: "God answers knee-mails." Prayer doesn't work; praying does. Not sure how else we breathe in the God of unfathomable compassion if not by our own spiritual practice and silent solitude. This allows us to land on God's oceanic shore and it organizes things for us.

Lucia gave birth to twins but one died at birth. Many months later, she wanted both baptized. Needless to say, every church office had told her no. I have known her since she was a teenager. So, she brought in her live baby and the ashes of the dead twin. Baptized them both. The parents could not stop sobbing. When push comes to shove, we all know how to breathe in the God of unfathomable compassion.

The false images that Exodus cautions us against aren't about statues in a church. Rather, it is the false image of God that allows you to separate children from their parents at the border or permits you to pack a church during a pandemic or excludes anybody at all. Jesus did not come to start a religion but to present the most expansive understanding of his God. I saw a billboard in Indiana once: "Jesus: Your Only Way to God." Fortunately for all of us, both God and Jesus disagree with this billboard. These are false images we ought not to have before us.

This may seem odd, but I have had many folks pack up all their belongings from different parts of the world and make the trek to Homeboy, wishing to live and work here. I'm moved that they find themselves so moved, but still. "God put it on my heart" is usually how they make the proposal to cast their lot here with the homies in Los Angeles. I'm always wishing God had put it on their heart to send me an email first. One couple from somewhere in the South told me, "Then the Lord brought us to Los Angeles." I remember thinking, Hijole. *The Lord is no more your travel agent than he is my barber.* When it comes to how we see God, we have work to do. Once we attach magic to God, we expect magic. God planning our itinerary.

There are many cages that hold us still. The "will of God," for example, is never different from what we most deeply want. Ensuring, then, that we never are strangers to ourselves will give us access to our deepest longing. This is God's will. Not sure God puts stuff on our heart, but rather opens our hearts so we know what we most deeply desire.

Comfort with one another can give birth to bright images of the God we have. José will enter my office with "What's crack-a-lackin'? . . . besides the bottom of my feet." When we banter and I get off a good one, he'll look at me with admiration and say, "Touché, pussycat." Meister Eckhart saw God's identity in laughter and affection. Essentially, "God laughs to us. We laugh back."

Often, when the two of us are speaking, say, in my office, if there is ever a break in the conversation, José stares at me and says, "Damn, G . . . I love you . . . so much." Certainly, part of it is an unalloyed expression of love. But mainly it reminds me of God, filling every break and breath. God inserting the same line whenever we've stopped talking. Exactly the same. We are all immersed, as Hafiz writes, "in the Soft Brilliance. We are all just waiting to break camp—into God." Saint Ignatius called this "devotion," which he defined as "an ease in finding God." It is a self-deprecating God who is never saying, "Look at ME," but rather, "Would ya look at YOU!"

A homie at a very low point once stared at me and asked, "Has God disowned me?" The question startled me. Before I could reply, he followed with, "Have you?" And you discover that the only way he'll know that this is NOT on God's mind is that it's not on yours either.

-◇◆◇-

My spiritual director, Sergio, a homie, sent me an email: "I was driving home . . . I always get caught in a moment of peace and joy . . . and today . . . before I could give God thanks . . . God beats me to the punch and . . . thanked ME . . . for allowing myself to be loved. Really, G—it felt so real." And THAT is the God I believe in: the one who beats us to the punch and thanks US. Like many Hindus who visit temple after temple not to see God, but to let God gaze upon them.

I was at an international conference in Rome, and every morning a different global continent was responsible for the prayer service to begin each day. Africa had the last morning. And they danced. They spoke of a God who dances. They suggested that in the Prodigal Son story, the father runs to his kid. The man leading the service said it's the only time "God runs." But he thought God was really dancing. Above all, God doesn't await the arrival, since we're all "a long way off," but dances toward us with delight at the sight of us.

There's an old Native American saying: "He who cannot

dance claims the floor is uneven." Our God dances toward us. Don't blame an uneven floor; agree to dance. Feel this God beating us to the punch.

We always need to abandon "performance" when it comes to God, and walk instead into the arms of encounter. Sure, "the floor is uneven," but our self-improvement resolutions should be jettisoned since they keep us from dancing. The arms of encounter are held out by the Tender One, who wants us to gravitate in that direction.

Joel and another homie took their first plane trip with me, ate food requiring bibs at Fisherman's Wharf in San Francisco, and shared their stories before a gym filled with high school Catholic boys. I had heard Joel's story several times at that point in our trip, but I noticed the detour he took in the middle of his presentation this time. "So, there I was . . . at home . . . cleaning my bathroom." I was amazed that he ventured to tell this story. I had heard it the night before at dinner.

"And as I'm scrubbing the sink, Marvin Gaye is singing on the radio, 'Let's Get It On.' You know the song." Joel began to sing. "'Let's . . . get it on.'" The gym exploded in hollering and raucous laughter. Without a shred of inhibition, he repeated his singing of the line and added a kind of cholo-shuffle dance. "'Let's get it on.'" The packed room could not be contained.

Then Joel began to speak other lines from the song and the boys grew quiet. "'Don't ya know what I'm dreamin' of? Don't ya know how sweet and wonderful life can be?'" He paused and communicated with certainty that the story was downshifting to a slower, deeper velocity. "I realized . . . it was God . . . dropping me a hint." Tears fell down his cheeks as they did at dinner the night before. This was not lost on his audience and they were completely still. "'Ain't goin' ta worry . . . won't push ya, baby. If you believe in love,'" Joel continued, "'then . . . let's get it on.'" His crying now was just this side of derailing his entire speech.

The gym was absolutely hushed. "So . . . I said yes . . . I surren-
dered to the love . . . to God . . . Yes . . . let's . . . get it on." He
stopped there. Echoing applause punctuated his story's end.

--◇◇--

A gospel singer once said famously, "My goal in life is to make
God famous." Not sure God shares the same aspiration. It is
more akin to loving us with all God's heart and then thanking
us for accepting that love. Meister Eckhart writes: "How long
will grown men and women in this world keep drawing in their
coloring books an image of God that makes them sad?"

Ran into a homie at the CVS, early in the pandemic. He's
pleading with me from behind his mask. "Please, G . . . marry
me and my lady . . . fast . . . cuz we want to get right with God."

I tell him in the aisle, which is empty of hand sanitizer and
toilet paper, "Son, you've never been wrong with God."

Or when homies comment on how perplexing things
can sometimes turn out: "Funny . . . how God works." This
kind of statement always feels like: "Funny . . . how long and
white . . . God's beard is." God is just loving us, no work in-
volved.

My friend Pema Chödrön, one evening at UCLA, said the
quiet part out loud. "While you were speaking, Greg, I kept
thinking: *I wish he'd stop talking so much about God.*" This came
in the moderated discussion following my remarks that may
have included a few things I believe about the God we actually
have. She later told the crowd that perhaps her discomfort was
a residual holdover from her own Catholic upbringing. I get it.
I ended up saying, "Obviously I don't think it's preposterous to
believe in God. I'm just hoping that people stop believing in a
preposterous God."

When I was a kid, I could not stomach liver or lima beans.
Not a big fan now. One evening, my mom served up both for

dinner. All my many sibs had cleaned their plates and left the table. I refused to touch these two food items. So I sat there with my arms crossed, stubborn and still. Hours passed. I couldn't leave the table until I ate my whole dinner. Finally, my mom said in exasperation, "There are thousands of children in China who are starving and would love to eat that food."

I looked at her coldly and said, "Name one."

We often hear, "Great people are tested by God." Name one test sent by God. "God will not place a burden on our shoulders that we cannot carry." Name one burden. Just one time that God placed a burden on your shoulders. God does not test nor burden us. Ever. We need, Teresa of Ávila cautioned, to "overthrow any government inside that makes you weep."

The only God we have is the God of this world and the only world we have is the world of this God. We don't measure to God's pleasure—we just meet God's pleasure in us. And we are "God's delight" who is endlessly pleased with us, who always, as Hafiz reminds us, "is playing catch with your soul." And so humbly generous is our God, that union itself with God is not the goal, but rather oneness, with one another, in this world of God's. Our God has no interest in fame.

Octavio is next in line to be called into my office. He walks so slowly, dragging half of his body with him, with his right arm crimped up, folded, and pinned to his chest. He tells me his name with great difficulty, and I ask him to sit. His head is the most startling array of scars and dents. It took him forever to say, "I got shot in the head." And to the extent that he can shrug at all, he does. "A blessing . . . or a curse? . . . I don't know." He poses this question a total of three times while in my office. "You," he points at me. "Con . . . fir . . . ma . . . tion . . . camp."

"I confirmed you? In camp?"

"Yup," his upper torso nods so that he can gesture affirmatively.

"Which camp?" I ask. He thinks for a bit. "Football."

"Oh . . . Camp Kilpatrick." (The famous sports-focused probation camp.)

Again, the top half of his body nods in agreement.

"Work here," he says, holding up his recalcitrant arm, trying to indicate this location.

"Son . . . you need this place. This place needs you. You'll love this place. This place will love you back."

He takes it all in, and says, for the final time today, "Blessing . . . or curse? . . . I don't know."

"Blessing," I tell him. "All blessing."

Meeting God's pleasure in us where there is no need to distinguish blessings from anything else. Just finding that spacious heart connected to all things. God playing catch with our soul. Soft brilliance.

Sharky moves all the time as a kid. His dad gets saturated in rock cocaine and in PCP paranoia, and even with restraining orders he always finds Sharky, his mom, and his sister. Sometimes they are even living right under his dad's nose. Invariably, he finds them and threatens to kill them all and they are forced to relocate yet again. Nine different schools before Sharky is eleven.

At twelve, Sharky comes home only to find his crazed father hiding in the closet. His dad begins to interrogate him beyond the kid's ability to take in any more terror. Sharky races out of the house, gets to a neighbor's phone, calls his mom at work, and sobs to her as she tries to quiet him down. "Meet me at the Hollenbeck Youth Center in one hour."

She just holds him there, in the gym bleachers, as he sobs all the more and her only message is this: "I'm so sorry you had to go through that."

Once Sharky moves from a tagging crew to a gang, to active gang violence and drug dealing and addiction, he lands in his more-than-predictable prison tenure. This is not what he wants his future to hold. Some old *veterano* tells him that he needs to ask forgiveness from God for all his sins. And so, he dedicates himself to this task and sincerely prays for forgiveness. In the heart of his prayer, alone in his cell, comes a message from God not of forgiveness or even reconciliation, but rather a singular expression of tenderness. God holding a sobbing Sharky and saying only this: "I'm so sorry you had to go through that."

Sharky tells me later that this has become the notion of God that holds him still. It fills him enough to say finally to his own father, "I'm so sorry you had to go through all that." Consequential.

The Tender One keeps trying to rearrange our thinking. We keep being led to the utter fullness of our hearts aligned with this One tender heart. This One is sorry that we go through what we do. "You're here," God says, holding us in the bleachers. We can rest in that.

Chapter Two

————◆◆❊◆◆————

The Soul Clapping
Its Hands

The Blessed Virgin Mary nuns at Saint Brendan's gram-
mar school had us all memorize this little ditty: "Good,
better, best . . . never let it rest . . . until the good is better and
the better . . . BEST." They meant well. The mystical view sees
what's lopsided here: the starting point is really not "good," but
"bad." We were all thrown out of the garden because we were
bad, so now we are desperately trying to become good enough
to get back in. It's really about, I suppose, original sin, and the
progression is from BAD to good to better to best to holiness
and sainthood. Bad is where we always seem to begin.

When homies say they are trying to be "better people," I
tell them that they "could not be even one bit better." A homie
texted me recently, just this: "Pops . . . what can I do to be a
better man?" It felt more heartbreaking to me than some as-
pirational expression. We never say to the homies, "We believe
you can change," but rather, "We know you can heal." I saw
a sign in a store behind the counter, meant to pump up their
workers: "My goal is not to be better than anyone else, but be
better than I used to be." Jesus uses the word "hypocrite" and

its original meaning is "performer." Which is to say, goodness is not about a measurable performance, about being better than we were yesterday. Jesus uses this term when folks make a big show of things, which is why he says we should fast and pray and give alms in private; don't perform. It has been ingrained in us, however, that our "performance" needs to move always from good to better, finally, to achieve best. In the mystical view, goodness is our starting point, and realizing it, not becoming it, is the task.

In prison, folks panic about appearing before the parole board. I suspect at Homeboy we write many thousands of letters each year assuring the boards that a homie has a place with us upon his or her release. The boards hope for a "finding of suitability." Homies have to comb their lives for traces of character defects, feel remorse for their actions, never minimize their crimes, and convince the board that they are no longer the person they were at the time of the crime. Never mind that the people locked up are as much victims as perpetrators.

We want to hold the wounded AND the person who did the wounding—because we are all always both. The deincarceration movement can't make much headway unless we reconcile ourselves to this truth. Prosecutorial overreach, I suppose, is the very opposite of the mystical view, since it is unable to see the whole picture, and can't get beyond (or underneath) the criminal act. Hence, the freedom they have to imprison whomever they want for as long as they wish. They don't see the goodness.

It unlocks some door, however, to embrace this mystical view. It will keep us from seeking satisfaction in revenge. It frees us from thinking that peace will come from humbling others, or that being stern with our children makes them gentle, or that justice is pain doled out to those who behave badly. It holds us back from believing that our righteousness arrives when we prove someone wrong. We will praise someone and then say, "with all his flaws." What are flaws, anyway? It would seem

that flaws are what only other people have. Not me. Turns out, judgment is blind, only love truly sees, and only an understanding heart speaks the whole language.

Ignatius said that his "last defect" was that when he walked the halls and saw another Jesuit, he would laugh because he was so filled with the other's goodness. He finally "reduced this" to a smile. Such an impulse comes from knowing that the Tender One has "pitched his royal tent inside of you," as Hafiz writes, "So I will always lean my heart as close to your soul as I can." A smile is hard, then, to contain.

A senior staff member asked me once, what was a force more powerful than death? I said to her that I thought it was inhabiting your true self in loving and thereby no longer being a stranger to your own unshakable goodness. Homeboy is the Lost and Found Department. We all lose ourselves and find ourselves in the other, and then so find our true selves in loving. A powerful force.

It's not about discovering your good qualities and making them better. Nor is it about finding your potential for good. A donor once said of me that I didn't see "gang member" when I saw the homies, but that I only saw "potential." Not quite. I only want to see goodness. None of us want to settle for reaching our full potential when we can inhabit fullness. We find our true selves IN LOVING—in the verb of it. Otherwise, we get stuck in the noun of it. What seeks perfection is not our self but our love. We need to, each day, if you will, "log on" with our username and password, fully agreeing (to the cookie policy) and allowing the free flow of tenderness in the world. If it stays a verb, tenderness doesn't seek or care about its return on its loving investment. It just finds its full measure of goodness in this loving.

I have a framed photograph in my office of Victor, a young homie, receiving a bouquet of flowers from the queen of Sweden—in Sweden. (Long story.) A very smart kid. I had met him in a probation camp and he later told me that he taught himself French in the camp. "Why'd ya learn that?"

"Cuz . . . I was bored as fuck." After that picture was taken, he flew home and came straight to the office, jet-lagged and giddy. He stopped me three times that day to hug me and say, "THAT was life changing. I'm even gonna remove my tattoos." Later he would tell me, "I'm gonna try and dress differently now—less gangster. In fact, I wanna dress more like you."

I tell him, "You mean old-fashioned and out of it?"

"Exactly," he says.

Some months later, having decompressed from the experience, he tells me, "Damn, G—I'm in love and it feels proper."

"Who ya in love with? "I ask him.

"Myself," he says. Victor had been invited into his own gracious heart and RSVP'd. Transformation is not just a destination, but a process. He saw his own goodness and then could repurpose himself for positivity.

Before mass at San Fernando Valley Juvenile Hall, we were awaiting the arrival of the kids and I was speaking to one of the Catholic volunteers. She lamented, "There just isn't enough time here with them to teach them. What do we do?" Surely her heart was in the right place.

I found myself saying to her, "But there is plenty of time to learn from them." A willingness to be reached by them is reflective of the God we actually have. If we insist on "teaching," it signals that God doesn't think they are enough. Lifelong learning is, of course, magnificent. Yet, it will be difficult for these kids to shake the already solid sense that they are deficient because they don't measure up. But if we learn from them and cherish them, and one another, all of us inhabit the truth of our unshakable goodness, and with it, our common dignity and noble hearts.

Dwelling deep within all our souls is this undeniable, inexhaustible wellspring of love, wisdom, and goodness. If we can't uncover and see this essential purity in ourselves, then everyone we see is ugly, limited, and not measuring up. So how do we make contact with this?

A homie I met in camp expressed a common lament. "I mean . . . my *jefito* [dad] just doesn't get me. He does . . . not . . . understand me. I mean . . . he thinks . . . I'm good." How easy it is to believe and invest in our impoverished identity, to believe that the injured self is who we are. We never want to be who we are. Yet one doesn't "become" noble. We locate our nobility. The hard part is embracing our inner nobility, beauty, and goodness. Unfortunately, so often for all of us, it is the frightened, damaged self that takes center stage. We can learn to catch ourselves. The homies think that this is their truth. They get caught in the downward spiral and repetitive cycle of unworthiness and shame. The flip side of this is developing a positive facility for a different way to define. To define oneself in donation rather than deficit. It's not that they have forgotten their original goodness, but that they have never been properly introduced to it.

Endlessly, though, we keep trying to rid ourselves of our selves. We just won't let go of this grudge match that we carry on. We sidestep a satisfaction with who we are and how we are and we try to get rid of the parts of ourselves that we find odious.

I met Candelario when he was fifteen and "running amok" (as he called it) in the projects. He got shot in the chest once and a very large medallion of Our Lady of Guadalupe deflected the bullet nicely. Unharmed and breathless at this whole moment of magical thinking, he showed me the dented medal. "This woke my ass up proper." Some years later, though, he wrote me from prison, "*Yo no soy malo* (I'm not a bad person) . . . ask God." Such knowledge is a gift from God, and it is a gift God longs to give. Once I know, "*que no soy malo,*" I see this goodness wherever I look. And yet, this "finding of suitability" always seems to elude us.

When drug use became a problem for homies in the late '90s, there was a slow gradation from drinking, to bud, to crack. Meth is most pervasive now, but in the old days, there was this "It's only Thunderbird" or "*El Presidente*" or the constant "It's only bud." Gang members sold drugs but didn't so much use drugs. Manuel was a full-blown alcoholic as a teenager, then graduated from selling crack to being consumed in using it. When I would visit him in juvenile hall, he would downplay his alcoholism when I brought it up. "I just drink gin and juice . . . maybe a Thunderbird once in a big while." This ushered in a crying jag and an emphasis he wanted to make. "I never drink beer. Cuz of my mom." She had four kids, left on her own, after being abandoned by Manuel's father. "When I was a kid, I'd wake up early after a night that my mom got really drunk and I'd go to the fridge and take out all the beer left and one by one I'd open them up and reach high up to the sink and pour them out. That's why," he finished proudly, "I never touch beer. *Me da asco.*"

I got him into a rehab to address his crack habit some years later. He left after one month, for one day only, to attend his younger brother Paul's funeral. Paul shot himself in the head. We talked a lot about his brother on the long drive home. After the funeral, returning to the rehab, I asked how his recovery experience was going. "You know, G . . . I'm not gonna tell ya it's been easy, cuz it hasn't been. It's been real hard." Then as soft as he can be, he said, "But I'm learning wisdom every day. In fact, now I want wisdom to be my best friend."

I pulled into the rehab parking lot and Manuel asked what I suspected had been on his mind since his brother's death. "G . . . where is my brother now? You know, they say, that when you kill yourself, you go to hell. What's up wit' dat?"

I did the best I could. I said that God knew the wholeness of his brother's life and the greatness of his loving heart and understood his struggles. "So, *mijo* . . . there is no doubt at all that, right now, he's resting in the loving stillness of God."

Manuel heaved a huge sigh and said "YES!!!" He turned to me and explained. "I asked God last night, as I stood and watched the stars, to give me a sign today about where my brother ended up." He stared at me. "And the sign was going to be . . . whatever G says." Drug rehab kept Manuel from sliding deeper into substance abuse, but it also freed the deck so that he knew who he was, so he could allow that place to be fed. It is the very wisdom of God that could look at creation and say: This is good. Learning wisdom for Manuel is to know that God says the same thing about him.

On Good Friday in Cochabamba, Bolivia, where I worked, the Quechua Indigenous people would each grab a huge rock, which represented their sin, and they would carry it up this hill and place it at the foot of this huge, bleached-white cross towering over our town. The larger the rock, of course, the more admired you were for your humility and honest self-appraisal. As I look back on this, the rocks, heavy and arduous to carry, didn't represent their sins, but rather, their notion of sin. This idea of sin kept them from themselves. It was self-estranging. And certainly, "public sinners," criminals released, drug addicts, prostitutes, felons, gang members, were all estranged from everybody else. Truth be told, Jesus hardly mentions "sins," and I'm not sure he'd say he died for them.

In John's gospel, when he speaks of the "sin of the world"— it is singular. And the sin is the division we create, the scapegoating, the otherizing, the striking of the high moral distance. But Christian love resists the scapegoating agenda by remembering the humanity, "the other." We hear about the separation of the sheep and the goats in Matthew 25. Surely, this is a pretty good list of things to embrace and do and care about (hungry, thirsty, stranger, in prison, etc., and you tended to these folks. Which is to say, you were tender to them). But it's the "separation" that departs from how God sees. Inclusion IS God. Separation ISN'T. There are no goats, just sheep—all sheep.

It is a message of radical, mystical kinship that addresses the singular sin of the world. It aligns with the original covenant that invites us to a preferential care for "the widow, orphan, and stranger." Theologian Ron Rolheiser points out that, in the original language and context, the widow, orphan, and stranger were those folks whom society looked at and said, "We can live without you." The singular sin of the world? To fail to see with God's eyes. To see goats, when, really, we are all just sheep.

It's the mysticism of Jesus that looks to the widow, orphan, stranger, gang member, homeless person, the undocumented, the felon, the mentally ill, drug addict, the returning citizen, and all those excluded, and says: We will not live without you. We don't tell homies, "Stop being a goat and become a sheep." We say, "You are sheep. We all are." Raul cries in my office: "I take myself to court every day . . . and every day . . . I find myself guilty." This line induces a crying jag from which we both wait for a respite. "Why do you love us so much?" He continues. "If you knew what we've all did—it would dissuade you. I signed on the bottom line of everything I did." Still, if we see Raul's wholeness, he begins to see it and takes up residence there.

I have baptized all of Horacio's kids, and today it's number five. I watch Horacio masterfully corral everybody, the kids, the *suegra* (mother-in-law), and his siblings, and deftly bring the proceedings to order. He's a pro. A scrappy gang member with overly pronounced ears—he's so skinny it makes you wonder how he managed to defend himself on the streets. (Trust me, he managed.) Once I saw him and his kid brother, many years ago, in the middle of the day walking in the projects. I asked Horacio if he had ditched school that day. He was insulted. "Noooo," he said, "we didn't ditch school—we just didn't go." My apologies.

A Navigator at Homeboy aptly said of Horacio, "He is a mansion. He has many rooms." Horacio is an incandescent soul.

As grace tends to do, while winding down the baptism, I am filled with the utter fullness of Horacio's bright goodness. I recall Mary Oliver's words: "That you have a soul—your own, no one else's—that I wonder about more than I wonder about my own. So that I find my soul clapping its hands for yours more than my own." Indeed, Horacio is the whole accomplishment, and my soul is clapping its hands.

While folks are taking postbaptismal photographs, I call him aside. I'm brimming with such love for this kid with whom I've logged many years of memories and heartaches.

"You know what I was thinking about . . . all during the baptism?"

"That I gotta stop having kids?"

"Nooo."

"Cuz I'm thinkin' a gettin' a vasectomy."

"No, dawg . . . I was just thinking . . . how thoroughly good you are and what a beautiful job you've done with your life. Serio."

And both our eyes get flooded when we allowed the soul to quicken at hearing what it didn't know it already knew.

Micah 6:8 fills most of us with a sense of clarity as to what we are to DO with our lives, generally speaking. "To act justly. To love mercy. To walk humbly with your God." I saw a translation recently that framed the second part this way: "To love goodness." It suggests that love is more like a Geiger counter. It doesn't want Horacio to meet his potential (or even get a vasectomy). It just wants to zero in on his goodness. Our deep center is indeed saturated with divinity. Love will always find it there. The discovery is that we are the magnanimity of God. Then it is no longer about "doing good," but loving goodness.

I just saw a ketchup commercial. A couple with two kids

walk into the creepiest of diners. The place is dark and empty but for a menacing clown sitting alone in a booth. We see the cook, a huge, scary-looking guy with a black eyepatch. The family is scoping out the place and wondering whether they should dine here. The viewer already thinks they shouldn't. Right then the wife spots on the counter . . . a bottle of Heinz ketchup. Cue the glorious music; the parents smile and nod to each other. The final shot is them sitting at a table, eating. The moral of the story is written in big letters on the screen: "Find the Goodness." We can be mindfully awakened in loving awareness of our fundamental dignity and goodness. Beyond creepy clowns and menacing chefs, there is goodness. Then our grief and trauma are mere visitors, but not who we are. The goodness puts the thumb on the scale.

I had said once in a talk that "God didn't want anything from us—only for us." An elderly minister, afterward, said that he liked the talk except for that part. He said, "I mean, what about the Ten Commandments?" Of course, what is there to say to that? So, I said, "What about 'em?" I would think that loving goodness covers every base. Yes, there are urgent things to do, but God loves us into doing them. Once this is our heart's compass, no one needs to tell us not to covet our neighbor's goat.

What saves us in the present moment is being anchored in love and tethered to a sustaining God who keeps reminding us of our unshakable goodness and the goodness of others. I suspect that when Jesus said, "Your faith has saved you," this is what he meant.

I make my way to Pelican Bay State Prison at the top of the state of California, near the Oregon border. The Catholic chaplain, a gentle soul named Sam, made the arrangements. Pelican Bay has long been considered the repository of the "worst of the worst." It has forever been the last stop of all the stops. Sam walks me through a segregated unit, one-man cells, holding the most "incorrigible." He announces me to the cell ahead: "It's Father Greg from Homeboy Industries." Many become little kids in Juvenile Hall again. "G-Dog, remember me. You used to throw mass at Central . . . at Eastlake?" After Sam would announce me, I would step up and carry on a brief conversation and end with a blessing. One guy says, when I arrive at his door, "You're Father Greg?"

"Yeah."

"Huh . . . you look skinnier on TV." I thank him for pointing this out.

I celebrate mass in the gym on A-Yard. Sam has secured a large group to gather and has also been allowed to take pictures, which is not a permission typically granted. After mass, inmates pose with me—one, four, sometimes groups of twelve or more. I meet a guy named Louie with every inch of his face covered in tattoos, a calling card for a seriously traumatized human being. Tattoos like this can often be a "Keep Away" sign, meant to keep all comers guessing as to the mental stability of the tattooed one. Louie "has all day," sentenced forever and will never leave prison alive. He is goofy and charming, and not at all off-putting. He becomes the phantom, ever-present photobomber. He manages to insinuate himself into EVERY picture. Though never invited, he steps into the shot, and no one rebuffs him. He's just a tender part of the scenery.

As Sam and I walk from the gym after mass, I mention Louie and laugh about our intrepid photobomber. Sam tells me that some months earlier, he had planned a concert by Eric Genuis. Eric has performed at Carnegie Hall (and later, at Homeboy Industries). He plays the piano and has a couple others who accompany on strings. Sam had "ducated" (secured permission) for two hundred inmates, but only sixty showed up and Sam was a bit disappointed. Eric had planned to play for forty-five minutes, then engage in a question-and-answer session for fifteen minutes. He began to play, and something descended on these folks gathered in the same gym where I had celebrated the Eucharist. There was a reverent stillness thick in the air. Inmates and guards alike were held in this music's spell. It was the most glorious thing Sam had ever witnessed at Pelican Bay. He looked at the prisoners and soon they were all sobbing. He saw that the guards were discreetly flicking tears. The magnificent music had detonated some release so welcome and unexpected.

Eric finished and turned to his stunned audience and asked if there were any questions. There is only silence for some time. Then Louie, our photobomber, rose. He had something to say but he was still crying so hard, it was momentarily a struggle for him to locate his question. He could only utter one word: "Why?"

Eric began to cry as well and said, "Because you are deserving. You are worthy of beauty and music. And because . . . there is no difference between you and me." And here, I suppose, is the faith that saves . . . when we are anchored in love, tethered to a sustaining God and ever mindful of our undeniable goodness. That's why.

⬦

The Incas would greet each other every day with a recitation of the moral code lest folks forgot: "Don't be a thief. Don't be lazy. Don't be a liar." The response of the one greeted was: "Don't you be either." Still, dedicating ourselves to finding and loving goodness in each other puts "avoiding evil" out of business. The "moral code" is even replaced by what Saint Francis called "the city of love." For "no one lives outside the walls of this sacred place . . . differences exist, but not in the city of love. The priest and the prostitute—they weigh the same . . ." The pianist and the "worst of the worst" photobomber. The same.

People settle for saying that every human being is "worthy"

U-tube Epic
Genus

or "valuable." But these ideas are still stuck in the "measurable." "He is a valuable member of our team." "He is unworthy to be president." But goodness is unshakable. Solid. The truth. There is not a thing one can do to make this not so. God does not hope that we become something other than what we are. The Pharisees kept trying to be somebody, but they didn't know they already were. You teach children that they are valuable by valuing them. Not by insisting that they prove their value to you. There are lots of things and toxins and blindness that keep us from acknowledging this and seeing it AS true, but nonetheless, it is immutably certain. Before we can love goodness, we need to find it, and see it. It's there. It's there.

Here's a bad example. In prison or jail, if a "fish" or "new booty" is asked by another inmate, "What size are your shoes?" and the new guy says, "Size eleven," the inmate takes your shoes away. The correct answer to "What size are your shoes?" is "My size." There is an ownership to your goodness that needs to happen. It is a "My-sizing," if you will. People inhabit their dignity, nobility, and utter goodness and make it their own. (I told you it was a bad example.)

-◦|◦-

When we allow entry into our hearts the very tenderness of God—soaked as it is with hope, joy, and delight—we say what we say to friends in the same situation: "You're just telling me what I want to hear." Well, yes. God IS just telling us what we want to hear. Then we land on the shore of this oceanic God, and it organizes everything for us.

I'm with Dame Julian of Norwich, who found the mystical view and did away with sin. "I believe," she writes, "that sin has no substance, not a particle of being." More than a hundred years later, John of the Cross ceased to believe in sin. You put on the mind of Christ—then sin doesn't exist. And yet, for a long time,

Amazing!

we've been stymied by the idea that God needs to take a wire brush, if you will, to scrape away the barnacles of our soul. We all are glib when we announce that there is wickedness in the world, and yet, if we try and see as God does, we just notice how unwell and damaged people are and they can't, just yet, get at their goodness. It's not about fault, but impediment. Wholeness and health ARE what holiness is about. People aren't "wicked," they are just strangers to their own goodness.

How long have we trotted out this chestnut: "Love the sinner, hate the sin"? Yet, hating the sin hasn't gotten us very far. It has kept us from the love of our understanding hearts. We've reduced morality to just a high level of horror at hating the sin, rather than helping the ill, healing the traumatized, or bringing hope to the despondent. No one needs to stretch very much to know this aligns with God's heart and longing.

Saint Ignatius, in his autobiography, describes his wild scrupulosity and he realizes . . . finally . . . that it can't be sustained. Because once he came to know the expansive, spacious God we really have, once he found that mystical view, he moved beyond altering behavior and measuring up and chose instead to live in this generous light of God's outsize love. My size. He fired the other gods. He found the goodness.

Every homie is a quaint city in a land you've never been before. We don't save homies, we see them. We don't measure people, we meet them. "See me for the first time," a homie told me, "and I won't forget how I look." We all want to see who the other person is and quit staring at who they aren't. It's a truism at Homeboy to say: "The homies are used to being watched. They aren't used to being seen." An inmate at Mule Creek State Prison told me, "I was violent so people would see me." Exactly like the Zulu greeting. When you meet and welcome someone, you say, "I see you." The other person says, "Now that you see me, I'm here." You're here. You're here.

Sin as a notion estranges. Not sin, but the notion of sin. It keeps you a stranger to yourself and it insists on distancing us from each other. The "sinful" behavior becomes the identifier that separates and divides us. Moralism has never kept us moral. It's kept us from each other. There are mythic narratives that Americans like to tell themselves about right and wrong and good and bad. Thich Nhat Hanh speaks of behavior not in terms of "good and bad," but "more or less skillful." That's closer. I would say more or less healthy. I saw a billboard in Toronto: "Mental Health IS Health." Yup. In any case, believing in "demons" is the gateway drug to "demonizing" and that is always untruth. It keeps us from each other.

Often, a homie will call me and only identify himself in this way: "It's me." I told a homie once, "If you had any idea how many "me's" I know." There's a pause and the guy says, "Wow, G—you used to always know who 'me' was." You really can't win. But the homies always think they need to become a "me" other than the person they are. The problem, of course, is not that God does not think we are good enough, but that we don't know how good we are. We are distant from this truth. Homies, when they share an emotional experience they once had, instead of saying, "I cried," they always say, "Tears started coming out." (Another one said, "I got sweaty eyes.") Distance. We simply can't shake the narrative that we were tossed out of the garden for being bad and our only hope of return is to become good. How do we replace the god who wants us "to get our act together" for the God who just wants us to "get it on"?

"[God's] love thaws the holy in us," Teresa of Ávila said. Love is God's meaning and being. Create a culture of this, then homies can suddenly move from invisibility, from unspecified "me," to the wide-open spaces of our common truth. Kierkegaard writes: "To be entirely present to oneself is the highest thing and the highest task for the personal life." They can see as

God sees, then be entirely present to that. "Try," as Hafiz tells us, to look "upon your self more as God does. For He knows your true royal nature, God is never confused and can only see Himself in you." They can move from that miserable place that dissociates from the unspeakable things done to them to the quaint city of their true selves. "My problem is," Mikey says, "that I get new information, but it's processed by the old self." Out with the old. In with the true self. Wisdom: your best friend.

Famously, the Dalai Lama was interviewed in English and was asked to comment on "self-hatred." He just couldn't understand the question. He turned to his translator, to no avail. Finally, he said, "I just don't understand this question." Then he paused, gently tapping his hand on his chest. "Everybody has Buddha nature." To borrow from Obamacare, goodness is our "preexisting condition."

Eastern spirituality teaches us that once the surface mind and disordered desires are still, the true self awakens in love and compassion as its natural movement. Tyler is beginning his first day with us. He is a seventeen-year-old Black gang member and because of his age, the position with us is conditional on his being enrolled in school. He tells me he's a high school grad already. I'm incredulous. "At seventeen?"

"Actually," he says, "at sixteen."

"Damn, at sixteen? You must be a genius."

He smiles faintly. "I would like to think so." Tyler locates his "royal nature." "Oh nobly born, remember who you really are."

A homie named Lefty, "going through it" in jail, ends a recent letter to me with, "PS: I'm not feelin' so fuckin' noble at the moment." I suspect I had once called him noble. Nothing erases your goodness. There is no canceling of it. I never use the term "basic" goodness or "essential" goodness. Those words seem to hedge our bets. Unshakable goodness is our royal nature.

It's about seeing differently. We then undertake the search

for innocence in the other. We cease to find the guilty party. We no longer divide into camps: Heroes and Villains. We end up only seeing heroes. We look for the unchangeable goodness that's always there in the other. Love as the Geiger counter watching for any sign of light and strength. This goodness is a heat-seeking force. Love always sees how far we've come. You see Lefty and presume "he's up to all good." This real self, truly the Christ self, is experienced as expansive and huge.

It will always be less exhausting to love than to find fault. When we see fault, we immediately believe that something has to be done about it. But love knows that nothing is ever needed. Ever. As the homie Stevie says daily: "Love, love, and more love." Only love sees.

Joey was always and forever grouchy. You could never catch him in a good mood. He went to prison and, sadly, is still there. But there was a kid in the projects, Evar, who would get eternally picked on by everyone. I started to get letters for him from Joey in prison. Joey knew him from the projects and was aware of how he was constantly tormented by his peers. Evar shared with me, sometimes with tears in his eyes, the very moving, supportive letters that this surly, grouchy homie would send him. I wrote and thanked Joey for his kindness and told him of the impact it had. "I'm a bitter person," Joey wrote me. "When I do things for people . . . it makes me feel good." More love; the selfless action born of it frees us all from sorrow and fear. It ventilates the very place we get stuck.

A *New York Times* journalist, commenting on the twentieth anniversary of the death of Guinean immigrant Amadou Diallo, who was shot and killed by four police officers with forty-one shots, said, "We realized that the police had not been trained for innocence." All of this is a way of saying that they hadn't been taught about the unmistakable goodness and innocence of everyone they encountered.

A shouting match broke out in the reception area of Homeboy Industries between Cyca and her lover, Lola. I raced out of my office just as Cyca threatened, "I'm gonna kill you."

Lola returned, "You need professional help."

Cyca bellowed all the louder: "Then I'll hire a hitman."

The whole room paused a little to allow the words to land softly on us. Peals of laughter suddenly transformed the fracas, and we were all able to trade in the exhaustion finding fault for the Geiger counter locating goodness. Even Cyca and Lola couldn't resist.

I guess I met Joker in a probation camp. Hard to retrieve the memory of our first encounter. He's tried a few times to begin our program, but has difficulty being in the vicinity of other human beings. He also "blazes it" constantly to calm himself down, so it's hard for him to test clean for us. He's more than a "daily communicant" with me. He texts me at least four times a day. He often shoots me pics of meals he has prepared for himself and shots of his arm donating blood. I always call him my son and try to inch him one step closer to seeing himself as God does. One just keeps hoping against hope that he will find love as his true identity and deepest dignity. There are always glimpses of the movement from isolation to relationship and I watch as Joker's fears get transformed. "I'm fond of you," he texts me once, from left field. I write back: "Well . . . I'm fond of you, too—and I'm grateful to God that you're in my life." His response is immediate: "The feeling's neutral." I'll take it.

There is the greeting "Namaste," which means: "I greet the Holy One in you." I acknowledge the fullness of God and the solid goodness at your core.

My grandmother had two peculiar pronunciations in her repertoire. She pronounced "spaghetti" like "sperghetti" and the word "beautiful" came out as "beauty-full." As in, "the sperghetti was beauty-full." We see the Holy One, we "train for innocence," we look for the sheer, utter goodness in the other and deem it "beauty-full." In this, we find the unbearable beauty of our own life. It's there and we can actually choose it.

Even if we talk about "evil" as eclipsing our human nature, we feel the ham-handedness of this. Isn't it more sophisticated to say our blindness, or our mental disorder, or our wound or pain or injury or PCP use, is what eclipses our human essence? Why is it necessary to call in the "Boogie Man" (evil) as the thing that prevents us from seeing our thorough goodness? We could say that when we are exiled from our very selves, a sadness envelops us. Satan need not be called in to help explain. This just in: God does not have an evil twin!

We can, I suppose, set off on some journey to renounce and eliminate those things that divide our hearts. I guess. Or we could just give ourselves to relatedness and the search for goodness in ourselves and others. We can break loose from the cocoon of our habitual habits—the ones that have a sneaky ability to rob us of our palpable experience of God and our own exquisite truth. What my friend Pema Chödrön calls, "propensities." Identifying these inclinations is more of a movement toward health than a fleeing of sin. If who we are is love, then we just transmit love. Love, then, is all we teach, communicate, and put out in the world.

Even in the Advent readings with John the Baptist and "Prepare the way . . . make straight the path," we think this is about cleaning up our act and slapping ourselves into doing the right thing (for once). But what really wants to happen is this: God will show you your splendor. Clear the path for that.

Nicky showed up for work wearing this wild and brightly colored pajama top. I flagged him into my office. "Hey, dawg—you do know that's a pajama top?"

No beat is missed. "No, it ain't—it's a the-cops-won't-mess-with-me-if-I'm-wearing-it shirt." God and splendor shaking hands.

We will consult either fear or love (since fear is love's opposite). Then there remains no justification for our fear, ever. Thich Nhat Hanh doesn't speak of "original sin" but "original fear" or even "original wound"—that begins when we enter the world gasping for air. That is closer than sin. Thomas, the doubting one, is out in the world and he is loving who he finds there. All the other disciples are trembling behind locked doors. Then love makes fear illusory and our outpouring is other-centered and rich in joy. Our decision is firm: to search for innocence in the other.

There was a nomadic tribe of aborigines in Australia, being observed by anthropologists. They were traveling in the desert and would stop for no apparent reason—not to get food or water or to pee. Finally, they were asked, "Why?"

"We stop to let our souls catch up with us." When we consult love instead of fear, our innocence and goodness catch up with us. Take a moment—hear the souls clapping. It fills us with our truth. Then, God wants us to continue walking.

My great-great grandfather founded a dairy in Los Angeles in 1913 and called it Western Farms. It lasted over a hundred years until it finally closed shop. My grandfather, all my uncles, my dad, and every male Boyle worked there. It was, of course, thoroughly sexist in that none of my sisters (nor any other Boyle female) worked there. I loaded milk trucks every Saturday and every summer and completely paid for my own tuition at Loyola High School. My father was the vice president of the company, which mainly distributed milk to all the Catholic schools. He used to say, "All I have, I owe to udders." He repeated this groaner on *Family Feud* along with saying he had eight kids: "three hits and five misses." As you can imagine, my sisters loved that one.

Every late afternoon, before he came home, he'd call my mother to get a read on how stocked we were with milk and eggs and butter and such. He brought home every imaginable dairy product. Invariably, my mom would tell him, "We need eight cartons of milk." My exasperated father would always say, "Don't tell me what we need—tell me what we have." It was his surefire way to assess what to bring home. Not about deficits or what we lack, but always what we have in abundance. It's always more illuminating to see what you have rather than lament your need. There is an abundance of goodness and innocence—focus on that.

Something liberating happens when modifying our behavior ceases to be our first priority. Mystical love accepts with peace and isn't on the hunt for things to criticize. The Geiger counter of our heat-seeking love has no interest in "weakness and short-comings" (or what we need), only light and strength. It is our practice at Homeboy to do this and see in this way.

Since God persists in love, no matter how dark things get, God is not preoccupied nor enfeebled by our "sin." This is true because God doesn't see sin but wholeness. God sees right through it. A homie texted me, sending a YouTube homily by a bishop who spoke of sin and the need for a "contrite heart." This gave the homie a passageway to deem himself, really, "a worthless piece of shit." I texted back only this: "God doesn't see sin. God sees son." The relief in his next text was palpable. His notion of sin was self-estranging. He wanted to accept that he was "son" but didn't know how to dare to believe it.

Erich Fromm says we have two main fears: losing control and becoming isolated. During World War C (the COVID-19 pandemic) while we were all staying at home, these fears got activated. But the homegirl Carizma texted me during our house arrest: "Yeah . . . love is stronger than any virus." Everyone asked themselves: "Is that true?" How quickly the answer came: "Yes. Of course it is." So, we set out on the task articulated by Teresa of Ávila: "I have stepped from that region of me that did not love all the time." The antidote to our fears is to live in the "region" of that singular focus.

-◇|◇-

I took Manuel and Todd to Chicago with me to give a handful of talks. Both trainees in the sixth month of their eighteen-month program with us, combined they had spent more than half a century in prison.

It wasn't until I experienced their stony silence in the car, on the way to the airport, that I realized these two were gang rivals. Fresh out of prison, the racial divide was also pronounced. I braced myself for a very long five-day trip.

As we stood in line to board the plane, Manuel seemed to have lost the knob on his volume control. He asked me, "CAN I USE AIRPLANE MODE?"

I modeled a lower setting and told him in a near whisper, "You're okay right now, but once we're on the plane and the doors close, you have to shift to airplane mode."

Then to a total stranger, a woman behind him, he said with large enthusiasm, "I'VE NEVER USED AIRPLANE MODE BEFORE!"

The woman looked startled. "Oh . . . okay."

Later, I reflected that Manuel was inviting this woman and me "to the infinite moment where everything happens." He was anchored in the luminous now. And we were just occupied with propriety and volume control.

We all gave many talks, including one in a packed church that had a musical prelude to the event. Manuel leaned into me, finding yet another infinite moment to delight in, and said, "I've never heard a live choir before." All of their presentations were hugely moving, and on our final afternoon in Chicago, I gave them each cash to bring back gifts to their womenfolk and kids. They went to Navy Pier. The following morning, while we were awaiting our ride to the airport, they both produced from their packed duffel bags teddy bears made to order from the Build-A-Bear Workshop store on Navy Pier. They'd taped their own voices into the bears, activated by pressing a paw. Manuel's bear said this: "I love ya with all my heart, baby. Come here, give me a kiss." Manuel was loud and bouncing in the hotel lobby. "Do ya think my lady will like it?"

"Oh, hell yeah," I told him.

Predictably, as their bags went through the TSA machine, we'd hear, "I love ya with all my heart, baby." And as Manuel forced and squeezed the bag into the overhead compartment: "Come here, give me a kiss." These two, separated by race and rivalry, found some particular song in our dissolving laughter.

We drove home from LAX and Manuel, in the backseat, leaned forward. "Hey, G, you know what the best part of this trip was?" Then he grabbed Todd's arm, who was in the front passenger seat. "Getting to know him." I turned and watched Todd smile and nod. My friend Sister Peg Dolan used to say, "Each of us is a word of God spoken only once." God spoke loud and clear during those days together.

Some weeks later, Manuel stepped into my office and announced that his father had just died. He had been deported many years before and Manuel had not spoken to him in over twenty years. Until, that is, five days ago, after someone alerted Manuel that his father was dying of cancer.

Manuel and his twin brother, when they were nine years old, made a pact. "When our dad comes home from work tonight, and he's drunk and starts to beat on our mom . . . let's . . . defend her." They shook on it.

The twins' father came home, predictably drunk, and began to whale on the mom. The twins flew into action, leaping on the back of their dad like a couple of marsupials. They toppled their stunned father to the floor, until he became enraged and flung the boys off him. Then he grabbed them by the backs of their shirts, opened the front door, and dragged them to the street, where he tossed them. He told them they were both dead to him now. They were never to enter this house again. And so, they didn't.

They ended up living in a park down the block. "Every night, we'd pull a garbage bag out of the trash can, then tip the can over, and the two of us . . . would slide in . . . and sleep in each other's arms. Every night." They got jumped into the local neighborhood gang, locked arms with other orphans, and sold drugs to survive. Manuel's twin is still in prison, and Manuel himself was released after twenty-four years.

"So, someone told me my dad was dying and I got his number. I needed to call him . . . to forgive him." Manuel's eyes moistened in the telling of this. "Yeah . . . I just didn't want to carry this around anymore," he said, patting his heart and composing himself. He paused, then shifted gears. "You know something, G . . . in my six months here at Homeboy . . . I'm enjoying the man I've become . . . like I've never enjoyed anything before."

"Enjoy" is an odd word. It's a right-this-second word. It's a word soaked in abundance and the resurrection . . . and the infinite moment. It's saturated in one's own unshakable goodness. Mystics enjoy God's longing to fill us. We then enjoy what we've become: filled. Like ancient Israel, in the exodus from Egypt, we stop morning and evening. Our souls catch up. We are fed by supernatural food. We are delivered by manna from the sky. We see ourselves and each other and find the goodness there. Our souls spoken only once.

Chapter Three

The Thorn Underneath

We have long been saddled with the notion that mysticism is some otherworldly escape, above and beyond this earthly existence. But it's not "escapism," it's "dive-right-in-ism." The binary mind is just unable to see wholeness. It might see an individual's unique gift that we each possess, but that will always be secondary to "wholeness." The great equalizer is that we all share this one gift: our true selves in loving. Therein lies our wholeness.

Saint Ignatius always encouraged folks to trust their own experience. Mystics are joined to their experience in a nondual consciousness. Their experience is both/and, not either/or. My friend Jack Lipscomb, when he was a child, would be asked if he wanted chocolate ice cream or vanilla. He'd say "both of each." Mystics are "both of each" people. In Ignatius's autobiography he says that even if the Church and Scripture said otherwise, he'd still believe his experience. He believed what happened to him.

I was invited to preach and preside at a parish in a beach town in Southern California. After mass, I'm shaking everybody's hands, as one does, and a young guy stops to greet me and says his name is Jerry. He says he's been to Homeboy before. He points to his arm and I don't really understand. "This is where my tattoos aren't," he says. "And that's because you guys removed them completely." The homie hands me his card. He's an "import analyst." Now, I don't even know what that is. I tell him that he just made my whole day. He counters with, "Homeboy Industries made my whole life." Maybe it's more true to say it helped make his life whole. And he believes what happened to him.

In our Jesuit tradition, Homeboy Industries has always found resonance with the House of Saint Martha, founded by Ignatius in the 1530s as a refuge for prostitutes who were trying to reform their lives. Like that population, our folks are frozen in survival brain and need to settle into a more integrated brain that leads to belonging. The demonized, marginal folks all know what it's like to have been raised where attachment didn't happen and basic needs weren't met. We don't aim to ready folks to survive as the fittest, but to thrive as the nurtured. To be nurtured is to be reverent for what is happening to you. This softens how we see things and leads to active cherishing. A job is good, but healing is forever. Joseph said on his first day with us, "I know how to work, but I don't know how to live. And this is the first time . . . I've ever tried trying." To try trying is a by-product of nurturing. When he was in middle school, his friends would call him over to a car with steamy windows and laugh. He'd stare into the car, then wheel away at the sight of his drug-addict mother "servicing" a homeless man. His friends toppling over each other, howling. He said to me once, "Everything around me is dark—even when the sun is shining. And it hurts all the time." Being nurtured and thriving took some time.

Moses saw God "face to face." It is how we are meant to see God and each other. "Face" in Hebrew symbolized the entire person. The winner of our 5K T-shirt slogan contest was Angel. "Homeboy Gives Us a Face and a Place." It got the most votes.

Angel explained, "Face means we are all human beings." A mystic sees the whole person and speaks the whole language. It is the "piety of the open eye."

Judgment, however, keeps us stuck in the partial view. All of us get up in the morning, place our feet on the floor, and hit the ground . . . judging. We can't help ourselves, though we can catch ourselves. Consequently, at Homeboy Industries, mysticism is our "core competency." The therapeutic mysticism at Homeboy chooses love as the architecture of our hearts. The world will focus on outcomes or behavior or success. Mysticism glances just above what the world has in its sights. It puts judgment on check. It develops a warmth for everything that comes its way and rests in the center of it. When we are whole, that's what we see in others. We choose to live in our hearts. Homie Stevie Avalos says, "We see the homie's heart until they can see their own. Then they leave here, and they see other hearts." Mysticism, then, sees connectedness.

It is the absence of relationship that leads to isolation. In fact, relationship building IS crime prevention. You can tell when a potentially provocative gang member walks in—there's a look and body language. From my office, I always wait and make eye contact with the guy. It always softens and works. Even if I don't know the *vato*, it establishes a connection even before we've exchanged a word.

José Arellano and Steve Avalos oversee the Case Managers and Navigators. Their business cards say they are in charge of "Culture and Community." Often, in nonprofits, we dedicate ourselves to a certain amount of strategizing on our processes and structure. All very necessary. But strategy, process, and structure must be at the service of culture and community, not the other way around. Because culture is about holiness and wholeness. Culture eats strategy for breakfast; processes for lunch; and structures for dinner.

We can rest in being reactive and relatively adept at responding to situations that arise. We can sit around and wait for the need that comes up, the trainee who seeks us out, the crises that present themselves. But rather than settle into reactive dexterity, we want to always be attuned to being proactively relational. We need to walk the halls and floors of HBI and not just wait for the alarms to go off.

In the probation camps where I say mass, the staff sits in the back of the gym and can only see the backs of heads. Invariably, as the presider at mass, I see the gathering storm. I catch the kid mad-dogging the *vato* across the aisle. I notice the throwing of gang signs. I see that guy mouthing sweet nothings about his enemy's mom. And the staff in the back misses it all. Like clockwork, things jump off, fights break out, and the staff "responds" to the pandemonium. Many times, I've asked the staff, "Why do you sit in the back?" I'm always told, "So we can respond when something jumps off." I always gently suggest, "Of course, if you sat in the front, nothing would jump off." The eye contact alone is the hope of relational wholeness. Staff "watch" them from the back of the room, but "see" them up front.

A little homie walked down the aisle of the San Fernando Valley Juvenile Hall chapel, hoisting high the red gospel book, with all the pious seriousness he could muster. Then he bowed with reverence, placed the book on the altar, bowed again, and returned down the aisle. But before he passed the front pew, he seriously bombed on a guy sitting there. The whole moment was calmed this side of pepper spray. Yet, it's clear that the more proactively relational we are, the less likely that things explode.

As the homies filed out of mass at San Fernando Valley Juvenile Hall, an especially tough kid scowled at me and asked me for my "credit card." I handed him my "business card" and his scowl intensified. "There's nothing on this!" I reached over and turned the card around, revealing all my vital information.

"Oh," he said. Seeing is hard when you've been disconnected and there is a severed belonging. In fact, our eighteen-month training program mirrors the eighteen months it takes for an infant to attach to the caregiver. It is not a time period calculated to capture how long it takes to locate another job or get a GED. Healing takes a lifetime but surrender to this moment can carry you. And headway gets made and attachment repaired so that people can finally see.

Jesus asks the blind guy, "What do you want me to do for you?" As audience members, we're yelling at Jesus (in our heads), "HELLO??? He's blind." But Jesus won't give us sight unless we say, "I want to see." Any number of "blind" homies walk into our place, bumping into each other, and sight comes when they request it. It's what surrender looks like. I asked a homie once, "Why should I hire you?" He responded immediately. "I need a family—cuz I ain't got one." I suppose it's how a homie asks to see. He would later say: "This place gave me some eyes."

As mentioned previously, we call forth the unshakable goodness that is already there. This culture of mystical tenderness holds every soul in high regard. This palpable cherishing revives folks in love, trust, and patience. There is a theory that a newborn baby stares into their mother's face as a sort of mirror, which helps them form a self. It is precisely this "mirror" tenderness at Homeboy that makes homies feel less far away. A homie with me at a restaurant says with glee, "I am at a restaurant and I feel important—I may order a salad and a beverage." A soul in high regard. Above all, homies wake up, not shape up. Homies come to us with a severed belonging and feel cut off from their very aliveness. Wholeness is not the arrival at good behavior. Though it might contain it, high performance is not the goal, but rather, a surrender to healing is. Then everyone finds this gentle road and practices, with each other, the pathway home.

To get into our eighteen-month program, you take a drug test and if you are clean (though, frankly, we have wriggle room), you are approved for the three-person "selection committee." Then the decision is presented to the council and once they all approve, a candidate awaits the "start date." All depends on the ebb and flow of our "head count" and how much money we have. More often than not, homies will come to me to get a start date.

Moises comes in and this is the first time I'm meeting him. A lone tattoo straddles his neck and he's like a fullback; he doesn't have much of a neck to begin with. "They told me to check with you about a start date." I can't tell the tonal temperature of his statement. I ask a few questions and tell him I'll check with the council about bringing him in. "So, you're a father," he says, then half turns in his chair to point at everyone in the packed reception area, "and these are your children." Before I formulate whatever I am to say next, he cuts me off. "Now I will tell you why I came into your office." He looks to the floor, and I wait for him. "Can . . . I . . . be your son?" His stocky body leans forward and he grips his face with his hands. I sense the crying may take some time.

But before too long, I, too, lean forward, and whisper, "Imagine what a gift it would be, to have a son like you."

The crying accelerates and I let him be. Finally, he looks at me, and I hand him several Kleenex. "The one thing. The one thing," he says, "THAT . . . is the one thing . . . I only . . . ever . . . wanted to hear from my own father." I give him a start date. No better place to begin than here. When you enter the program, a homie told me once, "You need to bring your pain with you." It is often true that the pain a homie has caused hasn't been able to keep pace with the pain he feels. And people who know suffering are trustworthy.

Jesuit theologian Karl Rahner said, "The Christian of the

future will either be a mystic . . . or he will cease to be anything at all." He's not suggesting that "we see visions" but that we be "visionary." We are asked to see as God sees and this changes all we view. We see wholeness, and it helps all of us rewire, not just the traumatized. The mystic's quest is to be on the lookout for the hidden wholeness in everyone. Then we can remind each other that we are made for loving, and that the true measure of our love . . . is to love without measure.

Homies who know me will tell you the one thing that pushes my button is if you walk away. Stay in the fight. Roll up your sleeves. Don't walk out on the discussion. A young, certifiably knucklehead homie named Humberto comes at me "sideways." This part I don't mind. I'm trying to underline some issue that came up in his interaction with his co-workers. But then he storms out. Button pushed. I storm right behind him and now we're on the street. I did my "Get your ass back in here" and, well, yes, I'm madder'n hell. "Don't walk out on me."

Humberto, seventeen years old, turns and stops fleeing. He's sobbing. "My dad's a drunk and beats my mom and I don't want . . . to go back home." There you have it. Part of our longing to be "visionary" is to truly see and not get tripped up by "sideways" behavior. It's speaking a language. It is a particular dialect to which we need to be attuned.

Homies can, indeed, initially speak a rarefied dialect. I remember it acutely from my stint as chaplain at Folsom State Prison, and certainly in my decades at Homeboy. Manipulation is the peculiar dialect, the base language of survival and stress. They aren't exactly trying to pull a fast one—they are just going through a hard one. You brace for it and don't allow it to topple you. You accustom your ear to it and recognize it always as the local dialect of those cut off.

I ask Gus why he missed work the day before. "I was having technical difficulties at my house." (Say what now?) Then he tries to make a turn to extract money from me. "I'm in my last critical stages." Still, I try to press him on his many absences. "I want to verify you of the actual situation." I question his drinking. "I drink for a reason. I have probable cause."

I ask, "Are you also getting high?"

"None of the above," he says. Dialect spoken here.

Rigo comes in for work, sporting the largest of hickies. We have a hickey policy, inasmuch as you're not supposed to have them. You can be sent home for this violation. *"Tiene mal aspeto,"* it doesn't look right, and besides, I always tell them, it just means your lady doesn't trust your ass.

So, I ask Rigo: "Is that a hickey?" "Oh . . . no . . . ," he says, "it's a black eye."

"Even though," I tell him, "it's not near your eye and it's on your neck."

"Yup," he says, "a black eye."

Pulling a fast one is only a shallow reading and hasn't gone deep enough.

In the old days, when I'd give a talk somewhere, I'd have homies sell our merchandise at a table in the lobby. Sammy and Alex accompanied me to a talk at the Bel-Air Country Club. I tell them it's kind of a fancy place, "so, everyone on best behavior. You know what that means?"

Sammy says sheepishly, "Good posture?" The two were pulling the large duffel bags out of the van. "Give me that bag, dick," Sammy directs to Alex.

I feel like I need to intervene. "Can't you talk nicely to each other?"

Sam straightens and modulates his voice some. "Excuse me. Would you be so kind as to hand me that bag . . . dick." In the car before arriving, I ask the two of them how they will peddle the goods to their customers. Sammy says, "You touch—you buy."

Alex pipes in, "Hey, you gonna buy somethin' or what?"

"Yeah," I tell them, "we may need to work on your sales pitch." Though I suspect they were yanking my chain, severed belonging comes in as many shapes and sizes as wholeness does. Both of each.

Mireya's tattoos were alarming and she was barely sixteen. Her face had such an arrangement of ink that it was hard to decipher. So, I asked her about it. "When I was more younger . . . my older brother would practice on me." I let this settle in.

A famous director on Broadway would tell his actors: "If you forget your lines . . . if you get lost . . . drown in the other's eyes." I was glad to have forgotten my lines and lost my place. All I wanted to do was drown in Mireya's eyes.

At a fathers' group I ran at Folsom prison, the gathered were speaking about how they managed to get their kids to "behave." One inmate, I think a bit irritated at all the back-and-forth, said this: "I go get my gun. I hold the gun to my kid's head. And I say: 'Behave.' Trust me—he behaves." No one spoke for what felt like a very long time.

My favorite moment in the Tom Hanks movie about Mister Rogers happens when the journalist, the main character, is watching from a distance as Mister Rogers greets fans in a rope line. The journalist turns to the woman standing next to him and introduces himself. He discovers that she is Mrs. Rogers. "So," he asks, "how does it feel to be married to a living saint?"

Mrs. Rogers winces. "Yeah, I don't much like that word. It suggests that his way of being," pointing to her husband, "is unattainable. He's not a perfect person. He gets angry. He's learned how to deal with it." She now looks at the journalist. "He works at it. It's a practice." The gentle road home. You don't chase happiness, you cultivate tranquility. Turns out no emotion is final if you dedicate yourself to this practice. Mister Rogers could, as they say, allow himself to be carried by the river of feelings, because he knew how to swim. He practiced at it.

Researchers will say, for example, that mentorship helps teens overcome trauma. But they will take the wrong message from their own findings. The presumption will be that it is the "content" delivered by mentors that is so compelling. Truth be told, it's the context that matters. Youth, as they say, rarely remember what they've been told, but mainly recall how they were made to feel. "Make better choices" is the battle cry of the "content driven" and they principally hope to insert this message into the ears of struggling young people. It's not about message, and it's not even about the messenger. It's about a nurturing culture and context that allows everyone to move into their own dignity and nobility. We can work at this and make it our practice. We can help each other to locate the warm sunlight so that folks can bathe in it.

I ask Gato, released from prison after two years, if he knows how to drive. "Of course. OPC." I didn't know this one. "Other People's Cars. G-rides." Now he cruises down memory lane. "I remember it like it was yesterday. I was fifteen. My first high-speed chase. It was a yellow Astro van. We were on the freeway. I was going eighty." He gets to the warm sunlight eventually. He is nurtured into a new way of seeing. "Now I drive like I have a license. Windows are down so the cops can see the kids. No loud music." Progress.

Honestly, human beings insist that it HAS to be about good choices and bad choices. We want to feel superior about the good choices we've made and point out the bad choices others make. An extremely well-intentioned woman, a volunteer at a prison, was asked by an inmate: "Do you think we are evil?"

She answered: "No. We are all the same. I just made a different choice." Ouch. We were so close there. We tend to think that things are mainly about choice, when they're really about chance. And, of course, not all choices are created equal. It is so difficult for us to see layers and angles that we just can't catch

with our either/or minds. Both of each. We need a mystical knowing and consciousness that God offers to us always.

I call Bandit and I can hear his lady yell for him. He was on the crew of homies who helped build our child-care center in the earliest days of Homeboy. In the background, the *Jeopardy!* jingle floats in the air. He arrives at the phone. "Wow," I say to him, "*Jeopardy!* I'm impressed."

He wants, even more, to land the mount. "What is a brontosaurus? What is a hermaphrodite?" I laugh. "You can learn some shit on this show," he says. Then he leads me to a philosophical insight. "I discovered something—your brain—you can do a lot with it. You can decide which way your day will go." He proceeds to tell me that one can choose to be positive and decide to have a great day. "Now," he says, "if opportunity doesn't knock, I'm gonna build me a damn door."

It was not always smooth sailing with Bandit. People in recovery will tell you that they've been to many rehabs and it never "took." But, of course, it takes what it takes and it never works unless you work it. Bandit was summarily fired from Homeboy Silkscreen for telling Ruben, the guy in charge, "Well, fuck you, then." When I asked him later about it, he said, "Well, he forced me to say it."

I sit him down. "Look, you're the boss of you. Ruben didn't force you to say anything."

Bandit thinks for a beat. "Yeah, well, he had a great influence."

The outsider's view on gang prevention and intervention is to offer content. The thinking goes like this: If only these folks knew more, were trained more, had better character, had classes in values, and the like. The outsider's belief system rests in information. What's different at Homeboy is that content and information are always secondary to context and transformation. Our cultural context is the accepting community of tenderness that receives them. This is primary. Content is offered once this is established. Transformation happens where this is afforded.

-◇|◇-

It was not in Jesus' DNA to be violent, to punish, or to exclude anybody. But even with our unshakable goodness, there remain traces of this in our DNA. The gospel challenge, then, is to alter our DNA. We now know about neuroplasticity and have found new capacities to change neurons—and to heal the brain. Neuroplasticity says it's all possible and workable. Richard was told that he was not accepted into our eighteen-month training program. He was in his early thirties and had established himself as somewhat belligerent and erratic. Generally speaking, these are the folks we want. But his girlfriend worked with us (a complication), and he was still struggling with a pretty virulent meth addiction, and so was given a "no." He stormed out.

The next day, Fabian, a wisdom figure on our team and former gang member and recovered drug addict himself, resurrected Richard's cause. He convinced the council that Homeboy exists for the likes of Richard and so the council relented, and Fabian called him.

"We've reconsidered, dawg, and we want you to start tomorrow. We will be drug testing constantly." When Fabian finished, Richard told him with all kinds of surly laced in his voice, "Fuck you. You can take this job and shove it up your ass." Richard abruptly hung up.

Recounting the story some months later, Richard said he then stood at the phone he'd just hung up and stared at it. *Please call back. Please call back.* Tears cascaded down his face.

When I questioned Fabian about HIS version of the story, he told me that he walked around the block twice, to gather his shaken self, and then indeed . . . he called back. Richard answered on the first ring.

Richard found his footing at Homeboy. Once, a Navigator, Robert, trying to calm Richard down after one of his fleeting outbursts, asked him, "Have you ever thought that maybe you don't love yourself?"

When Richard told me of this exchange later, he said, "Damn, G. That question got me to open the hurt locker. I realized I didn't know what love WAS. So, I went home and googled it. I found all these other foreign words, like affection . . . kinship . . . tenderness." If we listen carefully enough, that's the sound of DNA being altered. It happens when a person finds the thing that afflicts them so that they will no longer be stuck there. As homies feel their hearts and minds closing, it is the cherishing community that asks them to stay with the raw material (the hurt locker), so they can remain curious about it and bravely touch it.

◦◦◦

We get many thousands of visitors a year. Tours are part of the daily experience at Homeboy. A couple from somewhere in the Midwest had Homeboy Industries on their bucket list. The wife couldn't speak after spending several hours taking in the morning meeting, getting a tour, and talking to folks. It took her a bit to compose herself and say to me: "This . . . is the Sistine Chapel." We all knew what she meant. There is something of a sacred shrine to the place, where homies find a power that says no dark fate determines your future. You can sit in any chair in the house and be captured by a noble spirit and you watch folks embark on a journey to fullness, a broad-shouldered resilience and wellspring of joy. Michelangelo could not have painted it better.

Homeboy Industries has no interest in punishing misbehaving trainees, only in encouraging their liberation from sadness. It's not about pointing out their "bad choices." To be sure, this

liberation requires their cooperation. In any case, WE don't lib-
erate them. We can only create a place of liberation. The locale
where the bodhi heart is awakened. It is an open heart, no longer closed in sadness. A culture of tenderness that fosters long-
term, redemptive relationships will alter the larger culture and
its structures.

I hadn't woven together the whole of Louie's journey thus
far, except for one piece of understatement: "I lived with my *jefito* in Mexico for a while, but then, we got in a fight. Well . . . I
burned down his house." He shrugs. "I messed up." Soon he is
crying, lost in the sea of it.

"What do you want, *mijo*?" I ask him.

After a brief wait, Louie finds the words, "I just want, one
day, to look forward to . . . looking forward to something." Principally, we want to create an environment that transforms fear.
Then the future can happen.

Be not crushed, the prophet Jeremiah told us. I suppose, easy
for him to say. Chuy, when he can retrieve memories at all, con-
jures up repeated beatings with the plug end of an extension cord
delivered by his mom to him and his older brother. "This lady
made that dude Chemical Ali look like a damn saint." Harder
to call to mind are the countless times he was taken from school
by his mother for a doctor's appointment or some other invented
excuse. Then he would be delivered to a strange motel room
and a strange man would hand cash to Chuy's mom. She would
return in an hour, after the man had done anything he wished
to with this boy. "I've survived things people don't survive. If my
mom raised me right"—Chuy's crying has now turned to gasps
of sobbing—"I'd be a fuckin' doctor by now." Chuy would act
out wildly during his time with us, challenging us all to find a
larger embrace to hold him. With tenderness as our nurturing
stance, Chuy could, eventually, build up great reserves of con-
tainment, and an ability to self-regulate. Homies have to start

where they are, not where we'd like them to be. Somehow, Chuy was able to forge a new path of meaning, finally able to choose connection over alienation.

As a society, we are often self-congratulatory when we address some issue "head-on." But it's never about "head-on"—it's always about underneath. It's about something else. What's underneath and behind Louie's and Chuy's sadness? Most valuable of all is their vulnerability. This is the Velcro of attachment. It is how we adhere and connect to each other. Homies work with the "Inner" and it transforms the "Outer." Speaking of this inner work, a homie said to me: "If you don't work on something, it will return and it will be humbilizing." And let me just say that being in the presence of gang members going on forty years has been deeply "humbilizing," and I mean that in the truest sense of that word that doesn't exist.

After my speech at our gala fundraiser, Lo Maximo, I bump into Pedro, one of our trainees. We're heading to the parking lot, riding the escalator. "You made me cry, your speech," he tells me. "And I embarrassed myself. There I am at this table—with all these homies—cryin' like a bitch. And I'm afraid one of these *vatos* will turn to me and ask, 'What kind of cholo cries?' and I'm gonna hafta say . . . A transformed one.'" Velcro. We all want to become transformed people—not just folks with answers.

A tease on a CNN report said, "Coming up, one man is taking on hate." I thought during the commercial break, *Well, how do you do that?* "Head-on," I suppose. Of course, if it's about "hate," then you argue with it and hope to win someone over. "Don't you see? Don't you see?" "Love, instead of hate." But it's never about hate—it's always about hurt. So now what? You create the place where healing can happen. A homie, Robert Juarez, says, "God knows how to look underneath, to find where the thorn is."

Driving to work, I see a billboard: "Racism Is a Public Health

Issue." These words are written above, and I think, *Yes, true*. But written underneath is: "Stand Against Hate." They were so close to getting this right. It's not about "Hate," it's about "Health." A university, after the tragic shooting in Pittsburgh's Tree of Life synagogue, started a seminar called "Hate." But surely we'd make more progress if it was named "Health." If you talk about health instead of hate, there is no severed belonging. If you say "Terrible" instead of "Evil," there is no severed belonging. Not "Erase the Hate," but "Increase the Health."

I was invited to the FBI Academy, a training center in Quantico, Virginia, to help train members of Latin American Chiefs of Police and other officers about the gang mentality. The first day featured lots of FBI folks who were touting, I suppose, their expertise to this group. As you might imagine, they painted quite the alarming picture. We received a tour of Quantico, and at the end of one hallway was a huge wall dedicated to the FBI's Top Ten Most Wanted Fugitives. Number one was Osama bin Laden. I suppose I didn't make any points with my small group when I signaled that number two was a homie I had known since he was ten years old.

I was slated to be the last speaker of our three days together. After hearing endless presentations of diagnoses that were so far off and demonizing, so outsize, I chucked my talk and just addressed almost all the misinformation that had preceded. I had taken pages of notes for two days. There I was, the proverbial turd in the punchbowl, but I felt I needed to put some human face on the gang member and try to present the thorn underneath. I braced myself for blowback from the FBI agents who had been with us these days. Yet, one came up to me as we were all leaving and thanked me. "We don't really know this stuff," he conceded.

I was signing books after a talk I gave in a church in Florida. A man approached me and said he had read both *Tattoos* and *Barking*. "I notice you never mention forgiveness in your books."

I thought for a second and found myself saying, "You know, you're right. I never thought about that before." I paused and said, "I think we settle for just forgiveness, when we're being offered mercy. I think mercy is more spacious. Let's embrace mercy." In this way, as my friend Jack Kornfield says, we "set the compass of our heart."

Many can recall when some family members of those gunned down in Mother Emmanuel Church in 2015 appeared at Dylan Roof's bond hearing. They stood before the man accused of killing their loved ones and forgave him. Some applauded them for doing this. Others derided them for extending an act of kindness and glossing over a culture of racism that daily endangers Black Americans. Some would claim forgiveness as a requirement of faith and an act of closure; others said it perpetuated an expectation leveled at the Black community who had endured racism since the seventeenth century.

But no one chooses mental illness. The torment is too great. It chooses members of our community, all of whom belong to us. A court-appointed physician deemed Dylan Roof fit for trial, and he was sentenced to death. It in no way turns a blind eye to a horrific act to say that I don't need to consult a doctor to know that Dylan Roof was not healthy. No one mentally well does what he did. I said this once in a ballroom of psychiatrists and they expressed their horror, suggesting that the mere mention of this view would stigmatize the mentally ill. I wasn't sure what the alternative was, except to not talk about it. That didn't seem whole. I suppose you could talk about racism, but it doesn't get you very far. Systemic racism, yes. But racism was how Dylan Roof's mental illness presented. It was a big, gaping wound that he never chose. How do you punish a wound, or even forgive it? Our designations are stumbling blocks. Good people. Bad people. Blame people. But whole people don't go to prison. Nor do they gun people down. Nor do they carry tiki

torches in Charlottesville, chanting, "Jews will not replace us."
Nor do whole people demonize anyone, ever. Wholeness and
health are worth our aspiration.

The father in the gospel runs to his son while he is "still
a long way off." Find me, anywhere in that story, where the
father forgives his son. He doesn't. He doesn't settle for forgiveness; he rushes to mercy. He just says, "You're here!" The
father has the mystical view—he sees the trauma, the wound,
the pain, the PCP addiction, the mental illness in his kid, and
he saw all the things that led his son to take off in the first
place. The father's hope (and our invitation at Homeboy) is
that this son will touch the center of his pain, go through it, not
avoid it, and come out the other side.

Mercy is better because it is always reverent of complexity.
Forgiveness is the step toward mercy. "Mercy," Pope Francis says,
". . . that's the name of God." It sees the whole person always
and is never derailed by the egregious act. This is how God sees
Dylan Roof. And yes, the guy was right—I don't write about forgiveness.

When we embrace relational wholeness at HBI, our divisions tremble. When we all aspire to be on the lookout for the
secret beauty in each other, separation is a folly. My friend, the
late Senator Paul Wellstone, used to say, "We all do better, when
we all do better." Same thing. Then the goal is not holiness, but
more like the Buddhist notion to engage in the wholesome. Not
Little House on the Prairie wholesome, but a profound sense that
our being whole is indeed beauty-full and God's hope for us.

Listening to and receiving people is wholesome. Yet we
think that our listening needs to produce a result. But the listening is the result. I met a man who volunteered in prisons and
brought the Kairos retreat program inside. They seemed to have
a mantra that kept the volunteers centered where they needed
to be: "Listen, listen . . . Love, love." If we receive love, we are

all brought to a place of mutual vulnerability. Suddenly, there is room for everybody. Even for number two on the FBI's most wanted list.

Recently, a homie emailed me: "You were in my dream last night. Someone was sitting and talking with you, and you were listening. I don't know who it was, though, but I've never seen you more calm and focused." How I wish this dream would become a reality for me. Listening IS the result. Room for everybody.

We sent Tavo up to UC Berkeley to jostle his imagination and coax him some to consider further education. He was in a large group and the only representative of Homeboy up there. "This lady told me," he said upon his return, "that I was an ambassador for Homeboy Industries." His posture corrects itself, and he stands tall. "Damn, G. It sounded proper—and I don't even know what an ambassador is."

There is this "hermeneutical shift" at Homeboy where we are changed by what we are focused on. We focus on therapeutic mysticism and it transforms us. You can't help but become an ambassador. The mystical itinerary that we wish to follow leads us to humility, in the best sense, and then to a greater relinquishment and surrender, and finally, we no longer live "God-fearing lives" but rather "God-seeing lives." We see as God does. This is the mystical trek. It's written in *The Cloud of Unknowing* that "the humble feeling never lies to you." It's not the heat. . . . it's the humility. Not so much "seeing God" but seeing as God does. Humbilizing.

In my daily communication with my spiritual director, Sergio, he comments in an email about a video that went viral about a sixteen-year boy who threw a cat as hard and as far as he could against a wall. Flinging the cat broke its leg. The internet exploded with a unanimous chorus of "Off with his head." Sergio is sober and clear. "When ya think about it . . . we're all just one mistake away . . . from tossing a cat." People would rarely guess that this is the sound of mystical compassion.

You have to heal before you can have hope and be utterly convinced that happiness is an inside job—aligned with God's own heart and tender aspiration. David came home from East Los Angeles College and couldn't wait to tell his aunt the good news: "I made the Dean's List." His aunt, who raised this kid, shook her head, "*Ay*, David . . . even in college, you get in trouble." David grew into the privilege of a lifetime to be who he was. Kind of like Virgin Mary, he started to "hold all these things in his heart." Not passive, quiet, or silent. Like Mary, who wasn't silent, but centered. So, too, David. You hold these things in your heart so that you can live these things in your life. "No, *Tía*—the Dean's List is a good thing."

⟡

Bugsy told me, "I joined a gang at thirteen. I was angry cuz my dad died when I was eleven—he drank himself to death. I needed someone to say, 'You matter,' and when my dad died, I knew I'd never hear that." Bugsy doesn't need to measure up; he just needs to heal up. Republicans used to speak of "the soft bigotry of low expectations." How about no expectations? Just healing—just relational wholeness—just the tender glance. This is what restores and that's enough.

A graphic artist, Karen Toshima, was on a date in fashionable Westwood on January 30, 1988, and got caught in gang crossfire and was killed. Her death set in motion hundreds of officers pumped into this area where gang shootings didn't happen. A special task force of twelve officers were selected to expedite the investigation into her death. A reward for $25,000 was offered for information that would lead to the arrest and conviction of those responsible for her tragic death.

As I write this, I will, in a week's time, bury my 247th young person killed because of gang violence. His name was James. I can't recall, in over thirty years, officers redirected, special detectives designated, nor rewards offered for any of these souls lost. No victims' lives matter, until all victims' lives matter.

The former employer of Toshima devised a campaign to address the issue of gang violence and its random, tragic consequences. He coined the phrase "Turn the Tide" as both battle cry and the name of the effort and solicited the help of community organizations, churches, and KABC as a cosponsor. All these well-intentioned folks set their sights on a gigantic march to be held in Exposition Park with a hoped-for 100,000 participants.

KABC advertised for the event by devoting a weeklong series of spots on their late afternoon broadcast. The five-minute pieces each evening of that week underscored various aspects of gang life. They featured "Gangs in the Valley," "Girls in Gangs," "Preschool Gang Prevention," and the like. The closing piece was focused on the strategy and approach of Dolores Mission with gangs.

Nearly thirty gang members from different gangs packed into the Rectory TV room to watch each episode. They watched with interest and not uncritically as they endured many caricatures and false representations of how gang members actually see themselves and operate. They would jeer and boo if a correspondent incorrectly deemed a tagger's scroll as gang graffiti. They endured these spots, night after night, waiting to see themselves in the final evening's piece on Dolores Mission.

And a most unfortunate piece it was. Of course, this was thirty-two years ago and reflective of the demonizing that was in overdrive at the time. The final spot chose to point/counterpoint my approach with that of law enforcement. The captain of the local LAPD precinct derided me as "part of the problem and not the solution. He allows them to fly their colors on the church property and doesn't say a word." The gathered homies saw themselves on the screen and hooted and hollered as they mercilessly bagged on each other. "Nice *orejas*, Flaco," they comment, as their homie's ears get special play. "Orale, you're baaaad, homes," they'd mention as the camera catches Travieso, whose "bad-ass" posturing is in high relief.

This last episode ends as the previous ones had. The news anchor reappears and pleads with the folks at home. "Please join our efforts with Turn the Tide and you, too, will help us wipe out gangs." She further invites folks to attend the rally; a 1-900 number flashes on the screen and assures the audience that their donation will subsidize this campaign to "wipe out gangs."

The TV goes off and I head to my office, and the homies follow and fill every seat there, while some go outside to smoke a *frajo*. I'm clearing my phone messages and Flaco places his hand on my shoulder as I sit at my desk. "Gotta talk ta ya, G," he says, looking as grim and serious as I've ever seen him. I don't think I exactly snapped to, so he leans in with even more insistence. "*En serio*, G—I gotta talk ta ya, *orita*." There is no mistaking his tone now and I usher everyone out of the office. My office at the rectory is a tiny square and we sit opposite each other. I lean in, "What's up, *mijo*?"

Flaco, whose real name is Adan, is seventeen years old, dark, with an open, humorous face. His ears ARE pronounced and his mouth a tiny etched thing that reveals a bright set of teeth and a generous smile. No teeth or smile today. He is a reliable mischief maker and champion "bagger." If I'm chewing out one of the homies in the parking lot for some *cabezon movida*, he'd sidle up to me, put his arm around me, eyes focused on the wayward homie, and say in an easily heard whisper, "Git 'em. Git 'em." In those early days, I'd play oldies in my car and he was adept at lyric changes. There is an oldie called "Just Because" sung by Lloyd Price. "Just because . . . your forehead is so large." My hairline seemed to be good source material for him.

"That TV thing really got to me, G," he begins, cradling his Locs (sunglasses) on his knee and handling them with both hands. "I mean . . . they wanna wipe us out. They even have a number you can call if you want to wipe us out. They're even asking for *feria* . . . to pay . . . to wipe us out." He seems genuinely perplexed by all this. "What d'ya think they want to do, G?"

"I don't know, dawg. I guess they want to wipe you out," trying to keep it light, but he's not having it. "I wish they'd help ya out, son," I assure him. "I wish they'd fix your schools, give you a job, and a place to kick it. But . . . I guess they just want to wipe ya out."

"And they were talkin' shit about you too." More hurt than confused this time. "How come, G?"

"I don't know, *mijito*. I guess . . . it's because they want me to hate you." I pause and our eyes meet. "Should I hate you?" He shakes his head "no" and I'm unprepared for what he does next. Rusty grabs his Locs resting on his knee, puts them on. He stares over my head and to the bookshelf behind me. We sit in silence while something seems to catch hold of him. His head rests on the wall and he explodes in sobs beyond his control. The crying is full-bodied. He's bawling and struggles to breathe. This goes on until it finally subsides into choppy, shallow gulps of gasping. I really wait before saying anything. "Do you want to talk about it, *mijo*?" He shakes his head, and we settle into the silence.

"I love you very much, *mijo*, you know that?" He manages an affirming nod. *"Aquí tienes tu casa.* And no matter what, I'll always be there for you. You can count on that. *Tu sabes, mijito.*"

"I know, G," he whispers as he returns to himself and quiet. "Damn, G. You don't even have any DAMN Kleenex," as his eyes do a quick search of my office. The sleeve of his black sweatshirt comes to the rescue. We hug each other, and he darts into the hallway bathroom, washes his face, and joins his homies in the parking lot.

Two months later, I tell that story at Flaco's funeral.

Flaco was bright, wildly imaginative, tender, and courageous in his affection, and so keenly humorous. He also had become so alienated from his family and ceased to reside with them for about the last two years before he died. His alcoholic father was particularly unskilled in communicating his obvious love for his son. The fighting grew all the more intense, and Flaco's father was rarely capable of saying the right thing. Try as I had to effect some reconciliation between them, so much damage had been done that Flaco finally refused to make any attempt to bridge the gulf.

I recall sitting Flaco down with his younger brother, Lil Flaco, also from the same gang, with their parents in my office. They all cried as they struggled to put words to their confusion and baffling rage. Clear in all this was their love for one another, but many missed opportunities and shattered feelings later had thoroughly muddied these familial waters and none of us could see our way clear to swim to shore.

Many years later, the youngest of the brothers, Samuel, helped me understand the source of Flaco's disaffection. "My brother was born in Mexico and he was the oldest. When he was about two, *mis padres* went to LA to start a life, and they left Adan with my grandma. Seven years later, they came to get him. By then, they had already had my sister, my brother, and finally me. Adan thought my grandma WAS his mom. Just before Adan left our house for good, he kept asking my parents, 'Why did you take so long to come and get me?' He'd cry when he'd ask them this." The thorn underneath.

I identified Adan's body as the police pulled back the sheet and revealed his slight, sprawled torso on Mott Street, with a single bullet to the head. I knocked on the door of his parents' home shortly after three in the morning. His mother, Blanca, a tiny, youthful, and pretty woman, appeared behind the screen door. "*Sí,* Padre." She was breathless and, I suspect, well aware of what was coming.

"I'm so sorry. Adan . . . is dead," I told her in Spanish as she opened the door and let me in. Blanca let out this yelp, like an indigenous cry from her soul. It came from a place known to mothers. It is chilling and as horrifying a sound as I've encountered in my life. I've heard it many times.

Before Adan tragically left us, he had found the tender glance in a community that held him into belonging. Adan was caught in the notice of God and on the cusp to find what was beneath the pain that was his constant companion. He was beginning to know the contours of being cherished, and it softened him into seeing differently. He was starting to see his parents in their wholeness and unshakable goodness. To have that fill you IS like supernatural food dropped from the heavens, as unexpected as it is nourishing.

Adan was nearing the moment when he could forgive himself for all the things he did to survive. He was on this side of mercy. Everything was about something else. He had undigested memories that, as a child, he couldn't handle or process. And what remained unspoken, certainly, was dangerous and did damage. Surely, the thorn underneath. Still, he began to surrender to the magnetic pull of the God who cherishes, and it started to free him and give him a broad-shouldered resilience. His whole being seemed to say, "I want to see."

Chapter Four

❧⟡❧

The Eighth Sacrament

I t took three hours to get from O'Hare Airport in Chicago to the Hilton Garden Inn in Springfield, Illinois. Carlos and Ricardo slept most of the way, since we had an early rise. We were scheduled to speak the next morning to a retreat center hall filled with hospital administrators and board members. We arrived at our hotel by 4:00 p.m.

As we pulled up to the Hilton, Ricardo in the backseat mentioned to Carlos in the front, "Hey, fool, there's a Hooters down the block. We can walk over there after dinner." I didn't say anything.

I found a restaurant in the heart of downtown Springfield where, trust me, no one looked like these two tattooed, Latino gang members. The restaurant was apparently the oldest in town. Abe Lincoln double-dated here shortly after it opened. Heads turned to us as we were led to our table. The heads remained fixed on us for some time. The waiter offered to explain the two house specials. An appetizer and an entrée. Each one came with a description, a fire-hose torrent of ingredients, and nothing was left out. "Our appetizer is a mussel gratiné, with a *woo-woo-woo* and a *la-di-da*, Spanish olives, shaved fennel, and parsley, sage, rosemary, and thyme" (though it was WAY longer than that). "Our entrée is a perch prepared in a *whooped-de-woo*, a pickled beet, au jus, red wine reduction, and parsley, sage, rosemary, and thyme." His descriptions were breathtaking, inasmuch as he didn't take one. Then the waiter looked at us and said, "I'll give you a moment," and walked away.

Ricardo looked at me blankly, and said, "What just happened?" Our table exploded in laughter and a new catchphrase was born. (Like the next day, when we flew from O'Hare to LaGuardia and the TSA agent confiscated Ricardo's ENORMOUS tubes of hair gel and lotion. "What just happened?")

Carlos and I had the beef Wellington, their specialty, and Ricardo had an enormous filet mignon, which he ordered "medium rarely."

We walked from the car to the hotel entrance, and these guys wanted to have a smoke. I made for the sliding door to go head to my room. Before I hit the door, I turned to them. "*Oye*—don't . . . walk . . . to Hooters tonight." Carlos, short, stocky, and tattooed, with a lit cigarette in his hand, chuckled. "Come on, G. We're not gonna . . . WALK . . . to Hooters . . . we're gonna . . . SKIP." He proceeded to, well, skip, in the most over-the-top, flamboyant, arms-flying way you've ever seen anybody skip before. His skipping activated the electronic sliding doors as he crossed it several times, and I'm not sure what the hotel staff inside were making of it as he encircled the entrance area with this wild, writ-large display of silliness. Ricardo and I found ourselves seeking support from our knees as we doubled over and cried laughing.

There's a word for all of this, of course, and it's communion. "Comun Union" as we say in Spanish. Walls are toppled, division reduced to nothing, everyone on the same page of connection, kinship, and exquisite mutuality. All of us feeling that it is probably past time that we acknowledge the sacredness of silly stuff like this. Playfulness forging new and bright neural pathways. The sanctity of this moment wasn't lost on us and we would retrieve it again and again during the course of our days of travel.

Sacraments elevate and exalt the most intimate human aspects of our lives. They also "re-member": they put us back together when we've drifted apart. I would be asked to do house blessings in Bolivia, and my part, the actual blessing with holy water, was always the last and seemed to be the least important. Before my ritual, these cholas, Quechua holy women, commence with a great passing of incense in each room and the pouring of a bit of Taquiña beer on the floor in each corner. This symbolized returning to the earth what belongs to Pachamama, the earth mother. Like our bus driver from La Paz to Sucre, who stops to buy a large forty-ounce Taquiña beer, pours the first *trago* (sip) to the earth, and boards the bus. When we safely land (*Ay Dios mío!*) he pours the last sip to the ground. The *tragos* were a simple reminder to remember.

In 1954, Rome outlawed the "worker priests," those Jesuits and others who, rather than sit in parishes, worked in the factories, accompanying the workers. Vatican officials evidently felt that such casting of their lot with the people and those on the margins threatened the notion of the "pedestal priest." In the Hebrew Bible, the word for "holiness" literally means "set apart, other." "Clerical" (*cleros*) means the "separated ones." So does "Pharisee."

Setting people apart, setting parts of our selves apart—all of this has kept us from locating the sacred in everything. Pedestals are impediments. They hoist folks high above everyone else. A breathless, admiring visitor to the Catholic Worker house in New York City asked Dorothy Day if she had visions. The story goes, she uttered an expletive and said, "Just visions of dirty dishes and unpaid bills."

How, then, to turn the world right side up? We long for a

movement from separation to oneness; from selfishness to love; from ego to God. The homies embody for me this tenacity to live this truth against all odds. David tells me, "I don't care if anybody calls me a punk or a bitch just as long as my kids call me Daddy when I come home, jumping and climbing on my legs." The world gets right when such choices get made.

Casting your lot puts you in people's confidence and they become remarkably comfortable in saying things to you. A homie leaves my office—he's buff and chiseled, *swole*, as the homies say, right out of prison—and Lety, the homegirl receptionist, enters my office just as this guy passes the threshold to leave it. She's eyeballing him with no regard for discretion. She hands me some notes and phone messages, vacantly, and shakes her head at this guy who has just left. "Damn, G. That *vato*'s lickable, fuckable, and all the other . . . '-ables.'" I suppose we could be horrified at this. Or we could be propelled into the sacred space of comfort and confidence where people don't hold back, because they trust you won't turn on them, no matter what they say. It's how you know the place is safe.

Eric rolls in at 11:30. "Why are you late for work?"

"Oh," he says, nearly startled by the question, "I got shot in the ass this morning."

I pivot from annoyance to concern. "WHAT? Did you go to the hospital?"

"No, "he says, "I just put lemon on it." He's nonplussed.

"Oh," I say, also not wanting to be plussed. "No onion or garlic?"

"Nah," he says, "Just lemon." Best to keep it simple. Safe at home. The world is crowded by God.

I see Pablo, who kind of disappeared on us this day and who pops up later, after 2:00 p.m. "Where you been at?" I ask.

"Oh, I went to my shoplifting class"—then holds two thumbs up—"Passed it!!!"

I tell him, "Passed it? You coulda taught it!" It is quite often at Homeboy that the playfulness in which we all engage forges a new and different neural pathway, quite distinct from their well-trod traumatic lane so familiar to them. A conversation with three homies in my office had bounced from crazy to hugely silly, and as it winds down, one homie turns poignant. "You know, G, how you've always been a father to us?" I nod reverently, as do the other homies. "Well . . . what about back pay and child support?" You can almost feel the brain rewiring.

Wino is standing in front of my desk and hesitant to tell me something. He's a large homie, well able to handle himself. Finally, he gets to it. "Well, I'm having problems—down there." I shamelessly don't make this easy.

"Your FEET are giving you trouble?"

"NO," he emphasizes, "DOWN . . . THERE." His eyes make a dive to his midsection. I finally let him off the hook and he explains. As near as I can tell, he has described something of a testicular torsion and now his scrotum has swollen to the size of a grapefruit. I take him to General Hospital and I get his name on the long list of numerous folks awaiting medical attention. We take our seats on a bench. Wino does this with difficulty.

After half an hour, I tell him that I have a meeting I can't miss back at the office. I stand and I tell Wino to call me when he is ready to be picked up. He immediately becomes "Whine-O." "Nooo! You can't leave." I ask him why not. "Cuz I won't know what to say to that lady," he says, pointing at the triage nurse as he intensifies the whining.

So, I give him all the vocabulary I think he'll need: Inflammation. Testicles. Grapefruit. Then I grab my imaginary clipboard and assume my imaginary attitude of the receiving nurse and begin my roleplay. "So, what seems to be the problem?" I can almost see the stars dancing over Wino's head as he reels with pain and discomfort. He tries his best and blurts out: "MY

BALLS ARE IN FLAMES." I become apoplectically undone as I laugh wildly.

"Don't laugh," he says, "it's not funny."

I sit next to him, "I'm sorry, son. But if you say THAT, to THAT nurse, she won't bring you a doctor. She'll bring you a fire extinguisher."

We remember the sacred by our reverence. Adoration for Ignatius was always expressed through reverence. This is the esteem we extend to the reality revealed to us. Jesus didn't abandon his reality, he lived it. He ran away from nothing and sought some wise path through everything. He engaged in it all with acceptance. He had an eye out always for cherishing his reality. A homie, Leo, wrote me: "I'm going to trust God's constancy of love to hover over my crazy ass. I'm fervent in my efforts to cultivate holy desires." This is how we find this other kind of stride and joyful engagement in our cherished reality. The holy rests in every single thing. Yes, it hovers, over our crazy asses.

For several years running, my entire Jesuit community of Casa Luis Espinal in Boyle Heights would make the long drive to Redwoods Monastery in Whitethorn, California, to make our annual eight-day silent retreat together. It is a glorious and serene place run by magnificent Benedictine nuns. Not sure I could live like a monk, but it's enriching while I'm there. We return home from retreat once to a Los Angeles stuck in a grueling heat wave. I make a run to the local Food 4 Less to get milk for the house. The refrigerated grocery store is a nice break from the 100-plus-degree weather outside. As I go for the milk, I see that to the left of me a crowd has gathered at the end of the aisle. The gaggle of folks are howling with laughter, and as I break through the group, I see the source of it all. There is a gang member, in full cholo, cut-off Dickies, hair net, tube socks pulled up to the knees, muscle shirt, and Nike Cortez, lying completely prone in the refrigerated beer section, on top of cases of brew, with his arms folded, eyes closed, in repose. And I think to myself, *This will always be my Redwoods Monastery.* The manger in Bethlehem proves one thing: God can be born anywhere. Even in the refrigerated beer case at a Food 4 Less.

Josue emails me from his deported perch in Honduras. He lives there with his lady, her mom, and their new baby. I had just met the Pope. There were two hundred of us from forty-seven countries at a Jesuit conference on social justice, and we had a special audience. I sent a picture of me shaking hands with the Pope and told Josue that the Pontiff wished him "a Happy Birthday."

"He said THAT?" Josue emailed me back. "*Serio,* though, what did you say to him?" I told him that I shook his hand, looked him in the eye, and said, in Spanish, "Thank you for your leadership." Josue came back quickly, "What he say back to you?" "I couldn't make it out entirely," I wrote, "but I think he said NEXT!!" He keeps at it. "Damn, G. You now have more juice than Sunny Delight! You not only have the juice card . . . you have the PLATINUM juice card!! Tell me how was it? Was it your wildest dream?" I write back simply, "It was surreal and a blur." He counters: "I know what ya mean. It's like yesterday morning when I came face to face with my *suegra* as she was stepping out of the shower—surreal and a blur."

I always liked that Saint Kateri Tekakwitha's name: "Tekakwitha" means "she who bumps into things." What if holiness is a contact sport and we are meant to bump into things? This is what it means to embrace a contemplative, mystical way of seeing wholeness. It gives a window into complexity and keeps us from judging and scapegoating and demonizing. If we allow ourselves to "bump into things," then we quit measuring. We cease to Bubble-Wrap ourselves against reality. We stop trying to "homeschool" our way through the world so that the world won't touch us. Hard to embrace the world, and speak the whole language, if we are so protective and defensively shielded from it. A homie told me once, "It's taken me all these years to see the real world. And once ya see it—there's only God there."

Years ago, I walked into my office and the homies had left me a pile of phone messages. There was this one: "Duke called. He needs to talk to you. He needs a million dollars. They're holding him ransom . . . He'll call tomorrow." With any luck, we don't protectively encase ourselves from surprising tenderness. We announce to each other that we are alive and kicking, ready to be bumped into. He'll call tomorrow.

We don't want to distance the secular but always bring it closer. It's only then that ordinary things and moments become epiphanies of God's presence. Some man said to me once, "I want to become more spiritual." Yet God is inviting us to inhabit the fullness of our humanity. God holds out wholeness to us. Let's not settle for just spiritual. We are sacramental to our core when we think that everything is holy. The holy not just found in the supernatural but in the Incarnational here and now. The truth is that sacraments are happening all the time if we have the eyes to see. Limiting them—seven for men, six for women— does not advance the kinship of God. In the time of Jesus, some people said, "No new gifts—we're okay with the old ones." The mystic is rapturous and ferociously attentive to the new gifts that show up every day.

It's the end of the day and Jeanette, one of the Navigators, is holding court at the "well," also known as the reception area. Many homies don't call it the well, but the "whale." (It's a pronunciation thing.) There are three of us standing outside the counter and two seated within. "I'm kinda impressed with myself today," Jeanette announces. I ask her why. "One minute I'm here at the well; the next minute I'm upstairs in curriculum; then I'm down here again. I mean . . . I migraine everywhere."

"I know," homegirl Ruthie deadpans from her seat in the well. "I have the headache to prove it."

The "whale" is not just a safe place—it's home. It is a sanctuary, but more than that, a sacred locale. It, in fact, cultivates an ability to find the sacred beyond this place. Jaime walks in. In my cell phone (to distinguish him from all the Jaimes I know), it reads, "Jaime Half 'N' Half," because whenever I ask how he is, he always says: "I'm doin' half 'n' half." Today he says, "I leave my house—it's a grumpy-ass place. But I come here—and I'm at home."

I can't for the life of me remember what word I corrected, but Moreno showed me his essay for school and I told him the word was spelled with a "ph" and not an "f." "Orphan," "phone," can't remember, but it set him off. "Why white people always be spelling everything with a 'ph' that they don't even need? Why is that?" Then he answered his own question, almost sneering at me, "Cuz they're so "PHisticated." Then he thought maybe he'd gone too far. "Don't worry G—you're not white. You're white-sican."

The homie standing next to him said, incredulous, "You used to be white?!!"

Folks always wanted to "stop the gang wars," but right here, in the belly of the whale, you wander into the place where gang wars start: in your heart and tender soul and, yes, in your grumpy-ass house. This sacred location keeps us from taking up residence in hatred and resentment, in judgment and competition.

I know I'm old when a homie whom I've known since he was a kid tells me he's going in for his first colonoscopy: "Wish me luck." I told my friend Bill Cain, and he called this "the Eighth Sacrament." True enough. Some deeply ordinary yet intimate thing is elevated, and in the process, we are "re-membered." Plus, it reminds us that the point of the Incarnation is that Jesus is one of us in the ordinary. Jesus is God's declaration that the Infinite is present in it all. Hafiz titles a poem, "Never Say It Is Not God."

I read once about a guy who, after a botched surgery to alleviate epileptic seizures, became unable to have memory. He was left in a permanent present tense—only always present. We want to rest in the reality of the present. We know that the opposites kick it with each other in the present moment. Then we stop being "spiritual," moving from here to there. Instead, we want to move from there to here. This is what it looks like when we choose to be "all there."

I got a text from a homie, Ernie, the other day. It was a video of him cutting the umbilical cord of his newborn son. After the clip ended (both clips), he wrote: "And now . . . life begins." And for those who still debate such things, apparently, life begins when a homie cuts the umbilical cord. The infinite, present and accounted for. When he relayed the moment to me in person days later, Ernie was exhilarated. "I was Tom Brady in the huddle . . . and then he came out." He told me how his wife drove him to the hospital. She told him, "I'm a better driver than you are." He said to her, "Kinda stealin' my thunder here." I asked if he got in the backseat and moaned all the way to the hospital. "My lady barrels into the ER and she says to the nurse, 'My husband will be needing a wheelchair, please.'" He told me how he loves his wife. "But, G, it's not about finding the right person. It's about being the right person."

Snoops and I are cutting it up in my office. Years earlier, we were having a heart-to-heart, after I caught him behind the dumpster blazing it. He was quite repentant. I looked at him and said, "You know, dawg, when God made you, he broke the damn mold."

Snoops shifted into verklempt. "Yeah?" His voice quivered and choked.

"Yup," I said, "God took one look at you and said, 'Naaaahhh, I don't think I'm gonna make any more of these.'"

Snoopy snapped out of it. "You're diiiirrrrty. You're not right."

This day, Snoops tells me that he's trying to find a side *jale* (job) because his wife is not working: "She's on eternity leave." I correct him. "No," he says, "eternity leave . . . feels like it's going on forever." He hands me folders with job possibilities to supplement his income. Out of the blue he asks, "What's autism?" I explain. "I think I'm autistic," he says.

"No," I counter. "You're probably just . . . artistic."

He considers it all. "Hmmm . . . artistic. How 'bout . . . handsome-istic?'"

I run it down to him. "First of all, there is no such word, and if there was—it wouldn't apply to you."

He stands and grabs the folders and starts to walk out. "That's DIIIIIRRRTY . . ." —then adds as he gets to the door— "-istic." Silliness, pure and simple.

Pedro Arrupe, the Superior General of the Jesuits, used to say that a man probably didn't have a vocation to the Jesuits if he didn't have a sense of humor. Part of this, I think, is not allowing the false (estranged or separate) self to be offended by anything. I had homies with me in the Bay Area for talks and one asked, "When do we speak at SFU?"

I tell him, "It's USF."

"What's SFU then?" I tell him I have no idea. Then he arrives on the answer: "Shut the Fuck Up." Works for me.

Our mystical "diving in" is at the heart of the Incarnation. Jesus ONLY referred to himself as the Son of Man, which means the Human One. It must be important. It shows up eighty-seven times in the Bible. "Never say it's not God," if it's human, in the flesh, and ever-present. I'm in my office talking to Oscar, and in the course of a conversation he says that some event "was serendipity." I'm deeply impressed that he has this word at his disposal. But then he has some doubts. "Is it 'serendipity' or is it 'synchronicity'?" I look it up and print out the definitions. Later, as he's leaving for the day, he sticks his head in my office and says, "Synchronicity is 'we're groovin' together.' Serendipity is . . . 'Fuck, how did THAT happen?'" Also . . . works for me.

A homie named Vince wanted to be brought into our eighteen-month training program. Often the name on a homie's birth certificate doesn't match what they are called at home. So, I asked Vince, "What do your people call you?"

He was quick but embarrassed. "Frijol." Needless to say, I wanted to know the derivation of this moniker. "Well, my grandfather is from Mexico and doesn't speak English. And he just couldn't pronounce Vince very well—he had a strong accent and it came out sounding like 'Beans,' so 'Frijol' was born."

When one of the emperors of China asked the Zen master what enlightenment was, he said: "Lots of space. Nothing holy." Which is to say, lots of room for synchronicity and beans.

Homies can "bag" and deliver you down to size faster than anyone I know. I come from a family of ten and before I met gang members, I thought I was pretty adept at this kind of banter and neutralizing. "Your breath smells like Similac," Garry says to Gabriel. On another occasion, Gabriel says to Garry, "Last time I trusted you, I ended up in TJ without my pants." One of the supervising homies says to a hugely belligerent trainee, "I know you're NOT a dick, but apparently you play one on TV." Or when a homie compliments me, like Manuel one day, and thinking I can't "take" the compliment, says, "It's raining cold, hard facts in here, Padre."

Truth be told, being reduced to your size is exhilarating. Lefty wrote me from prison and told me how he met this nun volunteering there. She was telling him how the Church makes saints. Then the letter turned wistful on me. "Damn, G . . . if I was Pope, I'd canonize you right away . . . with the biggest cannon I could find." He went on to say this would all happen in the Homeboy parking lot and we could charge admission.

I speak to a roomful of educators in a hotel ballroom in New Orleans. I'm the opening keynote, on the opening day, to five hundred folks. After the talk I go down the block to Café Du Monde. Almost a half century before, it was where, at eighteen years old, I had my first cup of coffee. Black with that distinctive hickory taste. I was driving around the country for two months in my '67 Impala with two great friends, Jim Rude and Colin Ewing. We were long-haired, bearded hippie types driving through the Deep South (what were we thinking?). I was nostalgic for the taste of this coffee.

I come back to the hotel and take the elevator to go to my room so I can check out and head to the airport. I'm alone in the elevator, when suddenly there's a rush of folks let out of the ballroom. They fill the elevator and I'm squashed in the back. They are all wearing the conference lanyards. The elevator door closes, and the last woman to board the compartment says loudly, to no one in particular, "You know that first speaker, that . . . Father Doyle?" I think, *Uh-oh—it's about to rain cold, hard facts in here.* I say from the back of the elevator, "Don't talk shit, I'm on the elevator!"

Gabriel is clutching his coffee and he hops in the front seat. His fiancée, Ana, is in the back. We're in the parking structure of a hotel in Charlotte, and it's 6:30 a.m. We have a speaking gig to teachers on their in-service day. Gabriel sips his coffee as I negotiate my way out of our parking spot. "Hey, G. Ya ever try Gold Bond powder?" I tell him I haven't. "Don't—burns like a motherfucker. My balls are on fire." I glance in the rearview mirror at Gabriel's future wife. She perfectly shakes her head and rolls her eyes. Lots of space. Everything holy.

I'm certain it was poetic license, but in his poem "The Forgotten Dialect of the Heart," Jack Gilbert writes that "a people in Northern India is dying out because their ancient tongue has no words for endearment." In any case, endearments are the containers of our tenderness. Sacraments delivered daily. They are the words and gestures that transport our love from one person to another. It is, I suppose, all we have.

Bobby worked for Homeboy Industries long ago and had some hard-knock relapses of late. The occasional stint at Men's Central Jail, the return to some meth use, some acute falling-out with family and friends, and now he was, yet again, estranged from his family and on the street side of eviction. Since often enough the woes of the homies who wander through our doors are outsize and intractable, it is a team effort to wrap around Bobby the numerous wrap-around services he needs. There is the secret handshake (from me) of funds and a gift card for clothes, and the finding of a sober-living roof over his head (Emily), and the transport from here to there, thanks to Marcos. It took the better part of a day to make all these things align as stars need to.

Finally, Bobby is ready to take his leave from us, heading to a warm bed and a protective roof. He's feeling grateful and full of emotion. He hugs me and is teary-eyed. He heads to the glass door of my office and before exiting, turns, and says this: "If your mom ever throws you out, G . . . you can stay at my place."

It was sweet. It was a word and a gesture. Never mind that it had been nearly half a century since I'd lived with my mom. It was an endearment. And it IS nearly all we have to get us from here to there. (But mainly, from there to here). To hold the tenderness long enough so as not to spill it en route. We all taste eternity when person merges with person. We need to find ourselves poised to enter into a relationship with anyone anywhere.

I'm walking on Lexington Avenue in New York City. It's nearing Thanksgiving, and Donald Trump has just been elected president. It's chilly, and I'm bundled, but enjoying the crispness of it. I pass a park and an old African American man has

commandeered a bench near the lip of the sidewalk. At one end is, no doubt, all his worldly possessions in a very large plastic garbage bag. It fills half the bench. He sits, semi-sprawled, on the other half. Our eyes connect for one brief moment, and he points at me and says, rather loudly, "NEXT TIME, I'M VOTIN' FOR YOU!!!" I, the man, and a few passersby nearly topple with our laughter. The Incarnational encounter—who knew?

Since it is the relationship that heals, our port of entry with everyone everywhere is the small thing, the tactile moment, the tender exchange. During the pandemic, it was difficult at Homeboy to keep stewardship over this tenderness while not being able to hug. It is the Incarnational encounter, Emmanuel—God with us—present in the tiny, whispered instance and warm embrace. And like Scrooge, we can say, "I will honor Christmas in my heart, and try to keep it all the year." This is the constant deciding to be endearing with each other.

Miguel, our homie head of security, pre-pandemic, is imploring me to stay home more and not travel so much. "I mean . . . we need ya here, dawg. After all, you're the Gumby of Homeboy Industries." I settle into that truth and I'm about to text him that I agree, when he fires one off quickly. "I mean Gandhi." Oh.

There's not much ironic sense among gang members. Fat homies aren't called "Flaco." Sane ones aren't nicknamed "Looney." And yet Looney and Flaco have a way with each other, a banter that is smart, openhearted, and never-ending. I'll be talking to Looney in my office and Flaco does not mind interrupting our conversation. He barges in to tell me what was so urgent and as he goes to the door, Looney will say to him, "Please come back when you can't stay so long."

Once I had Flaco sitting in front of my desk and Looney comes in, panting, staring at his cell phone. "I just got your text, G." Then Looney begins to read the faux message: "Looney: get in here now. Flaco is creeping me out. He's making me throw up in my mouth. Get in here, NOW." He stops reading, breathless. "I got here as fast as I could."

I buried "Manny 5 Dolla" this year. He was a homie who worked in the office and he'd always hit folks up with, "Hey, ya got five dolla?" Moreno christened him with this nickname, and I think he often referred to himself this way.

He asked me for money once and I gave it to him. "What are ya going to do with your five dolla?'"

He told me of his favorite Chinese restaurant at 4th and Soto. "They're not greedy there. And the rice is browner and the chicken more orangey."

Manny moved out of state, I think Indiana. He was gone for some time. Years later, he walked into my office and I was stunned. He was gaunt and "sucked up," as the homies would say. He had been quite a chunky kid. I knew this wasn't drugs. He asked me to do his wedding. The date hadn't been set yet. He requested a blessing before leaving. Though many homies ask for this, it was not typical of Manny to do so. His *abrazo* was long and lingering, also a display not usual for him. He turned to walk away, having said goodbye. He whirled around before leaving. "Got five dolla?" I happily gave him twenty. He was dead two days later. He had a heart condition few knew about. He just dropped in to say thank you and goodbye. At his funeral, we all remembered and laughed at the way he annoyed us, asked for money, and sought connection in the whispered thing. We left there wanting to honor him in our hearts and "keep it all year." Orangey chicken for everyone.

One day I'm on a bus in Berkeley. Two young boys, maybe brothers, are sharing a seat nearest the window and an elderly African American gentleman with gray dreadlocks sits next to them. The boys have a large shoebox with air holes carefully punched into the top. I'm standing behind, observing this all.

"Whatcha got?" the man asks.

"A rat," the boys say, in delight and in unison. They open the box and sure enough—a big old live rat.

"Does yo mama know you're bringing this home?"

"No," says one boy, speaking for them both.

"I'm sure she'll be thrilled," says the man in dreadlocks.

I watch as the man fully engages these two. He asks them questions and he waits and listens for their answers. He holds them in esteem, and I witness these boys float, elevated, in this stranger's high regard. It was downright sacramental. The man's stop comes and simultaneously, he offers his seat to a young woman. His farewell to the boys was this: "I think this lady would LOVE to see what ya got." And before he turns to leave, he looks at me and winks broadly.

Of course, Mark Twain was right, "Against the assault of laughter, nothing can stand." A homie named Tudy is shot and, as often happens, he is given not just a "John Doe" but a new name while he's in the hospital, to keep him anonymous, ostensibly for his own protection. For some reason, the name they put on his chart is "Muhammed Sharif." (He tells me, "I suppose it's because I look a smidge Middle Eastern.") A doctor comes in, sees the name, and proceeds to speak Arabic. I suppose Tudy could have simply said, "I don't speak Arabic." Instead, he waits until the doctor is finished speaking, glowers at him, and says, "What did you just say about my mom?" When Tudy shared this in my packed office, no one could "stand against it."

What is said of laughter is also true of affectionate endearments. They carry the power to reduce our defenses and unhinge all armor. Always on the Wednesday before Thanksgiving, at the end of the workday, there are racks of extra pies for the taking from our Homeboy Bakery. The homies fill their arms. A young gang member, Philip, is sitting in my office, oblivious to the bakery's largesse. "Don't ya want a pie?" He *tsks* and waves me off.

"You're my pie." An endearment. And one's own self-absorption can't stand up to such a thing.

Chepe had a greatly troubled relationship with his father. Like many homies, the "father wound" was deeply pronounced for him. When his father died, he came in to see me about arrangements.

"What's your father's name?"

"Manuel."

"What did people call him?"

"Lotsa names."

"What did your mom call him?"

"Nuthin' nice."

We stared at each other, then in unison, the assault of our laughter brought us into each other's vulnerability and shared humanity. This is what bridges our distance most of the time.

Playfulness, as well, is a sturdy boxcar of affection and a certain indicator that folks feel safe. It is how they know that the love around this place can be trusted. Sergio, a big, burly guy, would walk past my office as I was sitting with someone, and he was forever making faces and trying to break my concentration to make me laugh. One day he does this, and I mouth and mime, *There's a call for you,* holding an invisible phone to my ear, *on Line One.* I hold up the middle finger to indicate, with clarity, what line I think he should pick up. Sergio feigns horror at first, then laughs heartily.

Then the next day, he steps into my office and hands me a large manila envelope, saying, "This is kind of my life story. A continuation of our conversations. Open it later, though." I thank him and have no intention of opening it later.

Enclosed is a color copy of big ol' Sergio sitting at my desk, holding the phone to his ear, flipping me off, and written underneath, it says, "There's a call for you, G . . . on Line One." I look up from this and there is this tattooed character, who had once entered our place with more than his share of toxic stress and terrifying memories. Now he's collapsing at his own joke, delighting in the "safe at home" playfulness of our friendship.

We all engage at Homeboy in attachment repair. Every person is a practitioner who offers their time, tender consistency, and assured predictability. Everyone recognizes that attachment disorders result from problems with trust. Claudia is madder than hell and bounds into my office. "I'm just telling you now that I'm going to throw down with Gladys. She gets on my last nerve—but I'm keepin' it real with you. I'm TELLING you I'm going to fight her."

I calmly tell her how appreciative I am that she's honest with me. And if she fights, I'm going to have to let her go. She vents some more and together there is this clear willingness to initiate repair.

She hugs me before leaving: "I hate you, G."

I whisper back as we hug, "I hate you too." The coast is clear—and safe.

Every year I give a weekend retreat at the Jesuit Retreat Center in Los Altos, California. I always bring a homie or two to help me. I take Rafa this year, a large gang member with a vibrant spirit and humor to match. When we get to LAX, I tell him, "If we get lost, remember we leave out of Gate Seventeen." Immediately, he forms a fist and puts it to his mouth, simulating a public address system: "Would the faa-ther—of a three-hundred-pound baby boy, please come to Gate Seventeen." I think to myself, *How does he come up with this stuff?* Before the retreat began, the two of us had a morning talk in a large hotel ballroom of social workers. When we arrive, I tell him I'm going to get a cup of coffee, and "if we get lost, our talk will be in Ballroom B. "Will the faa-ther of a . . ." Again, he's on some microphone and we howl.

After the talk, he tells me that he's forgotten to pack virtually

all hygiene items, so we pull into a huge Walmart to get tooth-
paste and such. We both do some separate shopping. I have my
basket and I'm walking down all the aisles, trying to find him.
Suddenly, over the loudspeaker, is the cracking, adolescent voice
of some unsuspecting clerk. "Will the father of a three-hundred-
pound baby boy please report to checkout line Number Fourteen." I find Rafa there, doubled over, standing next to this kid,
none the wiser, who has just read, word for word, the script Rafa
prepared for him. Playfulness ventilating everything that needs
to be aired out.

I have never been much of a proponent of "scared straight"
or even "tough love." These ways of proceeding feel like a license
to be harsh. I think of the mother in *I, Tonya*. I believe in clear
love. So when I tell Joseph, who is out of his mind on PCP, "No,
son, we won't let you in the building. We love you so much. We
won't let you step one foot in here. But the minute you surrender
to your own healing, we got you. Not until then." Clear is better
than tough. Affection dresses up like this sometimes.

Jimmy comes in looking terrible. "You look like shit, son."
He corrects his posture some and says," Thanks for that positive
comment." He has lately been beside himself on "Zanny bars"
(Xanax) and has been missing from work without communication for enough days that he's been dropped from our payroll.
He's young and carrying a lot. His mom is in and out of the
hospital with a very serious cancer diagnosis and this has served
to unravel him some. I guess I had met him in a probation camp
and given him my card a year earlier. He appeared for the first
time in my office and said earnestly, "I've come here for unem-
ployment." I told him he came to the right place.

When the homies arrive, they have not been properly introduced to themselves. Before this introduction could be made,
Jimmy slipped into a self-medicating stupor. With a line I bor-
rowed from a homie, I told him, "Jimmy, you're cutting off my

arms, then asking for a hand." We tried different things with him so that he could see himself. They say, after all, that rules are for people who don't know how to think. Sometimes you need to throw out the book rather than go by it.

Our first office, after moving from Dolores Mission Church, was a storefront on First Street in Boyle Heights. It had a main reception area where four folks had desks, then my office, which didn't have a door. The whole place had been a butcher shop or something, and my office had a big old drain sloped in the middle of the room, where, I suppose, blood from the slaughtered would swirl down. In those days, we were called Jobs for a Future and a little homie, Richie, right out of probation camp, was sweeping the floors. Everyone was at lunch and Norma (who many called Auntie Norma) was the only one answering the phones and struggling to keep up. I was in my office, a stone-toss away. "Look," Norma said to Richie, "help me answer the phones."

The kid was flummoxed. "But I don't know what to say."

Norma picked up the receiver to demonstrate. "Jobs for a Future, how may I help you? Now you try."

She handed the phone to this little guy and he took it for a tentative test drive. "Jobs . . . for . . . a . . . Future . . . how . . . may I help you?"

Norma sat him down at the desk closest to my office. "Next call is yours."

His entire being was a clammy hand. The phone rang, he looked at Norma, she nodded. He turned to me and I gave him the thumbs-up. He grabbed the phone with gusto. "BACK TO THE FUTURE, HOW MAY I HELP YOU?"

Beyond my office was "the back," which had a small kitchen, a living room of sorts, a bathroom, and two bedrooms. The back door of my office connected to this part. A family had lived here before. I would let adult homies live in these rooms rent-free until they got on their feet. Many gang members stayed there over the five years we had that office.

I came in one morning early, with my coffee and my *LA Times*. Chuco and Gato were from different gangs and in their twenties. These current occupants of the "the back" emerge eventually from their rooms, and they see me at my desk as they prepare bowls of cereal in the kitchen. I question what purposeful tasks they will tackle today. They both land on the idea to wash their clothes at the *lavanderia* down the block. I encourage this, as I mainly want to return to my coffee and *Times*. They eventually take off to their separate rooms in search of ripe clothes for washing. There is blissful silence and the sipping of coffee.

Without warning, Chuco begins to sing from inside his room. "It's a beautiful day in the neighborhood, a beautiful day for a neighbor . . . won't you be mine . . . will ya be mine." I'm stunned away from the paper at the sound of this tattooed Mister Rogers from "the back."

Before I can recover, Gato joins the airwaves from his room. "Have you ever seen a dream walking? . . . well I have." The warbling from each room is unselfconscious and sweet. Gato spends some time sliding his "waaaaaalking" that I conjure him, fist on hips, insisting, in wooden shoes, half-skipping . . . "Well I have." Sometimes it's the retrieval of sweet songs that can properly introduce you to yourself.

I'm in Jack London Square in Oakland with two of our trainees, a couple, Ana and Efrain. Ana asks, "Who's Jack London, anyway?"

I explain, "He's a writer. Famous. He wrote *The Call of the Wild*. Every kid had to read it in school."

"Yeah," Ana quickly adds, "boarding school!" . . . which is to say, I suppose, "Not in any school I ever attended." The comeuppance was exhilarating. Endearments also come in this size.

A reminder of disparities and privilege and the gulf we need to keep bridging.

Tyrese asks me for a blessing before he heads out for the weekend. As with everyone, it allows me a chance to be sacramental with him. To see Tyrese as God does and then to remind him of it. This is such a foreign land for him that he weeps. "Damn, G," he manages to eke out before leaving. "You're like the Santa Claus of the ghetto." It's how you stay "dear" to each other even when that's not second nature.

"Love," Hafiz wrote, "will surely bust you wide open into an unfettered, blooming new galaxy. Even if your mind is now a spoiled mule." Jimmy and Neil are with me in the elevator. We're in a hotel in Knoxville. It's just the three of us in the elevator. They are surely trying to get a rise out of me as they practice their pickup lines. "How 'bout this one?" Neil says to Jimmy. "Well, I MUST be in Tennessee cuz you're the only ten I see." I get them to promise me that they will NOT use this in or out of my hearing. Yes, I AM a spoiled mule.

Every day, Percy Williams would show up for work. Robert Juarez would greet him in the same way: "Percy? . . . Williams?"

And Percy would beam and say, "Speak on it." Every day. Sometimes, multiple times each day. It simply was a routine that didn't age. It was always fresh, new, and vitally robust. Percy and Robert drew everyone near in this affectionate net and held us all for a moment. It was endlessly invigorating. A boxcar of tenderness. No expiration date.

Love transported. And it never got old.

I'm taking three homies, some thirty years ago, to pick up their tuxedos for a quinceañera celebration. Spider is the first to arrive back at my car, which I'm leaning against. He and I await the other two homies. Spider is the *chambelan de honor*, which means he accompanies the fifteen-year-old girl at the mass and in the "salon waltz" afterward. Consequently, his tux is different from the others. His is all white except for the cummerbund, which seems to be pink. "That's an interesting color, dawg. Pink?"

Spider recoils. "No, it's dusty rose!" Then his voice trails off. "Or some shit like that," embarrassed that he knows the actual name of the color.

I asked Smokey why I hadn't seen him at school. (This was in the early days, when our alternative school was located on the third floor of Dolores Mission's parochial school.) "Paulette [one of the teachers] said she put me on home study cuz I drove her crazy. But come on, G . . . she BEEN crazy since the day she got here."

A tough homie, Omar, was a "YA baby" (sent as a juvenile to the Youth Authority for a serious crime) who spent twenty years in prison. He was a boxer and quite accomplished in that realm. He loved his therapist at Homeboy and never had any trace of embarrassment in attending his appointments with her. He worshipped his father, who'd dropped dead of a heart attack when he was a tiny boy. Just the two of them were home, and he remembers finding his father dead in a hallway. He thought he was asleep and he was waiting for his dad to take him to a much-anticipated trip to the zoo that day. He saw his father and shook him, "*Apa*, wake up, we're going to the zoo." The father just lay there, and Omar climbed on top and settled in for a nap as well. He slept on his dead father until his mother returned home. As often happens in these abandonment scenes, Omar carried some heavy and unwarranted culpability that festered until gang allegiance replaced it.

At the office, he'd look at his watch and say, "Gotta go see my cuckoo clock doctor." He told me once that his therapist would sometimes just read to this six-foot-three man *Green Eggs and Ham* or *The Cat in the Hat*, and Omar would just curl up on the couch and sob. He told me once, "I've found poetry in my pain."

In the end, all great spirituality is about what to do with our pain. We hesitate to eradicate the pain, since it is such a revered teacher. It re-members us. Our wounds jostle from us what is false and leaves us only with a yearning for the authentically poetic. From there to here. Holiness as a contact sport, busting us open into some new, unfettered place. We are hesitant, then, not to call it God. Remarkable, incredible, and . . . all the other "-ables."

Chapter Five

Air of a Richer Kind

Johnny was probably thirteen when I first bumped into him. A gangly, goofy, wildly funny kid, he got into a gang but his heart was never in it. (Or as a homie said to me once: "Who really wants to be a gangster? In the end, nobody.") When a kid is this funny and quick, you know he's smart, no matter how he performs in school. "What ya learn today in school, Johnny, that you never knew before?" I asked him when he was in middle school. He thought for a beat, then said, "I learned that Maribel doesn't wear a bra. I did . . . not . . . know that."

When he came to work at Homeboy, before we did drug testing, Johnny returned from lunch one afternoon, eyes all red and bloodshot. "Did you blaze it, dawg, during your lunch-break?" He threw a minor fit, offended that I would ask. "I've been meaning to tell the pool boy, 'USE LESS CHLORINE!!!'"

Johnny is nearing forty now and the undergirding mental health issues have wrapped their tentacles around his ability to operate in the working world. He self-medicates as never before, and his drinking has brought him to jail repeatedly and to the brink of deportation several times. That he has managed to navigate around all these calamities is a testament to his ability to talk his way out of nearly everything. I call it "pummeling."

He can be a fire hose of verbosity—one that I often have to cut short. "Quit . . . pummeling . . . me!" I'll tell him. Once, as I was trying to wind down a phone conversation with him, two phrases collided in a mind meld. I wanted to say both "Stay up" and "Hang in there," and these two merged into one and I blurted: "Hang up." Paging Dr. Freud.

I send him to rehab, but the benefits are short-lived and he's back at it. He is among the few homies whom, on occasion, we have to alert our security to prevent from actually coming into the office. He can be an exasperating and even a violent presence when "he's on a good one." This back-and-forth with him has gone on for some time, and the death of his mom, with whom he had a ferocious and complicated relationship, only exacerbated things.

He calmly texted me one day. "Hey dawg . . . kick me down with some *feria*, yeah?" ("*Como si nada*," like we hadn't been doing battle about rehab in our last pummeling session.) I wrote back, "My son for life . . . You know I love you. I will always help you, but I will ONLY help you. If I gave you money, that won't help you. You need rehab. I'll pay for it. Now, I know you've burned every bridge . . . with family and friends. But you'll never burn this bridge with me." I pushed Send. His response was immediate: "Fuck your bridge."

Such things can, initially, startle and sting. Then you settle into them like a very hot bath, and the sting becomes savor. And you catch yourself, not wanting to get separated from your kindness. In no time, I'm sharing it with my council, and suddenly it's a new catchphrase. My senior staff homies will now hug me and whisper in my ear, "Fuck your bridge."

And I feign verklempt. "Thank you, dawg—that means a lot."

At Homeboy, we try to maintain a high comfort level with homie resistance, the projecting of hostile intent, and a whole world of defense strategies. We are all adept at reading the "Do Not Enter" sign around some homies' hearts. As my brother Jesuit and spiritual guru at Homeboy, Mark Torres, says, "If you're in pain, you point." Understanding this is a way one speaks the whole language.

When we speak only half the language, we fail to see the whole person, and "Fuck your bridge" can derail you. It can lead to instantly become a New Yorker ("Fuck me? . . . oh no, no, no—Fuck YOU!") or feel tempted to recite "the litany" ("Here's where I've been for you . . . after ALL I've done for you . . .") Homegirl Inez says, "At Homeboy, we don't check boxes, we check pulses."

And if one of our trainees misses, we don't ask, "Where you been at?" but "How ya doin'?" Then nothing derails you.

Jesuit activist Daniel Berrigan said that "the great revolutionary virtue is endurance." Part of that endurance comes from abiding in yourself and choosing to stay on good terms with your life. We even accept the invitation to forget ourselves on purpose. I take Abel and Tavito to join me to give a Thursday evening talk at a parish in Orange County, not far from Disneyland. It is pouring rain, a rare thing in Southern California, and people are driving like they've never seen rain before. It takes forever to arrive. I tell the packed house that we left on Tuesday to get here. Before the talk, Tavito, a tad nervous, is vomiting quite a bit in the bathroom off the vestibule of the church and I'm trying to talk over his retching to our pleasant host.

Abel speaks first. His gait is uncertain. He drags one leg and one arm is curled up some. He was shot thirty-three times, in a coma for six months, and spent a year and a half recuperating in the hospital. Someone in the office once asked him, "Why are you smiling and laughing all the time?"

He simply said: "I've been through too much, not to smile and laugh."

It takes some time for him to reach the podium. He gets there and silently surveys his audience, moving his head back and forth. Finally, he speaks. "Well . . . G told us . . . we were going to Disneyland. . . . And we ended up here." The entire church roars with laughter that is quite sustained. *I'll be damned*, I think. *He has them exactly where he wants them.* He tells his story at some length. The audience is spellbound and indeed reverent. Abel winds down. "Well . . . I better end this, or . . . you'll start throwing tomatoes." A charming end to a gripping story that won hearts and minds.

The three of us stand up there to field questions after my forty-five-minute talk. The first question "out da gate" is for Abel. "What led you to Homeboy Industries?" We wait for Abel to make his way to the podium. Having all heard his story, there is collective admiration now for the difficulty of his pace.

"Well," he says, "I heard they were having pizza." Huge laugh. Then he says with some quiet gentleness, "Everyone loves pizza." Abel is abiding in himself and it is a revolutionary act. It turns the world on its head and people know the poignancy of this. That we are all connected and born wanting the same things. Yes. Everyone loves pizza.

Our vomiting Tavito does fine as well. Afterward, in the hall where I'm seated signing books, I can "ear hustle" a conversation between a woman and Tavito. She is distressed about her teenage son and she's asking him for advice. "Be lovable," he says, "don't yell." He rewinds a bit. "I mean, I'm not saying that you yell . . . but if you do . . . don't." Experience speaking. Tavito (not withstanding his vomiting) has begun to attend well to all that is alive and kicking in his soul and has found comfort and healing. Plus, he begins to forget himself on purpose. This is the wisdom of one who has finally learned to be on good terms with his life.

I'm in an airport, sitting and waiting for my flight to leave, and a tiny girl, maybe three years old, rushes past in front of me. The floor is sloped and so the girl is screaming with delight, because this moderate hill propels her forward in running glee. Then her mom appears after having chased her some distance. She grasps her daughter's hand and gets down at eye level with the out-of-breath toddler. And the mom says this with some anger: "Charlotte, there is no margin of error in this airport." All the adults in earshot look quizzically at each other as the mother marches Charlotte away. All our faces announce: *Say what now?*

The "margin of error" for homies comes dramatically in the form of intense trauma thrown their way. It is a degree of difficulty placed in their path. All brokenness gets intensified and eventual gang involvement ensured.

The Adverse Childhood Experiences (ACEs) study helps us to see this large margin. It is a questionnaire that identifies ten childhood traumas that have happened before one's eighteenth birthday. Five are personal: physical abuse, verbal abuse, sexual abuse, physical neglect, and emotional neglect. The other five are related to family members: a parent who is an alcoholic or a drug addict, a mother who is a victim of domestic violence, a family member in jail, one diagnosed with mental illness, the disappearance of a parent (divorce, death, abandonment). The experts say that if you are a 4 or 5 on the ACEs, the chances are high that you will have health problems and/or socializing difficulties. I am a 0 on the ACEs. This has more to do with my own white privilege and the winning of the zip code, education, sibling, and parent lotteries. Stressors weren't widespread like they are in the community where I now have lived for more than half my life. This does not make me morally superior to the men and women who walk through our doors at Homeboy.

Every single homie and homegirl who enters our place is a 9 or 10 on the ACEs. This is the margin. This is the degree of difficulty. This is the burden at which we all stand in awe.

Saul is imposing, but long ago he chose not to lead with imposition. He's on security detail today at Homeboy, which is more like a traffic cop. During the pandemic, the homies have put up for me a fairly nice, airy tent (think *Lawrence of Arabia*) in the parking lot. It is white, with plastic windows, a desk, a carpet, and several chairs placed more than six feet away from me. The homies are overly stressed that with my underlying leukemia, it would be too risky for me to be inside the building. I'm going with it. A homie stepped into my "casbah" and said, "Damn, G—feels like Afghanistan in here." Saul is making sure safety protocols are maintained: masks and distancing. He guides one *vato* out and leads another in. I watch him call the younger guys "Papa" as he points them toward the exit. "Papa" is what you'd call your son.

Rene sits in one of the chairs in front of me, discussing whatever the dilemma of the day is for him, and takes a moment to point back at Saul, who is visible but some distance from the tent. "G, did you know he and I are the worst enemies? Our neighborhoods hate each other. But just right now, he gave me the best advice I think I've ever gotten. Uplifting. Made me feel confident."

Toward the end of the day, I call Saul in and play back all the times he called the little homies "Papa" and note how tender that was. I also share what Rene said to me. In an instant, this big old guy falls into some rapid combustion of emotion and holds his hand up to his eyes. I'm struck by how immediate this is. Maybe he's as surprised as I am. "I'm living my purpose, G," he ekes out finally. "All my life I was running and running— until I realized I was running from myself. Well, not no more."

As a kid, Saul lived with his mom and brothers and a stepfather who regularly beat and tortured him. Three adult relatives sexually abused him repeatedly. The stepfather would throw Saul's mom through windows, and once Saul came home and couldn't find her. Saul finally discovered his mom, bound and gagged, in the closet. So, at thirteen years old, he killed his stepfather. He spent thirteen years in the Youth Authority and then graduated to prison for another ten years. Saul swims in a liberating clarity of mindfulness. His unconditional high regard for his own tough experience has issued in a spacious connection to all things. "I've decided to grow up to be somebody I always needed as a child." His awareness of everyone is nonjudging and respectful. Living your purpose looks like this.

Sometimes our compassion is lost through fear and trauma, but it is always a few breaths away. It can be reawakened. Saul's history was a life-denying landscape filled with shame, a sense of unworthiness and self-hatred. He now opens to life without his previous armoring. He doesn't push things away and can rest in his true nature. He has chosen wellness rather than settling for a life that's just less miserable. A breath away.

⋄⧓⋄

In the gospel, we see the Gerasene demoniac, and he is completely alienated. He is the object of fear and many "devils" possess him. After the miracle, he sits at the feet of Jesus. He's become a disciple. From nakedness to clothed, he's become a witness now. Restored to living his purpose.

I meet Lil Casper in the halls of Eastlake courtroom. He recognizes me from Juvenile Hall. He's awaiting an appearance before his judge. I notice an ugly scar on his hand. It is a tattoo that he has burned off with a cigarette. "I know that if I had parents," he tells me tearfully, "I could make them proud of me." The good news here is that we can be re-created. If we work alongside the energies of God, we become new, despite the margin of error into which we are born.

"Still a long way off," the Scripture says, as the father goes running. "Mercy within mercy within mercy," as Thomas Merton put it. Something merciful and healing happens when you decide that escaping yourself is no longer an option. Our re-creation requires this, and we rest in the merciful bath of self-acceptance. Not just a bath but mercy as the water we swim in. In German, the word for "mercy" translates to "warmheartedness." This captures I think, tenderness as the foremost passion of God— what Dylan Thomas called "unjudging love."

Timothy, a Black gang member who always held his cards as close as he could, put them down once and started to speak. "I've never been loved by parents. I don't know what it's like to be loved, or to love somebody else. I don't open up to people. I'm afraid I'd be too ashamed if I told anybody how I grew up." Hearing himself say such a thing catches in that emotional part of his throat that produces sound and he half-croaks the next words. "I bring flowers home to my lady, cuz I've seen that's what you do." He cries. "But I don't know what to do with them or what to say. So I just leave 'em on the kitchen counter and hope . . . she'll run into them." He cries all the more. "I just hope she'll know what they mean."

A judge sentenced eighteen-year-old Max to life without the possibility of parole. The judge knew this sentence was illegal, since Max was sixteen when he committed murder. "I don't care," the judge said, "I'm giving it to you anyway. I think you're a monster." To the judge, Max was the Gerasene demoniac. But he was quite mentally ill and, therefore, worthy of compassion. Folks who carry this unwanted burden of mental anguish hope for a kindness. Plato was right: "Be kind, for everyone you meet is fighting a hard battle." And Max was fighting a battle I've never been asked to wage. Society punishes people for bad behavior, and we call it justice, but real justice restores.

We've mistaken moral outrage for moral compass. Moral compass helps you see with clarity how complex and damaged people are. It is the whole language. Moral outrage just increases the volume and the distance that separates us. I suppose if I thought moral outrage worked, I'd be out raging. But rage just means we don't understand yet. Ten people were killed in the Santa Fe High School shooting in Texas a number of years ago. Senator Ted Cruz said, "Once again, Texas has seen the face of evil." But a teenage girl and fellow student of the shooter said, "The one who did this must have been carrying a world of pain inside." Understanding love is who our God is. Loving this way announces the Tender One.

-◇◆◇-

I first knew Juanito when he was a little kid in the projects. He was once on a mission to collect cans for his mom. Maybe he was ten. It didn't take long for our conversation to dissolve into his crying, head bowed, clutching at his half-full garbage bag. His mom was pregnant with the sixth kid to join the household. Juanito's dad, a gang member, had his homegirls beat his mom down yesterday, so she'd lose the baby. We think of the light loads a ten-year-old ought to carry, then we contemplate such a burden laid on one so young. You have to catch your breath. They say that when a rat runs right into a fire, know that it is being pursued by something hotter than fire. That was Juanito.

So, no one was surprised when Juanito found his way to becoming Grizzly, a gang member who drew "respect" for all the wrong reasons. When he was sixteen, I saw him in the projects and heard he had been gone. "Yeah, I got arrested, but I only did a week. A homie got shot and that was because nobody was watching the barrio. They're all 'scary' . . . 'Oooh . . . I'm on probation.'" As he told me this, he mocked his homies by trembling and doing the homie version of shaking in your boots. "So," he finished, "I went down to take care of business." The veneer is like marble, rock-hard and impenetrable.

Grizz was once chased by cops. "Not sure why I ran—I

wasn't dirty. I took off cuz I just didn't want to be hassled." He scaled a fence with some razor wire, and a finger got caught. He leaped to the ground, but part of his finger stayed on the fence. He told me that the cops saw the dismembered digit, were completely grossed out, and left. Grizz took what remained of his finger to the hospital and coldly said to the triage nurse, "Fix this." And they did.

After way too much time, Grizz found his way to Homeboy and it was this sacred threshold place for him. Grizz found Homeboy as a hallway between his old comfort zone (which, let's face it, was never that comfortable) and a new, bold answer to it. He found this safe area, a field of kindness, care, and attention. Somewhere between this old and new version was a fecundity of healing. Grizz had been convinced, like all the traumatized, that he only had three responses in his repertoire: fight, flight, or freeze. He could even recognize that his past behavior was not so much "bad," but rather the understandable reaction to his deeply felt traumatic stress. He chose to no longer be victimized by his anger. "Besides," as the homie Robert told him, "your past is like your ass—behind you."

Homeboy Industries isn't just a sanctuary and sacred place, it's a petri dish cultivating an ability to find the sacred beyond this place. Someone like Grizz walks in and can't help but attach to this cherishing community. He's held by a no-matter-what-ness. Only in such a culture can you reidentify and accept yourself with a mystical wholeness. You can then discard all those things that previously you held back. The places where you used to get stuck. "The point of Homeboy," one trainee told another, "is not just to pay your bills but to heal your ills." After that, it's not so much smooth sailing as it is resilient and integrated enough to deepen the sense of your own truth.

Finally, Grizz walks in and waves a paper at me. "I got my welding certificate." We both are jubilant. Then, quite randomly, he says, "All my life I told myself, I'm gonna get me a house." He pauses here to tame a rising emotion. "But how . . . how'm I gonna get a house?" He stops to cry. "Now I know how: WELDING." A re-creation brought to you by the energies of God.

"None of us are well until all of us are well." This was plastered on billboards and buses all over Los Angeles. It was a campaign for the LA County Department of Mental Health, but it is also a quintessential and hugely Christian message. It's about health and about bringing others along as we all grow into greater wholeness and integration. How do we help each other to measure progress in this? Psychologists might say you notice such health in our individual ability to negotiate conflict. You see this only every day at Homeboy.

Human beings can sometimes move fluidly from some kind of developmental immaturity and behavioral quirkiness to substance abuse to bona fide severe mental illness. None of us are well until all of us are well. You fill the culture with the presence of healthy, buffering caregivers. We are all, then, as my friend Pastor David Moore says, "medics in a war zone." These "medics" have an ability to self-regulate in such a way that it can reduce everyone's toxic stress—even their own. Sometimes, we are caught in a paralyzing trance of fear and anxiety. Rather than defend our life from what terrifies us, we find relief from our fear in acceptance of the terror and allow it to transform us. To just feel the pain, rather than rush to fix it.

Rayshawn, Cisco, and I stopped by the *Maid of the Mist*, a ship that takes you on an adventure where you get so perilously close to Niagara Falls that you need to wear a raincoat (which comes with the price of admission). We were about to board when Rayshawn said, "We aren't going near the water, are we?" I'm not entirely sure what he thought we had been in line waiting to do. In RAINCOATS, no less. It turns out, Rayshawn was completely terrified of water. Showers and baths were barely tolerated. Twice as a child, folks had tried to drown him. At that point in our boarding, it was too late to disembark. So, Cisco and I each grabbed an arm, marched Rayshawn to the front of the ship, and we were off. Anxiety attack. Anxiety relieved. We all hung on to each other as we inched closer than comfort should allow us to the very mouth of the falls. The grip of fear relaxed its command on us all. Our belonging to each other seemed to ask this question of us: "Is it okay for us to be here?" The "yes" was resounding and we were freed. We had settled into a safe haven of belonging and had actually found rest.

Lucila and Cuko were duking it out in my office. I was grateful that she could scream all she wanted at him. His drug use had been all-consuming and had now put them and their two kids in real peril. She was standing, pointing at him, dry-eyed and clear. He had melted into his shoes. "You took my TV, you sold it. You took my CD player, you sold it. And the only reason you haven't sold my ass IS CUZ IT'S ON ME!!!!!" Then she sat down. Some stranglehold got loosened and freed up. They could look at each other now and even back their way into some merciful soft spot. Then they both cried, and I was blessed they'd found that place here.

Famous, award-winning Italian novelist Erri De Luca somehow found his way into Homeboy Industries. After a tour and a meal at Homegirl Café, they directed him to my office. He sat there and measured what to say. "This place . . . is the nerve center of hope." It called to mind a homie, Joseph Holguin, who told me once, "Show me a place of struggle, and I'll show you a place of strength." Create the place, the culture that repairs attachment and reconnects severed belonging, then you have a place of strength, a nerve center of hope.

Brandon, by any measure, is too young to have a daughter. He's seventeen, a gang member, and estranged from his "baby mama." He steps into my office to tell me of his disappointment

at having been told his ex would drop off his daughter at Homeboy, and now, for the third time, she's failed to do so. What he
really wants to tell me is this: "I know how I used to react before.
I'd get lokky and crazy with her. I'd lose it. It would always
make things worse. Not now. I learned this here. I was calm,
didn't raise my voice. Tried to be understanding. It didn't change
things, but it didn't make it worse." Brandon learned a way less
exhausting than getting lokky. It was the culture of hope that
brought him so far.

Homies resurface many years later. It's often an occasion
in which they want me to be present or officiate. I hadn't seen
Keith in maybe fifteen years, since he was in his early twenties,
a huge African American gang member who lived in the projects and had no business being in a gang. Of course, who does?
But Keith was always kind and centered in his own goodness.
His strong mother may account for this. While most folks need
constant reminding of the divine presence forever within, Keith
always seemed to have a handle on this.

Keith wanted me to do his wedding, so I made an appointment to meet with the couple. I didn't know Yvonne, his fiancée, and our meeting wasn't long. We filled each other in on
our lives, did a perfunctory pass over the wedding ceremony. We
were set. I walked them to the front door of Homeboy, hugged
Yvonne, and then said goodbye to Keith. His embrace was earnest and intense. He would not let go of me. Then I realized that
this hug had released some guardrail to his emotions, and now
he was softly crying, resting his head on my shoulder. I waited
to find out what this meant. Finally, he whispered in my ear,
"I expected you to do my funeral, and now . . . you're doing my
wedding."

I was talking with Abel, the one who reminds us that everyone loves pizza. He's been one of our tour guides lately and we
always assign a newer trainee to shadow the more experienced

tour guide, like Abel. He was telling me that he saw this guy walk in one day. "He was the guy who shot me." And then he said, "You hired him." I don't know who he's talking about, but now the shooter is shadowing Abel and listening to the story he shares with groups, large and small. "You give good tours," Abel's shadow tells him.

What we do at Homeboy is restorative justice. We restore people to wholeness, health, and the fullness of their own truth. None of us are whole until all of us are whole. Surely part of this is what Paul Tillich believed was the core of Christian faith: "to accept the fact that we have been accepted."

Hoang came to this country when he was two, among the boat people fleeing Vietnam in the late '70s. Since he lived in the Pico Gardens housing projects, he, like many teenage males, felt the gravitational push into the Latino gang there. As was unfortunately also typical, they called him Chino. He went with me and Manny to give talks in New Orleans and Baton Rouge. He stayed relatively calm on his first flight ever, only freaking out once, when he spied the pilot leaving the cockpit and ducking into the restroom. "WHO'S FLYING THE PLANE?"

We did Bourbon Street and the French Quarter and we noshed on fried gator. Our first night was spent in an old hotel off the French Quarter, with an overgrown courtyard and fountain. Very early the next morning, there was a great pounding on my door as I stepped out of the shower and wrapped myself in a towel. "I CLEAN YO ROOM NOW!!!" I raced to the front door, which had a paned window with a small lace curtain. The knocking intensified. "I CLEAN YO ROOM NOW!" I pulled back the curtain slightly and saw Hoang doing his best possible impersonation of his own mother, needing to clean my room . . . NOW! I open the door enough to tell him to scat and skedaddle. The memory of it is like gum that doesn't lose its flavor, and the sweetness of it endures and makes me smile still.

We had several talks in Baton Rouge. Each time, tiny Hoang would get up and say, "It's a pleasure and an honor to be here in (insert Baton Rouge)." But for some reason, his brain just couldn't perform the gymnastics needed to deliver those two words through his mouth. What came out instead was sometimes "Beirut" or even "Babe Ruth." I finally had to tell him, "Just say it's good to be here . . . period."

In his last talk, he said, "The only other place like Homeboy . . . is heaven. I see the flowers bloom there. I arrived as a caterpillar and I wrapped myself in the cocoon of all their services, and now I'm a butterfly. In fact, I flew here this morning."

I took Myles to Memphis. I always take two homies (or homegirls), but when I went to pick up Matthew, Myles's co-traveler that early morning of the flight, he was missing in action. So, it was just Myles and me. In his late thirties, Myles was from a large Black gang and had spent a sizable portion of his young life in prison. Part of his story was a gripping tale of declining an invitation from his brother and his two best friends to go out one night. They left without him and all three were killed. Not one of them was a gang member. Myles shared this story in Memphis in front of audiences who held him with such care. He spoke of the spiral of drugs, despair, and incarceration that followed this pivotal tragedy. "I realized that death didn't want me . . . cuz I was already dead."

I took Myles to the Lorraine Motel, where Martin Luther King was killed, and which is now the Civil Rights Museum. He stayed for four hours. "That just changed my life, right there." We ate fried green tomatoes at the oldest soul food restaurant in Memphis. Dr. King ate there. We even did Graceland.

Once, out of the blue, while we were driving somewhere in Memphis, Myles asked me if I'd ever been in a place where "you drive on the other side of the road." I told him that I had driven in Ireland many times. "Have you ever been to a winery?"

"Lots of times," I told him.

"Damn, G," he said, with a large piece of punctuation, "What HAVEN'T you did?" So I turned the tables on him from his random questions and asked if he had a bucket list. I guess we always think this will issue in a lineup of places you want to see. "Hell yeah," he said, "I want to skydive, which is funny cuz I hate roller coasters and heights. AND I want to learn how to swim."

Right away, I turned and looked at him, wide-eyed. "I know, I know," he said. The previous day, he had told me how terrified he was of water. Like Rayshawn, he had once nearly drowned as a child. "I've decided that I want to be a try-er from now on." He looked out the window and said in a reverent tone, "Yeah, I wanna try . . . a gang a' things now."

At Homeboy, we talk about the Hope/Healing Index. We always want to stay less interested in making statements about hope. We want to generate it. In the Second Letter of Paul to the Corinthians, the word "encouragement" is mentioned ten times. "The Father of compassion and the God of all encouragement." And yet we can get stuck in this place where we are utterly convinced God has been disappointed. But, truly, we are meant to both feel encouraged by God and be a source of endless, hopeful encouragement for the downhearted. Generators of hope. Martin Luther King said that "everything that is done in the world is done by hope." When Myles stepped out of the Lorraine Motel, he hadn't settled for hope, but, rather, the vitality of hope. At our place, we call it "Homeboyancy."

I told this story once in a funeral homily for my friend, Pam Rector. She died of complications from her second kidney transplant. "The first transplant gave her life. The second transplant gave her hope," a friend eulogized. Pam had a daughter, Grace, and spent many years in the Lennox School District and then at Loyola Marymount University. She was a force of nature. A mutual friend of ours, Eileen McDermott, once was headed to Pelican Bay State Prison as part of a delegation of ministers. As I've mentioned earlier, this was considered the locale for the worst of the worst. Pam heard of this and insisted that Eileen check in "on one of my kids from Lennox." This "kid" was called from the Security Housing Unit . . . where the even "worst" are held. Eileen was on a phone, behind thick glass, and this very large tattooed Latino warily approached, thinking, no doubt, *Why has this white woman called me out?* In no time, Eileen got to mentioning Lennox and Pam Rector and the melting was immediate. This thirty-year-old man had been rushed to his fifteen-year-old self and grew teary-eyed at the mere thought that his former teacher held him still in heart and mind. It was a favorable return to a favored self.

We simply have this capacity to buoy folks in a hope that floats. Theologian John S. Donne speaks of a parable of sorts that takes place during the time of the great exploratory voyages. These Spanish sailors are aboard this huge vessel at the mouth of the Amazon River, and they are dying of thirst. And yet, they were floating, without knowing it, in fresh water. We think that we rest upon undrinkable salt water. Donne calls it "a parable of exhaustion and inexhaustible life." We can always be drinkable water for each other if we set our hearts to it. We can sometimes live our life dying of thirst, yet, unbeknownst to us, we are floating on fresh water that carries us.

Ricky had been a juvenile tried as an adult. He was as diminutive as homies come, but stocky and scrappy and shaped by his eighteen years in prison. Ricky was released when most of the juveniles given draconian sentences were set free. He told me that when he was six years old, a favorite and trusted uncle took him to the beach. Ricky had never been before. The man walked him out, and the water, thrillingly, rushed around his legs. Before too long, a wave knocks him over, and he was gasping for air and immersed. Ricky would pop his head up, crying for help, and he could see his uncle but was barely able to decipher what the uncle was yelling. A wave came again, and he was submerged. Ricky was certain he would drown. When his lungs reached the surface and he frantically took in air, he started to make out what his uncle was saying. "*Párate.*" Stand up. "So I stood up. I've come to realize that I never need to drown in the shallow end of my own beliefs ever again. Been standin' up, ever since."

Fabian was suddenly surrounded by five menacing gang members on the third floor of the Montebello Town Center. Gang members can sniff out a gang member, no matter how one attempts to hide the fact. Fabian was working at Homeboy and finding his way out of the "shallow end" of his own gang mentality. "Where you from?" one of the five said with the sneer that is meant to go with this "hit up." Fabian, somehow, had the composure ready enough to reach into his pocket. The five recoiled a bit. Fabian pulled out the requisite number of business cards. "I'm from Homeboy Industries. Come in. We'll hook you up." These *vatos* studied the cards but quickly said, "*Serio?* Really? Where's it at?" Everyone wants to stand up in the surf. It sure beats drowning.

-◦‡◦-

Part of the restoration is a return to parenting and connecting to one's kids. George is at a crossroads. "I'm in men-o-pause." I laugh, but George doesn't. He thinks the word means a fence straddler—between being a boy (gangbanging) and being a man (not gangbanging). He thinks it means a pause in your manhood. This clear choice of George's informed him as a father. George says of his daughter: "When I'm around her, I feel like I'm breathing air of a richer kind."

Another homie on our graffiti-removal crew tells me: "I love my crew. I love my job. I love my life." And all this, I suspect, leads him to say further: "I feel privileged to have been sculpted by the culture here at Homeboy. Then I bring this culture home." And cycles get broken.

José says, "We ask people to swap out their habits." Practice doesn't make perfect. It makes permanent. Surely, a principal habit is gangbanging itself and the clinging to the idea of having enemies. But a place and culture of healing will always remind people that God doesn't have enemies. God has children. So, Nico and Beto are assigned to croissant detail. They stand next to each other masterfully manipulating dough and transforming it into a roll. They are enemies. They won't speak to each other. Nico has a tattoo of Beto's gang on his face just so that he can cross it out with another tattoo. This is an event in the "Provocation Olympics." Huge.

Once, on Nico's day off, he walks into our Tattoo Removal Clinic, points at his alarming facial tattoo, and says, "I want this off." The next day, side by side with Beto, he lifts a finger to indicate this raised, swollen red reminder of his first treatment and says, "I'm getting this off. It's because of you. You're good people." He hadn't "worked out their differences." There are no differences. Only "samenesses" that bind us together. Jesus doesn't call us to be peace feelers, or peace thinkers, or peace lovers. Peacemakers. We are asked to create something. We begin by swapping out a habit.

Nico tells me this shortly after his metanoia, this change of heart. "I was telling myself the other day, like G always says: 'You're a fuckin' dumbass if you go back to the neighborhood.'" My eyes widen. "Well, maybe not in those exact words, but that's my interpretation."

I'm on my beach cruiser and I bump into Smilone, a sixteen-year-old crack dealer and gang member, standing alone at midnight in a part of the projects where one of his homies had been shot the night before. He just had a major fight with his lady. "I had to get outta there. She's all up in here." He puts three or four fingers in his ear. "She's all up in the eardrum." I warn him of the dangers of his current location. He shrugs and says, "Padre, I have nothing to lose." A few beats later, he begins to cry, trapped in the desperate habits he's finding hard to swap out. "Heal the wounds . . . warm the hearts," as Pope Francis says.

Jeanette rarely asks for an audience. I've known her since her gangbanging days, her getting-high days, and her in-and-out-of-prison days. She has her kids back and is a Navigator. She rarely asks to see me. "You know, G," she says, "I texted you this morning and you didn't get back to me."

It's now nearing 4:00 p.m. and I move quickly into default defense. "Yeah, kiddo—it's been a crazy day, and I get thousands of texts."

Jeanette stops me and even uses her hand to halt my words. "G . . . if you don't text me back"—now she holds her hand to her eyes—"I think . . . you're mad at me." This just slits my heart wide open, and I am on my feet, hugging her, also teary, doing my best to convince her that "mad" is not part of my vocabulary with her, ever.

That evening I had agreed to speak to a combined group consisting of the members of confirmation programs from various parishes. Seven hundred teenagers await my speech. I am standing off to the side, at the front of the church, near the altar, while the catechist is explaining future events and assignments. I have become the mad texter. With Jeanette's admonition still fresh, I'm getting back to everyone. So many of them say, "G . . . I gotta talk to you." I get ninety-three of those each day. I tell these homies when to come in. The rest I respond to as best and as quickly as I can. "Thanks, son. Hearing from you made my day." "Hey, *mija*, is the baby sleeping through the night?"

"Hey, dawg, how'd that job interview go?" I don't stop texting even while the woman introduces me.

After the talk, I'm in the vestibule and folks are crowding around. They say nice things; I shake their hands. I keep turning and signing books. When I turn to a woman on my left, she says, "I'm very disappointed in you." I think, *Oh gosh, here we go.* I ask her why. "The texting." I'm confused. I think she's mentioning a riff I do in my talk on texting and autocorrect, so I suggest that. "NOOOO," she's quite insistent. "You were texting in front of the tabernacle." It all came into place now.

"Oh," I tell her, gently placing my hand on her arm. "Aren't we lucky to have a God who doesn't care about such things?" And I turn to the next person crushing in.

Here's the thing. I drive home and feel this dark and heavy pressure forcing its way into my consciousness. It's a dread mixed with dis-ease. Then I land on it. My words to this woman. I didn't catch myself and I weaponized my response. I was defensive and I just wanted to win the argument. It reminds me of what restoration I need still and I feel called to be sculpted anew by the culture of nurturing and cherishing. The mystical view keeps us from justifying how annoyed we are and it topples our self-importance. I wanted to stand with a radically loving and undefended heart. In my mind, I heard myself tenderly apologizing to the woman, acknowledging her pain without judging it as out of step theologically or inconvenient to me.

We talk a lot at Homeboy about transformation. This, of course, requires the fullest cooperation and some mystical and contemplative savoring of everything that happens to us. Even the discomfort of people calling us up short. The way of our broken, open hearts is to try and respond to the hurt, not with more hurt, but with a nurturing touch. You choose, as part of your practice, a genuine and unconditional positive regard shown to all, even to those expressing disapproval in you.

Trayvon announced that it was his birthday. He was a multiple returnee to Homeboy, having drifted away a number of times to addiction and jail. He was there to get a start date. I slipped forty bucks in an envelope, with a note to present the following Monday: "I'm glad you were born." So I've probably said this to many thousands upon thousands of gang members, but I never got this in return: Trayvon, his face laced with tattoos, asked, "Now why would you be glad that I was born?"

I had to think. "Well, that's easy," I told him. "It's cuz you've altered my heart. I have more room in it now, because of you." I had never seen Trayvon cry before. Heal the wounds. Warm the heart. Maybe, I think, the time of transformation, for both of us, has shown up.

During the decade of death in the housing projects, there were eight distinct gangs, all at odds with one another. The strangest piece of it was not the segmented gang territories in these housing developments, but the divided households. There were many brothers who shared rooms with their enemies. Though their apartment might be in a defined gang turf, one sibling could befriend guys at school from an entirely different and rival gang and then get jumped in. We had lots of these pairings.

Late one evening I am sitting on a project second-floor landing with four homies from this one gang. As happens many times, a car goes by and shots are fired at the group of us. As always, I get the "Secret Service" pile-on treatment and the car passes. It never takes me too long to find out who is in the marauding car. Leo, one of the four I'm kicking it with, tells me that the shooter is his brother, Jerry. I go out of my way to find Jerry the next day. He is horrified to know that I had been standing in that group. He does not deny that he was the shooter. "The thing I really wondered about, son," I ask him, "was, if you had killed Leo, would you have gone to the funeral?" He cries. In the end, one can't really "reason" with any of this. There is no other

way to face a lethal absence of hope, except, I suppose, by telling folks you're glad they were born.

One of our lifers at Homeboy, who never thought he'd see freedom, looked out his window at San Quentin and marveled at the water glistening and separating him from San Francisco. He'd first picked up a gun at the age of eight, shot a gun at eleven, and had his best friend die in his arms that same year. He would stare at the water and tell himself, *I will never touch that water again.* This sentiment finally would guide him to resolve, *Even if I die here—I can change here.*

—◇|◇—

In our third headquarters, from 2000 to 2008, I recall mainly chaos. Homies would hover in the "well," the recessed area where there were banks of phones and computers. "Homeboy Industries, how may I help you?" Folks lined the walls waiting to see me, but I don't recall much order to the process. I'd normally step out of my glass-enclosed domain and signal for someone to come in. It was my informal triage method. If I spotted a homegirl with crying kids, I'd call her in. Usually, a semi-throng would crowd me as I stepped out of my office, like vendors at the Tijuana border, arms flailing and throwing out verbal hints on why they should be seen next. Nacho was particularly good at this and annoyingly insistent.

One such day, his arms are waving and his word salad is: "Judge—court . . . Thursday—gotta get enrolled—outpatient." Like that. I keep calling in other folks ahead of him, to his great annoyance.

Finally, I step out, folks crowd, I signal the next person, and I turn to Nacho, on the clamoring edge, and say, "I'm seeing you last." Nacho approximates a stricken look. Then I say, "I'm sorry. *Spensa.* I came at you sideways, Nacho." Then I say with a sameness, "I'm seeing you last."

Nacho registers shock: "You didn't change nuthin'."

Nacho, at last, is called in. He's in his late twenties, a whirl-wind of bloviation and high energy. You kind of have to be in the mood. He settles into the chair in front of my desk. But I continue to be bombarded by interruptions. Homies step in and relay messages. I get alerted to important calls through the inter-com. "Hey, G, line three—the mayor."

Then I'd say to Nacho, "Sorry, dawg, I really gotta take this." (Once, they "intercommed" me. "Hey, G, line two—Barbara Walters." I think, *Wow, Barbara Walters.* I pick up. It's home-girl Jessica Valles. "I knew you'd take my call.") Nacho is ever the exasperated, put-upon homie. Finally, rest. "Okay, you're on. You have my undivided attention. Start at the beginning and don't leave anything out." Nacho becomes the model of leisure. "Well . . . first . . . I got up this morning . . . and I . . . made me some breakfast."

I lean forward. "Okay, Nacho, leave everything out."

Nacho, some ten years later, struggled to see his way out of a difficult maze of addiction and repeat stints in jail. The homie Stevie says, "If you don't deal with your pain, you're in a car with-out brakes. Eventually you crash." Well, this was Nacho. Often a runaway car. His weariness with this pattern became palpable. "Sometimes I wish I was an old man already—ready to die." The brakes are so essential, for only then can you embrace your suffering, then land on a spiritual intimacy with yourself and others.

We are always astounded by the resources we can muster and our human ability to transcend whatever gets thrown at us. I rush one of our bakers, Sergio, to the White Memorial Medical Center emergency room. He was horseplaying with one of his co-workers and popped out his shoulder. Apparently, this was not the first incident of its kind in his life. He and I are in one of those barely curtained waiting areas in the ER inner sanctum, and he is screaming and writhing in pain. A nurse comes in and needs Sergio to sign a release form before they can pop this shoulder back to its original state. I figure, since he's in such unspeakable agony, that maybe he'll mark an "X" or scribble the faintest semblance of a signature. She holds the clipboard firmly with both hands so he can, I think, put a Neanderthal scratch on the release form. He proceeds, however, to sign "Sergio Rodriguez" in the most careful, ornate, Old English jailhouse script imaginable. We're humans. We rise to the occasion.

I bump into Lupita in the hallway and ask how she's doing. "I have my upside downs." Yup. Who doesn't? Lupita was raped and sexually abused by her stepfather from six years old until she turned twelve. At that juncture, she could no longer carry the secret and confided this terror to her mother. The mom didn't believe Lupita and promptly threw her out of the house. Before too many days on the streets, she began to live with an uncle who commenced to do the same thing to her. She begged her mom to accept her back and she relented. The stepfather's abuse resumed for another two years. It would have continued were it not for a female cop who lived next door and somehow suspected something, just by observing Lupita, now fourteen. She told the officer that this had been going on for eight years.

Lupita was a compelling witness and her stepfather got fifteen years. Her mom threw her out yet again, and this time, Lupita found her gang. Denise Levertov writes: "You step out on the rope and move unfalteringly across it and seize the fiery knives unscathed." What words are there to capture the courage of men and women who have faced so much, those who contend with the margin of error and such "upside downs"? The air of restoration is indeed a breath away. In the end, Lupita discovered that she was the self she always wanted. And it's the Upside Down God who helps us catch the fiery knives.

Chapter Six

House-Sitting for God

I suppose this is a chapter on Church.

I find myself at a fancy dinner in middle America, in a country-club ballroom with a fairly conservative Catholic crowd in attendance. I am the speaker this evening. A young couple in their early forties are on my right. The wife asks me a question: "I have a dilemma. One of my best friends in the world is getting married. She's a lesbian. Should I go to the wedding?"

The husband nearly leaps out of his chair, mortified that this question got asked, and his arms seem to move like he is collecting the words that left her mouth and wants to return them home. "Oh, honey, come on."

She insists on proceeding full speed ahead. "I went to my priest and he told me to ask five priests."

The husband tries to intervene again. "Honey, if you go to the wedding it will just usher in gay marriage"—this happened some years ago—"so you'll be cosigning on gay marriage if you attend." The wife doesn't take her eyes off me and gently puts her hand on her mate's knee to silence him.

I know to tread carefully, since I'm sitting there in clerical dress and this crowd has already established itself as somewhat traditional. "Well," I begin cautiously, "science and Jesus." I tell them that science shows us that some folks are born left-handed, and I ask them if they would insist that their left-handed child be forced to be right-handed now. They both shake their heads no. Then I ask the wife, "What would Jesus do?"

There is no hesitation. "He'd go to the wedding." Even the husband nods.

"When you think about it," I tell them, "that was all Jesus did in his earthly ministry: he went—to lesbian weddings."

My friend Mary Rakow says, "The Church is always trying to come to us from the future." So, we need to allow it. Jesus lived, breathed, and embodied a boundary-subverting inclusion. If it's inclusive and wildly so, then you know you're warm. You are close to it. Nothing is excluded except excluding. The Church speaks the whole language when it includes. It was intended, by Jesus, to be an alternative social vision. It is what Scripture scholar Marcus Borg called Jesus' "politics of compassion," which was counterposed to the politics of purity and holiness. Our demand that things change, and this "social vision" become reality, must be born from our compassion and not our contempt. It's mercy that softens us to always find room in our hearts. Turns out, this supple mercy can be kryptonite to how we sometimes see things in the Church.

I'm standing in front of T-Bone's house on Gless Street, enjoying the fiesta. I had baptized his two nephews earlier in the day. This is my last stop after having made an appearance at multiple celebrations in the neighborhood.

I hear a great commotion across the street in the projects. Even recalling the sound of it now is vaguely triggering for me. Screams and taunts and the dull thud of kicking. When I cross the street, I can see maybe ten girls pummeling a new member of their *clika*. They see me and finish and the yelling morphs into cheers of welcome. I start to walk back to the fiesta. Roscoe catches up to me and from behind wraps his tattooed arm around me so that his hand can rest on my chest. He leans his head on my shoulder as we cross Gless. "That pains your heart, doesn't it, G?" I tell him that it does. He won't let go of me even as we return to the party. How constantly we are offered the chance to say to each other, "I'm sorry you had to go through that." We allow Church to move beyond institution to movement, when mercy and compassionate love can pat you on the heart.

Certainly, the compassionate heart of Jesus was about healing when he bumped into lepers. But really, it was about inclusion. The healing was secondary. What was ultimately treasonous about Jesus was his inclusivity. He ignored boundaries. Jesus plowed right through them. If Mother Teresa is right, that we've drawn our family circle too small, then Jesus sought to correct that. "The excluded," Pope Francis tells us, "are still waiting." And above all, the gospel doesn't know what a sexual ethic is; it only has an ethic of love that longs to include and foster belonging. As a Church, we've allowed much to get calcified for us and we need to render it all less brittle.

Authentic Christianity never circles the wagons. It always widens the circle. It also knows that there is no need for an "in crowd" if everyone is in. Sinners were social outcasts in the time of Jesus. There was no practical way out of that. Jesus was from the middle class. He was not by birth or upbringing one of the poor or oppressed. He was, however, an outcast by choice. It was his compassionate response to the suffering he saw. Jesus talks about the gospel and not about himself. So, I suppose there is just no point in knowing Jesus, unless we're going to see as Jesus.

When I was chaplain at Folsom State Prison, there were three yards to tend to. B Yard was tough, always on lockdown. C Yard was more of a programming place. And A Yard was a special needs Yard. It had gang dropouts, high-profile inmates, wayward law enforcement officials, and sexual offenders. Guards would derisively characterize the three yards this way:

"On B Yard, you have knife fights; C Yard, fist fights; A Yard, pillow fights." I had many conversations with the former gang members on A Yard, who would criticize me for talking to the "chesters" (child molesters) and the "tree jumpers" (rapists). Everyone was welcome to the A Yard Chapel. I would listen to their criticisms and knew that their rejection of them (and perhaps me, by extension) was born of something specific. If you don't make a home for your own wound within, you will always despise the wounded. I would tell them that I was just trying to take seriously what Jesus took seriously. "Jesus called—he'd like his gospel back." The excluded are always waiting for us.

There is no place in the gospel where Jesus is defensive. In fact, he says, "Do not worry about what your defense will be." Jesus had no interest in winning the argument, only in making the argument. A follower of Jesus does this by loving in an open-hearted and always clear way. Our lives are supposed to make the argument. Being clear is better than defense. Clarity is authenticity and needs to be a hallmark of our faith community. I was at a march in the early days of the Trump administration. A very young girl carried a sign nearly twice her size and it read: "If You Build a Wall . . . My Generation Will Knock It Down." That's clear.

Defensiveness is human and understandable. I hired a homie named Julio once who was in possession of the worst attitude to ever walk through our doors. Julio was not the first homie who told me where to go and requested I do things with myself that I don't believe can be physically done. I do remember, as I hired him, that I deliberately chose to be intrigued by him rather than get defensive. Instead of dreading his arrival and the implications of his belligerence, I opted for curiosity. Way better. It worked out.

We can prioritize as "Church" things like vocations, marriage and family, religious liberty, and anti-abortion efforts, but it's hard not to circle the wagons while we do it. How do we remain clear without defense and protection? True followers of Jesus aren't under siege, but under the power of understanding love. It chooses to be intrigued by our world rather than threatened.

The fruit of such compassionate curiosity is that the fear, for example, that there won't be enough priests gets transformed into bravery. It asserts instead that there are plenty of priests out there, if we are willing to ordain them. It guides us to enhance the lives of couples so fully that they don't terminate their pregnancies. We don't see gay marriage as a threat to anything, but rather an honoring of Jesus and science. And I suspect that we will feel less threatened in our religious liberty the more concretely we live authentically Christian lives. We trade in sadness and fear for joy and bravery. The whole language. It's a game-changer.

Bill Maher points out that Martin Luther King never said that Southern sheriffs have a point too. "He said, 'I have a dream'... they have a nightmare." There is a clarity in knowing that we cut all ties to Jesus when we exclude, are violent, reject people, put conditions on our love ... and, well, defend the faith. Joy and bravery are the marks of our clarity. Sadness and fear tell us that we're holding back. We've grown accustomed in this age in which we live to think that thoughtlessness is telling it like it is. We mistake cruelty for strength. And exclusion has always masqueraded as a safeguarding of what is pure. Living the marrow of the gospel corrects our view of things.

After all, why would we shield and defend ourselves from anything? The antidote to the world's exclusions is to be anchored in a transcendent inclusion. We don't want to keep anything out, be defensive, and enclose our hearts. New wine. Old wine. The wineskins to match. The old wine is cosmetic piety and the new is real discipleship. Faith as decorative; Church as museum: old wineskins that we discard. The preaching of our lives may be expressed in the language of the culture, but the gospel we present will always be a foreign element to it. Otherwise, our discipleship is the lockstep of "Believe. Behave. Be saved." A decorative museum.

In the States, I've spoken to young people at gatherings called Theology on Tap. They have beer, you talk, young people meet each other. In Canberra, Australia, I did one of these in an actual pub. They called the evening God and Guinness. Before they quieted down the saloon to listen to me, a man handed over his cell. "Talk to my daughter. She's lost her faith." I mean, who doesn't love it when a total stranger hands you a cell phone and says that? Turns out, a terrible thing happened to her long ago and she blamed God and, well, game over. She "lost her faith."

"Actually, no," she told me. "I didn't lose it. I knew exactly where it was. I just didn't want it anymore."

But aren't we SUPPOSED to lose our faith? It's not different from our voices changing in puberty or hair turning gray. Like snakes shedding skin, aren't we always meant to break through to something more expansive? The mystics surely teach us this. Otherwise, we just dig in our heels, get defensive, and get stuck pledging allegiance to our elementary school God.

I think I was in the seventh or eighth grade when I was ready to shed some skin. We had to, as in the many years before, memorize from the Baltimore Catechism. So, I got it in my craw that such memorizing had little to do with actual faith and gospel living. I told the nun who was teaching this subject that I refused to memorize faith and I was summarily sent home. It was one of those "Wait till your father gets home" kind of moments. And when he did, I gave him my speech about how disconnected it was to commit to memory what should be experienced and lived in real and authentic ways. My dad raised his vodka water as if to toast, as he and my mom sat for their evening drink. He smiled and said, "Good for you. Good for you. I'm proud of you."

In *The Brothers Karamazov* (which I read for the first time during a pandemic book group), a young woman has lost her faith and she seeks counsel from a monk. He doesn't speak to her of God. He just tells her to go home and practice loving with those with whom she has contact. He assures her, "This way is tried. This way is certain." A mystical, loving way of life. That's it. Buddha didn't teach Buddhism—but a way of life. Jesus too.

Churches in second-century Rome fed twenty thousand of the city's poor. This is how they saw themselves: leading with their hearts, loving with their service. A Greek philosopher described Christians to Emperor Hadrian in this way: "They love one another. They never fail to help widows. They save orphans from those who would hurt them. If they have something, they give freely to the one who has nothing. If they see a stranger, they take him home and are as happy as though he were a real brother." Not a religion so much as a way of living and seeing.

◇◆◇

My spiritual director, Sergio, sent me an email last week with this one line: "Let us continue to unlock eternity for each other." When I could, I would have dinner with my mom once a week. I'd pour her a Manhattan with extra maraschino cherry juice. I would have a scotch and we'd eat cashews and she'd go over her weekly prepared list. "I won eight dollars and thirty-eight cents at bridge on Thursday. . . . So-and-so died. . . . Did you read Steve Lopez's article on Sunday in the *Times*?" Like that. Once, she reached the last topic. She just said, "Purgatory."

"What about it?" I countered.

"Do we still have it? I mean, I can see why we got rid of Limbo. But I think I'm gonna need Purgatory."

I told her that we don't go to heaven because WE are good, but because God is good. She seemed to buy this.

In that last week of her life, many of my brothers and sisters had gathered, and we are in the living room while the wonderful Dolly, her caregiver, tends to her. Dolly appears in the living room and summons me. "She wants to talk to you alone." Uh-oh. I walk the narrow hallway thinking, *Yikes— does she want to go to confession? Is there something she longs to get off her chest with me and no one else?* I pull a chair close and grab her hand, and she inclines her head to me. "You wanted to talk to me?"

"Yes," she says. The words have trouble but are pushed through with deliberation: "Make . . . me . . . a Manhattan."

I go to the living room, tell my sibs; we fortify our drinks (having determined earlier that it was 5:00 somewhere) and crowd around her bed, clinking our glasses with hers, which she could barely hoist but did. Laughter unhinged the armor around our hearts. No need for Limbo or Purgatory. It was a renewed discovery that "religion as social control," requiring Purgatory, was indeed bankrupt. "Believe, behave, be saved" wasn't going to cut it. For it didn't share the reverence for the complexity of things and the sacred chalice of the Manhattan with extra maraschino cherry juice. Jesus was all about the Here and Now, not the Here-After. Right now is gloriously transcendent with a God exceedingly good. Eternity unlocked. The marrow of the message needs to be clearly anchored in this. Like a map in a mall announcing "You Are Here." The arrow points to that.

We are always hopeful that the Church will see its Copernican Moment, when it decides that its center is not located in Europe, in white males, in mandatory celibacy. We all hope against hope that it will become the "wonderful adventure" that Pope Francis envisions. Church as movement and not decorative institution. The hope is that the Church will find instead that the very marrow of the center is with the God who stands with the powerless. Only from this center can we truly interrupt systems that keep people down. This is an essential task of the Church.

God stands with the powerless not to console them in their powerlessness, but to always remind them of their power. Hence, Jesus critiques all forms of domination and we are compelled to do the same as Church. Jesus invites us to this anarchy. To address what Martin Luther King calls "the triple evils of poverty, racism, and war." The social architecture that oppresses and the privilege that keeps this oppression quiet can be dismantled only if we stand at the margins compassionately. It is how we are meant to be Church. We locate those cultural values that need evangelizing. Even the urge to be successful and our addiction to measuring need to be critiqued in the light of the gospel. At the end of a weekend retreat given by myself and two homies, during the final Q and A session, a young woman lamented, "I can't leave the Church . . . then what will happen to the Church?" Her sense of ownership startled everyone in the room enough to elicit laughter. Richard Rohr says that for Saint Paul, "you do not live in the world and go to church. You live in the church and go to the world."

Adrian had been texting me nonstop. I was giving a talk somewhere in Los Angeles and he kept wanting to know my time of arrival. When I land at the office, Adrian is among "the Undulators," a term my brother Jesuit, Mark Torres, uses for those gathered in front of my glass door, waiting to be called in.

Adrian is seventeen years old and a gang member on probation. He has thick hair slicked back. And though he would not know this reference, he looks just like Eddie Munster, complete with a peak at his hairline. Like James of the gospel, he is without "guile." He is earnest, and his tongue is never lodged in his cheek. Sweet and affectionate, Adrian is not prone to teasing, and sarcasm is a foreign land.

I welcome him in and ask why his (Eddie Munster) hair is on fire. The litany he rattles off is a usual one. "My baby mama won't let me see my daughter . . . My PO be trippin' . . . And I don't even have money to get a haircut." I give him the "secret handshake" of twenty bucks. Then he levels in on me. "But how are YOU doing?"

Frankly, I'm not used to homies inquiring this way. "I'm good, son," I tell him, "and that's very kind of you to ask. But why do you ask?"

"Well," he says, shifting in the chair in front of my desk, "it's because of what happened." He leans in.

"What happened?" I ask, leaning toward him.

"Well, I barely heard right now . . . that priests . . . can't get married."

I whip off my glasses in horror. "WHAT??!!"

Without guile, he doesn't laugh, only leans in more.

"Yeah, I know. How ya doin' with that?"

Though celibacy always takes getting used to, I just didn't know how to explain that after nearly a half century as a Jesuit, I was somewhat acclimated to the idea.

The moral of this story: We don't all arrive at the same understanding at the same moment. So we might as well wait for folks. As much as we would want to accelerate everything and get folks to the moment of truth more quickly, people need to take their sweet time. To enter rehab; to leave gangbanging behind; to walk away from an abusive relationship; to return the Church to the marrow of its message. It takes what it takes. Live in the Church. Go to the world. We get "to the world," and we tend to feel that waiting is passive. It isn't. It's holy.

Like the gospel and Dharma teachings, we come to the truth of them at "different points along the river." We see them differently along the way. Things we already knew, but now see from a different angle. It's why probably no one ever says in church, "Oh no, not the Prodigal Son story AGAIN." Our ears are different today than they were yesterday. We find ourselves at another place along the river.

Waiting is holy and we need to expect that we will still occasionally speak past each other, our meaning missing the mark, overshooting, flying past and over our heads. Three Westside ladies are having lunch at Homegirl Café. Their waitress is Tarin, a towering Black gang member who stands ready to take their order. One woman asks, "What's the soup of the day?"

Tarin tells her, "Chicken lime."

The woman counters, "Is it hot?"

Tarin scrunches her face into a question mark. "It's soup." Expect to hear things differently.

It's a good thing that the Church finds itself most assuredly in a time of purification and dislocation. The gospel always wants to dislodge itself from the places where it gets stuck and embedded in the narrow, cultural structure. So, we all take steps to free it, find our way, again and again, to an expansive tolerance and a high reverence for paradox. We need to allow the Church to become a movement again. Jesus says if you're not gathering, you're scattering. We either pull people in or push people out. We attract in the same way Jesus did. You see the opposite of this in the Westboro Baptist Church folks who protested Mister Rogers's funeral because they found his tolerance intolerable.

Paul Tillich was right that the first theological task was to remove absurdities. Indeed, it's always been the absurdities, throughout history, that led to atrocities. Sergio says, "Get rid of all the stuff that puts Jesus to sleep."

There's the bishop who blames priestly sexual predation on the Devil. "We are dealing with Satan wandering the earth focused on tempting the most important of God's servants." Yikes. Or I was in Memphis once, on Ash Wednesday. The priest said, "We fast because our bodies lead us to sin." A side order of Yikes.

We all left the church that day malnourished. It's like when I see the homies feed their toddlers Flamin' Hot Cheetos. "Dawg, quit feeding your kids crap." Same thing.

At Homeboy we say that folks walk through our doors barricaded behind a wall of shame and disgrace and only tenderness can scale that wall. We hear in the gospel, "No room in the inn," and we think Motel 6 and "No Vacancies." But actually, Joseph went home. These were his people. So, everyone who said no were probably blood relatives. They were cousins and uncles, and there was no room for the shame and disgrace of Joseph's "fiancée," big as a house and ready to burst. Tenderness finds room. Church at its best.

When Saint Ignatius says, "See Jesus standing in the lowly place," this still is an appeal to our goodness and not our conscience. There is no shaming because God doesn't believe in it. I think it's perfectly fine to distrust any invitation to stand at the margins that enfeeble us with guilt. Nope. We keep thinking we are being called to DO something at the margins. But the real question is: Who will we become as we stand there? So warmly embrace any invitation to stand in the lowly place that reminds you of your abiding goodness and points the way to joy. We are beckoned to be a Church that does this.

The "standing" Ignatius speaks of is not a standing still. Pope Francis reminds us that the living of the gospel must be on the move, otherwise it becomes standing water that gets putrid. It's the movement that keeps it vital. Jesus would eat with the unacceptable outcast to render them wholly acceptable. This stirs the water in any time. I ran into a homie at Juvenile Hall. He was certain I'd remember him. "You remember me—you scrubbed my feet." This meant he must have been one of the twelve guys whose feet I washed the Holy Thursday some months before at Camp Miller. The outcast experience real estrangement, but it is equally true how indelibly they hold the moment of inclusion.

I pull up the car in front of a sign in Chicago that reads "St. Ignatius: A Jesuit Preparatory School." I have brought with me Hugo and Darrell. Hugo, a tiny gang member, is in the front seat. "Hey, Pops, what's a Jesuit?" I mention how it's a large religious order, of which I am a member, founded by Saint Ignatius in 1534. Now, homies are purveyors of urban legends and conspiracy theories. "Wait a minute," he says, "I heard that Jesuits used to chop off people's heads." I told him only if folks pissed us off. "Hang on." Hugo holds his phone in front of his face. "Google: Did Jesuits used to chop off people's heads?" We wait for the election results. "Huh," Hugo says, reading his phone.

"What?" I ask.

"It says here, people used to chop off . . . JESUITS' heads." The marrow of the gospel is always found at the intersection of God's unwavering love and this fecundity of healing. This field of kindness, care, and, yes, unbridled hilarity. The laughter is always a defiant triumph. Joy and bravery are on the other side of it.

We always want to stay close to the gospel bone. We want to move beyond the "lyrics" and get to the "singing." Pope Francis speaks of the freshness of the gospel, the *"frescura."* Avoiding the stale is what we're after. Our gospel living ought to energize the prophetic in each other. If we're honest, we will admit that sometimes the Church can find itself disconnected from that itinerant preacher from Nazareth. Mussolini used to say, "I'm a Catholic, and anti-Christian." If we're not careful, self-preservation becomes our focus, and the Church can find itself preaching the gospel without living it. The marrow of the gospel keeps hoping we will live out a love reflective of our tender God in ways that are healing and inclusive. In early Christianity, it was illumined love, not the law, that drove the vehicle. In this way, as Hafiz suggests, "we are house-sitting for God. We share His royal duties."

In the gospels, we learn that Jesus sent the disciples out, two by two, because we aren't supposed to go it alone. One Christian is no Christian, as I believe the early Christians used to say. No Lone Rangers. It's only in community that we can move into the world with authority to be a part of the healing of "unclean spirits."

Here's how it works, I think. Jesus enters into a relationship, a friendship, with us and then invites us into a community and, finally, sends us into the world. Then we become an emerging Church and focused outward. Live in the Church. Go to the world. We occasionally have these graduations of sorts when folks finish their eighteen months with us and we gather in the large classroom.

A huge crowd piles in to celebrate Sierra's goodness and time with us. Thaddeus is in charge of securing a cake. He arrives carrying a huge pink box from our bakery and places it on the table. When he lifts the lid, he reveals the tiniest of cakes sitting in the middle. The throng of folks lean in and peek. Silence. Thaddeus says, "Um . . . everyone gets a lick." We moved from lyrics to singing.

The disciples aren't sent out to create an institution fortified by uniformity, just another tribe highly defended against all outside forces. Certainly, Western Christianity goofed some things up: it fostered separateness; it bet all its money on the "sin" horse; and it relied so heavily on external religious exercises. Clearly, we are being propelled into the world to cultivate a movement whose ventilating force is an extravagant tenderness. The disciples didn't leave Jesus' side with a fully memorized set of beliefs. Rather, theirs was a loving way of life that had become the air they breathed, anchored in contemplation and fully dedicated to kinship as its goal. "And only at that shrine," Teresa of Ávila writes, "where all are welcome . . . will God sing loud enough to be heard."

Safe to say, the early Christians were considered very dangerous people. This was saying a lot, since the Romans were actually quite tolerant. But in some way, it became clear that just being a Christian was a denunciation of Roman life and the acceptable ways of living at the time. Too frequently these days our living the gospel gets punk'd, intimidated by cultural imperatives. Jesus critiqued all forms of domination, and so we are compelled to do the same. Systemic racism, for example, could not stand without the white supremacist Christianity that always held it up. House-sitting for God means that what goes unexamined will never be upended. We swim in a culture that is racist and hides in systems. Our clarity of purpose wants to unravel the toxic thread so woven into our nation's fabric. It is the faith of Jesus that wants to address this, not some liberal agenda. Consequently, we don't rest in a belief in Jesus, until it becomes the imitation of Jesus.

I was invited, somewhere in the country, to speak in a diocese on a day dedicated to evangelism. In the flyer and in my letter of invitation, it had a controlling idea for the day: "How would you start a conversation about Jesus with the person behind you at the checkout line at a grocery store?" I saw that and was heartened that the date didn't work for me. My answer would have been to hightail it to the eight-items-or-less express lane. Our lives should be loud and clear, not our words. The great Shirley Torres at Homeboy says, "We've become a culture that lectures more than listens." It's not about broaching a subject, but living clearly.

An old wise Jesuit said once: "Jesus tells us three things: 1) All humans are valuable. 2) You will live forever. 3) And if you find a better deal, jump on it." And yet, our life's search isn't really for a better deal, but for a more authentic way to live. We seem to accept the stance of the world articulated by the Four Horsemen of the Apocalypse: War. Famine. Sickness. Death. And yet Jesus says, well, how about peacemaking and feeding

the hungry and healing the sick and bringing the dead to life?
I'll have what he's having.

Pedro Arrupe, the Superior General of the Society of Jesus,
once urged Jesuits to live our faith "out of doors." Hard to be
authentic if we don't step outside.

Ramoncita was legendary in the Dolores Mission community. I think she was 103 when she died. When she was a spritely
ninety-nine, she did the readings often at the daily mass. She
was so tiny that she needed to pull out this portable step tucked
into the ambo. She moved quite quickly and with a storehouse
of energy as she galloped in her pink tennis shoes to read. Once
she elevated herself behind the podium, she turned to the tabernacle behind her, winked at it, and saluted, like she was the
president descending the stairs of Air Force One. When she was
done, she lowered herself from the step, turned again to the tabernacle, and shot both arms energetically in the air, like she was
announcing some gospel touchdown. And she did not own a
single tooth in her head. It made the readings a challenge for
the congregation, but never hampered her resolve to deliver the
message.

The word was that Ramoncita had at one time sported perfectly aligned dentures, until one day in the projects she spotted
a young mother trying to corral her kids. This mother had no
teeth. Ramoncita approached her, pulled the entirety of her dentures out of her mouth, and said, "Clean these up, they should
work fine. You need them more than I do."

At the end of the letter of James, he writes, "Let your yes
mean yes." There's "yes" for you, with authentic clarity. And all
of it out of doors.

The novelist Shūsaku Endō speaks of "Christianity as a
wife chosen for him by his mother." Instead, we want to find
our own true love, a binary-busting gospel living. As we assess
things, we tend to ask, "What would Jesus do?" But it is perhaps

more clarifying to ask, "Does God agree with us?" It is for this reason that Pope Francis warns of the "temptation of rigidity." It is a wholly unnecessary fear of change. As Church, we're always trying to catch up to mercy but don't want to go there because we're afraid. Spaciousness frightens us. God agrees when things are fluid and merciful and makes room in the heart for everyone.

Consequently, things need to eventually get tossed overboard so we can float even more freely on this spacious sea. There are operative principles under which we navigate that weigh us down as a Church: hierarchy, patriarchy, a clericalism that infantilizes the laity, careerism, and even the notion that somehow, at my ordination, I was "ontologically changed."

I did a backyard baptism for a homie once (I often did this when having it at Dolores Mission was perilous because of the gang dynamic). The tiny table with the bowl of water was in place. I threw my alb on. I noticed three little kids staring at me, mouths wide open, while I did this. I placed over my shoulders my multicolored stole. When this all was complete, the oldest kid of the three, without taking his eyes off me, said with whispered awe to the others, "And now . . . he is God." Ontologically changed.

◇◆◇

I wasn't sure how many folks to expect at Chucky's funeral. When there are just the cremains and not the body, people tend to stay home. But the place was packed for this giant of a man who was always so sweet even as he struggled with his own drug use and homelessness and gang involvement. His body took a beating and could not sustain itself any longer. Everyone wore a Packers jersey, Chucky's team. The place was packed with gang members, drug addicts, and drug dealers; women who had engaged in sex trafficking and those who had engaged and traded them. People in recovery and people who presently were high. Felons and revived folks and those barely hanging on.

Before I began the mass, I invited anyone up who wished to say anything to eulogize Chucky. There was silent reluctance and I started to think, *Maybe no one will step up.* Then an old *veterano* with a huge *brocha* (mustache), gray and rigid, ambled to the podium. He was wearing a muscle shirt and shorts. He surveyed the room, taking his time, until he finally said, "Chucky . . . knocked up my sister." This shocking sentence detonated such an outburst of raucous laughter that it took some time for it to subside. The *brocha* guy knew how to ride the laugh like an expert surfer with a killer wave. And it went uphill from there. There wasn't a wet eye in the house. All those who shared told stories filled with joy and tenderness. My heart sang at how melodious it all was.

At communion time, I did my usual invitation: "Pope Francis says that communion is not the grand prize for the perfect person, but food for the hungry one. We're all hungry." I invite them all to receive the Eucharist. They did, and communion took forever. People were weeping, old gang members whom I didn't know received communion and gently touched my arm as they returned to their seats. I was struck at how moved to tears they were by Chucky's death, when a woman, taking communion in her hand, looked at me with tear-soaked eyes and said, "Thank you for inviting us."

Jesus says in John's gospel: "I will not reject anyone." Jesus always wants to show us our own humanity and reminds us that we cannot be friendly with ourselves AND judgmental at the same time. So be friendly. We aren't ever called to some disconnected sanctity but fully engaged humanity. When we live close to the marrow of the gospel, we seek wholeness and not perfection. We seek to be balanced, integrated, and in harmony. You can't find a moment in the gospel where Jesus punishes, excludes, or demeans. Our wide hearts hoping to meet the wideness of God. Becoming whole to meet our wholly spacious God. We may keep score until we discover that God doesn't.

What unifies us as revolutionaries of tenderness is the longing to find our true selves in loving . . . in community. My friend Pastor Brady Rice says, "Church is a circle, not shoulder to shoulder." We want to find the marrow of the gospel in this ever-widening circle. The treasure and the pearl. To find our open hearts—warm and affectionate—capable of creating a community with no outcast. Only in community can we step away from the scapegoating of our times and humanize the "other" by loving them. Luis, a trainee, said once, "Homeboy Industries is the opposite of things." We all long to be lost in such a place.

We try and find our way together to Christianity as a loving way of life—not just as a system of beliefs, dogmas, and requirements, but as a tender disposition of the heart. If we were honest with ourselves, we'd find the longing to sidestep religiosity and move in the direction of mysticism. From piety, purity, and moralistic measuring to the expansive, deeper joy that comes from not judging. Christianity is not about morality, it's about mysticism. When we are fearful, we distrust mysticism. Then we fall back on morality. That always moves from the outside in. Mysticism is the light from the inside out. Anchored in a mysticism emanating from within living "within the withinness of God," we are transported from fast food to healthy nourishment.

With a modicum of cooperation, Jesus gladly sets the compass of our heart so that it stays robust and tender. We go to the returns department and trade in our small self for our true self in loving. Only in this way can the Church be not merely a stone in the riverbed, but the river itself.

I take Rascal to look at an apartment. It's a tiny place behind a house. A converted garage, really, with bathroom, bedroom, and not much else. Rascal has had no luck in finding someone who will rent to him. I sometimes get trotted out in the hopes that the presence of, say, an old white guy might convince a landlord to actually rent to a gang member with a bunch of tattoos and felonies. Rascal is skeptical.

We meet the landlord, who greets us both warily on the driveway. We don't even see the garage room. He asks us some questions in Spanish, and then signals to his wife, standing at a distance from us, up the driveway, that he will need to consult her. "We're fucked," Rascal says. "Now there is no way they're gonna say yes. I mean, look at his *ruca*'s mascara." True enough, the wife seems to be scowling and in Rascal's general direction.

Finally, the landlord breaks away from his wife and rejoins us. He looks at Rascal and says, after a beat, "Well, how will you ever know if you're a good tenant if no one rents to you?" He then shakes Rascal's hand. And suddenly, as homegirl Inez says, "God gets visual." We all got caught up in the mystical "verb" of it.

Marcus Borg, scholar and theologian, says that "churchianity is not supposed to survive." He makes the case that churchianity has no hospitality for mystery and uncertainty, and because it is reliant on hubris and has no humility, it can't seem to appreciate any gray area (or as the homies tellingly call it, "the grace area"). Like with Pope Francis and "his mercy before dogma papacy," there is comfort with the grace area, like the landlord with Rascal, who swerves around the dogma of renter rules and finds his way to the heart of mercy. Beyond the tyranny of dogmatic rules and regulations, humility calls the shots.

Good, healthy fear opens our hearts and we are intrigued by it. Like the Greek word uttered by Jesus when healing a deaf and mute man, "*Ephatha*"—"Be opened." The Church is always beckoned to this—opening up so that a connection can be made. The Church then becomes like Jesus, a parable of God's tenderness and gracious acceptance of everyone.

My dad used to write me every year, no matter where I was, on the Feast of Saint Gregory the Great. I don't know that much about him, but Saint Gregory wrote this once: "We are saved by the people we despise." The folks who create dis-ease within us, cause us to recoil and flee, to become defensive, the very people we disparage for disagreeing with us and who are on the polar opposite spectrum of our political beliefs—turns out, these are our teachers and our salvation.

We seek this luminous union with the one who is outside, the "despised one." We are Church in our essence when we welcome these excluded, who are waiting for us. The root of the word "mystic" means "I am silent." Which is to say "visible," without the tsunami of words. It is the mystical view that frees us to take the gospel seriously and not literally. The Church that wants to come to us from the future is about witness, not words.

We've settled for answering Jesus' question, "Who do you say I am?" by naming or blaming. Naming: "Jesus the Christ . . . and did I mention . . . Jesus the Christ?" Blaming: "You don't belong to us . . . You are Them . . . You are a heretic," etc. We've settled for a discipleship that names or blames. The requirement for "house-sitting" asks rather, "HOW do you say that I am?"

I am sitting behind my desk with four potential donors in front of me. I can see, over their heads, through the glass wall and door, to the beehive of the "well." There are four homies at the large, sweeping reception desk and folks are signing in to see me, to visit a job developer, or to check in for a tattoo removal appointment. All seats in the reception area are nearly full and CNN is on the TV. I notice this guy come in. Clearly a gang member, but I don't know who he is. I see that the faces of the four homies behind the counter are fixed on him. This may be due in large part to the fact that he has a soda can, and with every punctuation mark, a big dollop of soda flies and lands on the desk. A comma here. An exclamation point there. I recognize this as a combo burger of meth and madness. It seems inevitable that I will have to intervene. I'm about to stand when Miguel appears. He is the largest homie who has ever worked at Homeboy. He could play Chief Bromden in the Homeboy production of *One Flew Over the Cuckoo's Nest*.

Miguel is in charge of security, though he does not like to be known as the head guy. His business card reads: "Community Outreach Worker," but he's our head security guy. He was a juvenile tried as an adult who spent twenty-one years in prison and half of that time in solitary confinement.

I watch as Miguel gently puts his arm around the shoulder of the meth/madness guy and then deftly guides him outside. (Our informal rule: always get the troublesome outside. Our population can get triggered so easily that if something "jumps off," we want it at some distance from our folks.) Miguel tells me later what happens next.

With his kind and open heart, Miguel looks at our friend and says, "How 'bout you and me, we go to Placita Olvera and get us some tacos?"

The guy stares back at Miguel and slowly lifts his T-shirt, revealing a handgun tucked into the front of his pants. "How 'bout," he says, with steel in his voice, "I put a bullet in your head." He drops his shirt.

Miguel adjusts the setting of his heart. "Two tacos or three?"

The two of them begin to walk down Alameda and the four blocks toward Olvera Street, the oldest center of the city of Los Angeles. Miguel tells me that while they make their way to the Placita, our brother has a conversation with the voices in his head, but Miguel says, "The voices don't stay in his head." They leap out of his mouth like a bunch of frogs, and he turns his head and talks to himself. "Shoot his ass." And the voice turns in, "Nah, he's okay." "Ya can't trust him," says the one. "He's buyin' me tacos," finishes the other.

The pair arrive at the taco stand and Miguel hands him a plate of three tacos. Our friend takes the first taco and hurls it to the ground, dispatched to do so, no doubt, by one of the voices in his head. Perhaps a sacrifice to Pachamama to calm the torment ever accompanying him. But then he inhales the other two tacos, because he is deeply and thoroughly hungry. Miguel answers the question: "HOW do you say that I am?" That's how.

Miguel spoke the whole language. He was able to locate this guy in a net of mercy. He didn't warehouse his love, he let it flow and overflow. The river itself. Miguel resided in a place where nothing threatened him and everything elated him. God singing loud enough to be heard. He was able for a moment to puncture this man's isolation. Joy and bravery. The Church making the argument with his life. Two tacos or three? This way is tried. This way is certain.

Chapter Seven

───◆•⊰◍⊱•◆───

The Lining of the World

H egel thought that a slave was one who lived in fear of death. He thought "work" was the answer to the dilemma "I will die." But we all want to find the path that renders death a finished product and a fulfillment. We want to know that whatever happens is not the end of the story. After all, we will all be dead a lot longer than we will be alive. What we seek is not the end of something, but something we gain. We long to put it all together like the great Stephen Levine, who suggested that "death, like birth, is not an emergency but an emergence." He posited that it's more akin to a flower opening than to anything else.

A homie I don't know writes me from prison wanting help when he gets out. He closes with this: "PS: There's a rumor going around saying you have passed away. If so . . . I'm very sure you're in heaven and will have this letter answered." Condolences accepted. I'll inform my assistant.

When my mom was in her eighties and my father had been dead for twenty years, she received one of those annoying appeal letters for money from a nonprofit. Okay. Full disclosure. It was from Homeboy Industries. It asked for a donation and suggested that you might want to give in someone's name, honoring them. She thought this was a good idea. She writes my father's name, Bernie Boyle. Then it asks for the address of the person, so they can be notified of the gift. So, she writes, "Heaven." Then adds, "If you find the address, will ya let me know?" She thought this was hilarious.

Finding "heaven's address" is really about putting death, ultimately, in its place. A man named Frank Buckles turned one hundred years old and people asked him, naturally, about his secret to longevity. "If you feel . . . like you're going to die . . . don't." Awfully good advice. Death is always a comma with a side order of exclamation point. Punctuation matters.

The ladies from Dolores Mission had given me a plaque with a Scripture passage on it. T-Bone is reading it on the wall in my office while I'm on the phone. "You like that?" I ask him when I hang up.

T-Bone says, "Yeah," and I ask what is his favorite part. "This line right here," he says. " 'I was a stranger and you invited me in naked.' " I'm an old English teacher. Punctuation matters. Death is not a period. It's a comma. Commas say, "Keep going." Not done yet. Don't die. I've buried so many homies who didn't let anybody put a period where a comma belonged.

Like Jesus, who delays in getting to the twelve-year-old girl who is sick. Because he slow-dragged, she dies. But she doesn't have to stay dead for long. We don't have to stay dead either, nor stuck in the death-dealing things that hold us back. Jesus arrives. No one has to stay dead for long. Which is a good thing, since death is so permanent and none of us are really ready for that level of commitment.

I was invited to speak in the Black Hills of South Dakota at the Crazy Horse Memorial. I brought Joseph and his son, Joey, both workers at Homeboy, because they are Mescalero Apache. Joseph's middle name is Thunderface. The sculptor's widow presented me with an amazing handmade quilt I gave to Joseph

and his son for safekeeping. They both remembered that a year after the Battle of Little Big Horn in 1876, Crazy Horse, the war leader of the Lakota, was asked derisively, "Where are your lands now?" Crazy Horse just pointed to the distant Black Hills and said, "My lands are where my dead lie buried." He was untouchable. The admonition, as with death, is to find the thing no one can take. After all, there is no such thing as a dead person, only a dead body.

After a young man, Frankie, was killed, I went to his home. I had known him practically all his life. I was led into his bedroom by his sister and she retrieved a strongbox from a shelf in the closet. "He kept all his valuables here." When she opened it, there was only a small pile of prayers he had kept and written down. One said simply, "We conquer death by continuing." It was his "Black Hills." Indeed, his valuables.

Death is not to be feared—but deadness, go right ahead. When Lenny wasn't gangbanging, he was using heroin. I buried his father, who died of an overdose. Lenny's dad had made the acquaintance of heroin when he was not even out of his teens fighting in Vietnam. Lenny got up at the funeral and said, "My dad was painfully human." He even conceded, "I suppose I tried heroin myself, just so I could understand why my father loved it more than me."

Lenny wrote me from prison once, managing to keep "deadness" at a reasonable distance. "I've got good news and bad news," his letter said. "And since you're not here with me, I can't ask which you want first. So . . . the bad news: I just got a six-month add-on for a scuffle I got into. And the good news: I just saved $100 on Geico car insurance." We continue and death gets conquered.

In a later missive, however, from prison, Lenny wrote: "I'm not afraid of death, in fact, I'm curious. It's the only thing I haven't tried yet. I want to die—cuz I want to yell at God. I'm pissed at him. I want to look him in the eye and say, 'What was up with that?'"

We want to lift the veil on death. We want to pull back the cover and find what is luminous and victorious underneath it. We long to see now, the light, peace, wonder, and joy that is revealed past the devastation and disaster of death. I visited Ruben's mother. He was killed the day before while fixing his car in front of his house. She was crying when I arrived, and I suspected she hadn't stopped since her son left us. "I don't hate those who did this to my only son. I forgive them. But mainly, I pray for them. I pray with all my heart that their mothers will never, ever know this pain." Forgiveness conquers death. It is indeed luminous and we continue.

A Jesuit friend of mine went to a huge party for his grandfather, who, like Frank Buckles, also turned one hundred. They rented a hall, everyone ate and drank, and folks got up on the stage and told stories about the guest of honor. Finally, the old man himself got up to speak at the end of a very long evening. He made his way slowly to the microphone and surveyed the room. This was all he had to say:

"If . . . you're given a chance . . . to die . . . in your seventies . . . take it. Thank you very much."

Denial with death is a given. The human capacity to keep what is real at arm's length is astounding. A panicky homie called me once because he didn't know what to do. "We were all sitting in this living room, high as fuck, and there was a gun, and I had it and was playing with it and it went off . . . shot Monica's mom in the face. It just barely happened right now. I don't know what to do." I always counsel the same thing: Turn yourself in. I can't remember if he did or not, but the next day, he called collect from jail. "Can you believe it, G . . . they're accusing me of shooting Monica's mom in the face?" Denial happens. Sometimes the narratives we tell ourselves can be downright stupefying.

Once I had a homeless man stand in front of my desk and say, "As you can see, I'm in a wheelchair." He seemed pretty convinced of it and would not hear otherwise.

I was at a university some years ago, speaking to a class. I brought Hugo with me, a towering gang member near thirty. During his part of the presentation, he said that he ran away from home at nine years old.

During the question-and-answer period, a young woman asked, "Why'd you run away from home at nine?"

And he answered, "I just was tired of listening to my parents."

As we drove home, I asked Hugo, "Remember that question the woman asked, about why you ran away from home?"

"Yeah."

"Do you remember your answer?"

"Yeah."

"Well, what did you say to her?"

"I said I ran away from home at nine because my mom kept beating my ass."

"Well, no, actually, son, you didn't say that. You said, 'Because I was tired of listening to my parents.'"

He was shocked. "Really? I said that?"

I asked him if he had ever even met his father. "No."

Hugo had every reason to not only deny death but even his life up to this point.

His mother put cigarettes out on him. She put his head in the toilet and flushed until he nearly drowned. Tied him up in the backyard on a very long chain . . . for an entire summer. Many years later, Hugo was finally introduced to the notion of mental illness and how his mother had been plagued in this way.

Susan Cheever writes: "Death is terrifying because it is so ordinary. It happens all the time." Nothing more democratic than death. I called my ninety-year-old mother when I heard that her

101-year-old great friend, Emma, had died. "She died this morning?" I asked.

"Yeah," my mom said, and then added, "It was bound to
happen." I suppose so. Ordinary.

The cause of death is birth. Letter from a kid: "Sometimes,
when I think about death in the world and God, I can't even
stay thinking about it." We still want to live in the truth that
grief never leaves us where it found us, and this is a profoundly
good thing. Death, as Rilke says, is a great gift. But we never get
around to "opening it." We are not just supposed to make sense
of death when someone dies, but decide, always, to repurpose
our own living in the wake of it. We repurpose and become a
GPS that always knows heaven's address. If we "open the gift"
of death, it organizes things, finds our human temptation to ca-
tastrophize, and gives us permission not to sweat the small stuff.

Once I was at an airport, late at night, waiting for a flight,
and there was a guy several seats from me speaking to his wife on
his cell phone with a thick Southern drawl. "Honey, my flight's
delayed. I'll be gettin' in real late, so don't wait up for me." There
was a pause, he was listening, and then he said to her, "Ain't nuthin' but a thang." I had never heard this expression before. As
the conversation continued, I suspect his wife was venting about
the events of her day, and he listened intently. He would console
her several times with, "Ain't nuthin' but a thang."

I would pull this expression out of mothballs a couple days
later. I'm driving at 6:00 a.m. to the state park for my daily
fifty-minute walk. Out of nowhere, a white truck pulls into my
lane. He didn't even look, and it was, well, 100 percent his fault.
I pull over and I assess things. I'm okay. The car can drive. The
doors open. The windows aren't broken. There's a mean old
gash in the rear passenger door. Big whoop. I walk back to the
white truck, and it's a homie, shaved head, rivers of tattoos visible, gang attire. He's beyond himself with nerves. Seated in the

cab with him is an old woman, possibly his grandmother. He looks completely terrified. My Southern guardian angel whispers in my ear. "Hey, dawg, don't worry about it."

He lights up. "REALLY??? THANK YOU!" It is, in fact, our acceptance of death that repurposes us to keep our hair from igniting. This actually prevents molehills from turning into mountains. We are terrified by the ordinariness of death, but if we open the gift, we're freed to breathe and relax. "Ain't nuthin' but a thang."

—◇—

Moreno's brother, José, died in his arms. Moreno pretended he was dead himself when the shooters came back wanting to ensure that they had gotten them both. Before too long, he returns to work at our headquarters, and I overhear him snap at his homies suggesting they "will handle this."

Moreno barks at them, "No, God will handle it." Later, when I pull him into my office to talk about it all, he chooses to put death in its place. "Death is a punk," he blurts out. This is not dissimilar from "Death, where is your sting" or "Death has no power over us," or Paul saying of Jesus: "It was impossible for him to be held by death." God would want the same impossibility to be possible for us all.

I quote Moreno a year later, after he's been gunned down while playing street football. It is undeniably terrifying, to love what death can touch. And yet, to the sobbing gathered at morning meeting in our lobby, the day after he was killed, I echo Moreno's words: "Death is a punk." Impossible to be held by it. The samurai can identify himself as "the already dead one." Death has no power.

Since I think we are all invited to be bodhisattvas, to alleviate suffering as Jesus did, we are likewise meant to accompany people to the shore of liberation. Putting death in its place is what all great beings engage in with purpose and resolve. A homie writes me from probation camp after hearing of my leukemia: "You're a good man and now it's time to return to God." I'm touched by the "good man" part and at peace with the "return to God" section. I suppose it's the "now" part that gives us all trouble. When asked in an interview about his own death, the Dalai Lama shrugged and laughed, "Change of clothing." Bodhisattvas and authentic disciples of Jesus ride on the waves of birth and death, with arms outstretched to touch both with tenderness.

When it comes to our own death, Jesus seems to be against staring. We are not meant to stare at our watches, awaiting death's arrival. Nor are we meant even to stare at Jesus. On the occasion of Lazarus's death in the gospel of John, Jesus tells us, "I am the resurrection and the life . . . believe . . . and you'll have life." But even that assurance is not an invitation to stare at Jesus. Staring, after all, is kind of a paralysis. It is a trance-like state, mouth slacked open, and eyes glazing. Staring keeps us from looking where Jesus would have us focus. Keep your eyes on the prize: the luminous purpose and meaning in our eternal now. Jesus, in his humility, knows that "staring" at him diverts our gaze from where it should be directed.

Kafka said that the "meaning of life is that it stops." In the same way, one would not distract a woman giving birth with complaints of your toothache, because she has a job to do. Equally true, a dying person. We don't try and console someone on their deathbed, because the dying person will recognize it as YOUR need to be consoled. Don't. She's got a job to do. Like Pedro Arrupe on his deathbed who was already "on the last amen of my life and the first alleluia of my eternity."

Not that long ago, I spoke at the memorial service of my friend Blase Bonpane. I had heard him speak some fifty years earlier, when I was in high school and he, Tom Hayden, and Jane Fonda were speaking against the Vietnam war. It produced in me a zeal that eventually led me to join the Jesuits. In the late '80s, many times I was arrested with Blase, protesting the United States involvement in Central America. He was this positively gleeful and giddy presence in the holding tank. The rest of us had an edge of anxiety, but Blase would have none of it. He died at ninety years old. His son got up at the service and spoke of Blase's last words to him. Blase was in and out of consciousness and in great pain. His son asked him, as one does, in a fleeting moment of lucidity, "What's the meaning of life?"

Blase could barely speak but eked out, *"Exultet.* Latin," he tells his son, "for . . . Let us rejoice." The first alleluia of eternity.

The last amen of our lives can be disorienting. It's true enough that our minds are unemployed if we aren't continually puzzled. Befuddlement comes with the last-breath territory. I ask my mom in the last days of her life, how many kids does she have? "I have two kids." Actually, she has eight.

"What are their names?" I ask her.

"Eileen and Maureen." These are my two oldest sisters. "I love them very much. I'm very happy with them."

So I ask, "Any more kids?" She's emphatic: "NO WAY! Two are plenty." I had to break this news to my sibs. We ready ourselves in this life to be dead a really long time. So we celebrate impermanence, acknowledge that everything ends and that something new is about to begin around this puzzling corner.

Gabino wants to talk. "I'm broker than the bottom of my *suegra's* grill." He's having a bad week, having just lost his job. ("They quit me.")

"How ya doin', son?" I ask him, looking for something deeper than his empty wallet.

"I'm lookin' for God every day that he goes by." As a result of this search, he's managed to land on some true irrigation of his heart and excavation of his wound. He finally gets to the thing that's gnawing at him. He's been having dreams. These can be bothersome for homies because they charge dreams with such magical thinking. Gabino's dreams are recurring and they're about Speedy. Speedy was killed in the projects some months earlier. These dreams are on a continuous loop. Speedy throws tiny rocks at Gabino's window and calls his name. Speedy used to do this when they were both younger, mostly in the middle of the night. Invariably, Gabino, in the dream, would follow him and next find Speedy sitting up in his coffin, in front of the altar at Dolores Mission. Gabino is in the front pew chatting with Speedy, who is smiling and quite talkative. In the dream, Gabino is taking copious notes and listening with great attention.

I always ask homies, when they share their dreams, "How'd it make ya feel?" Gabino reckons with his memory. "Peaceful . . . and quiet . . . and happy."

"So, was Speedy telling you to go out and get the *vatos* who did this to him?"

Gabino seems to be reviewing in his head the many notes he took. "Nah—where he is now, he knows it's all stupid and a waste of life . . . and so he just wants me to get on with my life." Heaven's address.

Poet David Whyte encourages us "to remember the other world in this world is to live in your true inheritance." Paradise, then, is not a place but a full participation in our true inheritance. A Jesuit came back from visiting an old, great friend who was dying at home under hospice care. I asked how it went. "All we did was laugh our asses off. It was a really good use of time." You dive into your true inheritance. You don't stare at your watch and wait for it to arrive. If we wait to face death on our deathbed, it's too late. The earlier you die, the better. The inheritance is here and now. Then you decide that what is right in front of you is so magically special that you cease to care about what happens next. After all, the Risen Christ cannot be found among the dead. Instead, resurrection locates us in the here and now. Death becomes an eternal alarm clock. Then we can dedicate ourselves to attentiveness. Mary Oliver writes: "This is the first, the wildest, and the wisest thing I know: that the soul exists and is built entirely out of attentiveness." We are startled awake to this. It's not just about my own mortality and the fact that everybody's going to die. Death reminds us to make sure every moment is important. In this way, we notice the way God notices.

Prepare to die. It's not just a line repeated by Inigo Montoya in *The Princess Bride*. The earlier we attend to this preparation, indeed, the better. Just now, a homie called me, quite unraveled by the death of his eighty-seven-year-old grandmother, who long had dementia and had just died in her sleep. He came undone by this news. This is quite common among the homies. It is often less about loss than some unattended, accumulated sorrow held tightly within. Complex trauma such as abandonment can be triggered with a death. This makes the ongoing preparation for death so vital.

I asked a homie who was to begin our program about his parents. He never knew his dad, but his mom had just died. "She died on the Fourth of July. It was the most beautiful day of the year. In fact, they lit up the sky that night." We prepare for the darkness of loss and the soul finds a way to touch it and the hidden gets released and you are seasoned by it. Preparation looks like this. Like the mother whose son was killed: "Padre, I've been prepared for this moment since he was thirteen." Preparation need not be trajectory, but sadly, sometimes is.

Truth be told, I find that I am in no way afraid of death and dying. I know that once you're born you start dying. I am, however, frightened of being scared to death. I hate, for example, roller coasters. Why would you pay good money to have them supply you with that sensation? As much as I fly, I hate turbulence. It rattles me. The thought of the plane actually going down and me ceasing to exist, ruffles me not. Just don't frighten me.

I'm flying home to Los Angeles from Chicago Midway and shortly after we take off, we suffer some severe technical issues. We need to find an airport to land—now. We lost something—an engine—a wing—something. It looks like Indianapolis, the pilot calmly explains, is prepared to receive us. He tells us to expect "a very hard landing." The head flight attendant takes the microphone. "I need you all to listen . . . as you've never . . . listened before." Her tone now is as solemn a cadence as I've ever heard in the air. "You need to have nothing on your laps. Nothing around your feet. You need to fasten your seat belt . . . as tightly . . . as . . . you . . . ever have." Now she pauses. She formulates, with some heightened degree of drama, what next should flow from her mouth. "And all I can say to you is . . . we . . . love you . . . very, very much." I serenely turn to the two young men, strangers, seated next to me, to calmly console them, and say, "We're fucked." And yet, I've never felt more tranquil in all my life. Death is not the issue. And since we are descending quite smoothly with no terrifying turbulence, the prospect of dying fazes me not. Even as we see large fire trucks quickly move into position below. You realize that one of the purposes in living is to get ready to be dead a good long time. Everything that ends is the beginning of something else, so ~~you can decide to~~ celebrate our ~~impermanence~~. I just don't like turbulence.

Jesus conquered death—but he also vanquished the fear of death. Way better. Death just keeps us from life. But the fear of death keeps us from living.

Think of any disaster movie. Earthquake. Fire. Flood. Apes commandeering San Francisco. Aliens attacking the White House. In all of them, you have folks running in a panic and screaming, "WE'RE ALL GONNA DIE!!!" Well, news flash—we're all gonna die.

Don't think for a moment that you won't die. I find that this truth enhances my living. And you die alone; no one will be going

with you. I got called to MacLaren Hall Children's Center, a foster care facility. It was a holding ground before a kid got trans-
ferred to an actual place. A social worker I didn't know invited
me to speak to a kid named Luis. Since he was a gang member,
she thought I "could get through to him." Luis was sixteen and
had been eating at a Jack in the Box with his girlfriend when
"enemies" saw him and opened fire. The injury from the bullets
forced doctors to remove his entire stomach. When I met him, he
was connected to IV nourishment, requiring him to lie still for
twelve hours to get all that he needed. He was, understandably,
depressed. "I'll never eat again," he tells me. "And I REALLY
like to eat." When he came to work at Homeboy eventually, the
homies called him Tubos, because his liquid nourishment was
stored in a backpack that was with him always and connected
to his body constantly. He finally received a stomach transplant
at Stanford. This carried him awhile until it didn't. "I feel like
I'm a beat-up ol' *ranfla*. If it's not one thing, it's another. If it's not
the carburetor, it's the brakes." Before he left us, he told me, "I'm
entitled to be tired of this." Yes indeed. But not for a moment did
Tubos think he wasn't going to die. And no one would be going
with him. The backpack was the daily reminder. It managed to
enhance the time he had with us. And, yes, the backpack for him
had been transformed into a parachute.

-◇◇-

In the last five years, I've buried more homies who were either
killed by law enforcement or from a drug overdose than by gang
violence. I did Cesar's funeral recently. The drugs finally pre-
vailed. He was living in Tijuana, having been deported, and life
was indeed hard. Back in the day, if I pulled my car up where
his homies were gathered, he'd hop in the passenger side and say,
"Let's take a lap." He'd fill me in on his life and times. I remember how his mom would say of him, he was "*honrado y noble*."

Indeed, he was, and his humor was of the kind that coaxed you to a softened heart. "I'm tired of being gangfully employed," he told me once. He told me in the car how recently "enemies" came to his house, shot in the air, wrote on his walls. He cut my lecture off at the pass, before I even began. "I know, I know, G . . . I'm not gonna trip. Not even gonna tell my homies. *Ya estuvo.*" This last expression means "That's it for me." I was effusive in my praise of him and my pride was on full display. He got misty-eyed as we pulled up to the place where we started. He placed his left hand behind my neck. "How come I love you too much *un chingo* . . . and a little bit more tomorrow." He hugged me. He opened the door to leave and turned back to me. "*Sabes qué*, G . . . when I die, I'm going to take half of my heart with me and I'm gonna give the other half to you."

This other half of his heart daily reminds me of the other world in this one. And this is the mystical take: to see wholeness. To live in the flesh of other people, to enter their bloodstream and to be so alive there that even death is afraid of you.

Before mass at a detention camp, a kid named Omar was speaking about his father. "The first, last, and only time I ever met my *jefito* was at his funeral. Staring at him in a box. His family knew how to find me after he died . . . they just weren't able to find me while he was alive. I guess it was important to them that I be at his funeral—it just didn't matter to them that I was in his life." Living in the bloodstream of each other can't be deferred.

At John Lewis's funeral, my friend Reverend Jim Lawson, with whom I've been privileged to be arrested and who is one of the few remaining prophets of his generation left, began his eulogy with a poem by Czeslaw Milosz. "When I die, I will see the lining of the world. The other side, beyond bird, mountain, sunset." And yet, our inheritance now is to see the lining of the world. Mateo lamented to me, "I'm afraid of dying without becoming who I am." We all share this same fear.

One of the many funerals I did during the early period of the virus was Cuco. Actually, it was only a graveside service, which was all they would allow at the time. Cuco had a flag-draped coffin and full military honors. There was a twenty-one-gun salute and soldiers meticulously folding the flag before handing it to Cuco's mom. Cuco had drunk himself to death.

The last time I saw him alive was many years ago, when he returned from Iraq. He was one of only a handful of homies who worked at Homeboy who had been allowed to enlist. Usually there were too many impediments, like violent records or tattoos. Cuco was wildly personable—the homie version of hail-fellow-well-met. No room that he entered remained dark. His mom wanted a mass and meal to welcome her son home. Cuco was already drunk when I arrived that day. I did mass, had a taco, then took my leave. Cuco walked me to my car. He thanked me for being there, then he wrapped me in his arms and just would not let go. He whispered in my ear and between sobs told me, "I did and saw things . . . in Iraq . . . that I won't ever be able . . . to shake." They say that the wise person practices death, but the believer practices resurrection. Truth be told, we practice neither. Though I'm certain we could. That's where we'd find the lining of the world, in a palpable spaciousness that doesn't wait for the next life.

Society has long assumed that youth in gangs hope for something better beyond the barrio, a future full of possibility. These youth, goes the assumption, would want to avoid having those dreams cut down. Clearly that assumption is wrong and so is our reliance on it. Sure, gangs cause problems, but it's also true that problems cause gangs. We have a high regard for isolating symptoms and a very low regard for addressing undergirding problems. These young people can't just say no to gangs, unless we offer to help them to just say yes to life, to a tomorrow that holds something better for them. For it is equally true that no gang member goes on "a mission" (a foray) into enemy territory hoping to kill. They do it because they are hoping to die.

I met Charlie at sixteen years old and I asked him, "What do your homies call you?" "Jehovah's Witness," he said firmly. I asked him why that might be. "Cuz I always be going to the homie's house each morning, knocking on their doors." What gave him an early rise was a household filled with terror and heartache. What Somali poet Warsan Shire says about the plight of refugees could be said of Charlie: "No one leaves home unless home is the mouth of a shark . . . unless home chased you, fire under feet." Once I got to know him better, he confided, "I'm just waiting to die or get locked up."

Jaime tells me, "At fifteen, I OD'd on PCP. The doctor said I destroyed thirty-five percent of my brain." Then he considers all this and adds, "But we only use ten percent of our brains anyway. So, I think I'm good." We can wait to die, and it looks like this sometimes. The homies will say of someone, "He's chasing death." Our living can be cut off at the pass if we aren't connected to hope. Fire under feet. Death will come; no need to chase it. So, we decide to help each other find our true inheritance now.

We had a Good Friday service in a youth detention facility that included the reading of the Passion. The homies had the different roles, like Jesus, Pilate, and "the crowd." They kind of got into shouting, "Crucify him. Crucify him!"

Afterward, I was checking in a with a homie named Oliver. I asked how he liked the service. "First of all," he said, "I knew how the story was going to end." This really made me laugh and compelled him to say with a smile, "So, I made your Good Friday . . . even better?"

One must look death in the eye to affirm it as the most real and single most important event of one's life. We say yes to the necessary culmination of life. Freud had two reluctances: to confront death and to yield. The wise person practices death. The mystic practices and yields to resurrection. Good Friday . . . even better. "Life is a dream," the Sufis say, "and death is waking up."

Yes, the necessary culmination of life. It is said that Chief Roman Nose of the Cheyenne, and all his people, believed he was immortal. Safe to say, they were all right, every day of his life, except one. We were discussing death in my office and a homie turned to another and said, "Look, dawg. Have you ever opened the newspaper and read the headline: 'MAN LIVES FOREVER'? Hell no." Don't wait for your last breath but for your next breath. Toward the end of Saint Ignatius's life, he forbade himself to think about death, as the idea of it gave him such consolation. More like that.

I was a hospice grief counselor in Boston from 1981 to 1984. I only had two clients, Debbie and Jack, both of whom contended with cancer for over three years. Debbie was an elderly, sweet Irish woman and I accompanied her until she died. It was a privilege to come to know her family as well. My other client was a man named Jack who was exactly my age, married, and with a young son. Jack answered the door when I first visited, and when we both laid eyes on each other, in unison we said: "Oh shit!" We were a mirror image: same hair, age, glasses, body weight, and shape. Ten minutes later, his wife walked into the living room and said, "Oh shit!" It was a story we'd retell over the long two years before he finally died. It was a singular gift to accompany Jack and it was one of those heart-altering times of my life to pay attention to the dying of the light of him and of my own mirror image.

Show me a mystic who believes in hell, and I will think you've located someone who is not a mystic. But all mystics agree that there is another world and have chosen to see it in this one. I'm in an International House of Pancakes with Chino and Johnny. It's evening and they're ordering dinner. The waiter asks Chino, "Soup or salad?"

"Yes," Chino blurts.

Johnny leans over, "Fool, you have to pick one."

"Oh, well, a salad."

"Salad dressing?" The waiter's eyes are at half-staff, not one bit happy that Chino seems to be indecisive.

"What's that one called, G?" Chino asks me. "You know the one?" Chino commences to do a hula dance, right there in the booth, arms elegantly undulating to the left and right. I let this big, lumbering gang member continue his dance for some time, already knowing full well what he means. This has made the waiter's eyes widen to two fried eggs.

"Um, Thousand Island?" I venture finally.

"Yeah, dat one," Chino says to the waiter, gesturing for him to write it down.

Once the waiter has taken our orders and left us, I turn to Chino. "Okay, can I believe you just ordered a salad dressing doing a hula dance?"

"I can't help it. Thousand Island always reminds me of Hawaiian *jainas* [females]."

A mystical sense of paradise contained in the infinite present. It allows us to let go of the desire to expect anything beyond this moment. A hula dance in an IHOP booth or our next breath.

My office can be like that of a doctor, inasmuch as I don't leave until everyone has been seen. This usually takes me well beyond closing time—sometimes, several hours beyond it. I can see in the reception area that there are two left, Danny and Moy. They both are little guys, best friends who grew up in the projects. The two rush into my office and occupy the seats right in front of me and blurt in unison, "FINALLY."

Moy says, "We were waiting so long for you, our clothes were going out of fashion."

I laugh and say, "Well, you know what Jesus says about the first and the last?"

Danny says, solidly, "Better late than never."

With equal confidence, Moy says, "First come, first served."

I look at them. It's been a long day. "Close enough," I say. Our antidote to misery will always be to stay close to such moments. It is how we dwell in the oceanic, the ultimate, singular place where God wants to be found. We won't live forever, but we can always choose to live IN the forever.

In the spring of 1993, I was sort of in exile. I had finished my term as pastor of Dolores Mission and went on my prescribed time of Tertianship. This is a period of one year in the training of a Jesuit that comes roughly ten years after ordination. I was told that I would return after this year away and would do full-time work with gang members. Then, a sizable monkey wrench got tossed in the works and my Provincial told me this wouldn't happen. It was complicated. The gang issue had indeed become pronounced at this time, and well, the powers that be thought, "This town ain't big enough for the both of us." Sorry if I've turned the Vague-A-Fier on to its highest setting. Celeste Fremon's book *G-Dog and the Homeboys* goes into greater detail.

So, the Provincial had a meeting with the people in the parish hall, and I'm told it was heated. I was not there. I was chaplain at Folsom State Prison. He made the mistake of telling them I had never been told that I would return. They admitted that they didn't know what he had said to me privately, but they quoted back to him what he had said to them in a prior meeting. All the while, outside, a gang member was having a field day vandalizing his car. Yikes.

While I was exiled, I received a long letter from Edgar, a seventeen-year-old gang member, explaining in detail how he was now ready to hang up his gloves. Some years before, where, exactly, I can't recall, but Edgar stopped in front of the window of a swanky architect's office. There were elaborate and fancy models in the window, and he was captivated. I went back and stood next to him. He was hypnotized. "This is what I want to do, G. I want to design and build houses and shit." We stared in silence.

His letter says, "*Ya me canse* [I'm tired] of all this bullshit." He writes of how he wants to finish school, get a job, and marry his childhood sweetheart, Patty. About how he still wants to be an architect. He expresses effusive love for me at great length and asks me to do his wedding when the time comes. Then he apologizes profusely for being the one who trashed my "boss's car."

One month later, he was gunned down in front of Moon's Liquor Store behind the church. Because of my "exile," I was unable to do his funeral. But one of his homies, who was with him as he was breathing his last, wrote me: "He had this look on his face, G . . . like someone was talking to him."

Edgar had told me once, "I don't want to die without loving someone." He was secure in this hope. No worries. I suppose that, in the end, we all want to "design buildings and shit." We want to create and connect and love like there's no tomorrow. One day there won't be. How, then, to notice each other in the interim, so that we all possess that face, looking . . . like someone is talking to us. Still, it is this yearning of our souls that carries us in ways that are endlessly surprising and tenderly sustaining. Even death is afraid of that.

Chapter Eight

———◆◦❈◦◆———

The Finishing Touch

I see Adrian in his hospital room. Multiple gunshot wounds riddle his body, but he will survive. And he's too old for this. During the decade of death (1988 to 1998), when Adrian was "out there," you'd understand it more. But this is twenty years after that time, and Adrian is a family man who shows up for work every day. The places where the homies live remain marred and marked, despite these personal changes, and a car passes by. Anyone will do.

"Are you in pain?"

"Damn, dawg . . . this pain . . . be kickin' like Van Damme." He manages a laugh, and it relieves me.

"You just missed Tony," Adrian says.

Tony is his older brother by two years and also a gang member. Tony just got out of prison and had called me, collect, a couple of months before he was released. "Do me a *paro*, G . . . I need dress-outs. They don't gotta be new, but I don't want to leave here looking like Pee-wee Herman."

Tony and Adrian survived a severely mentally ill mother. The tortuous imprint of their mom left scars they still try to sort through.

"Tony saw me here, in this bed, and he just broke down

crying. It took him a while to stop." Adrian says that he can only remember one other time when he saw his brother weep like this. "I was nine; he was eleven," he says. "We fought over a toy and I told him, 'Then I'm not your brother anymore,' and he said, 'Then I'm not YOUR brother either.' And he cried just like he did right now." Adrian allows this story to find its place in the narrative of his life. "We shared a bed together, so that night, we slept with our backs to each other. Finally, I reached out behind me and touched him on his back and said, 'You're my brother.' And Tony said. 'And you're MY brother.'"

We reach back always to touch with tenderness, the reminder that what had us bound together in the first place still binds us.

The tender glance that "reaches back" is the revelation at Homeboy. The homies find the courage of their own tenderness. It creates a passageway that enables attachment repair. It restores a sense of security and mutual trust. Perhaps for the first time, resting in tenderness, the homies need not be defended, nor arm themselves for protection.

Many who have been in prison initially always have their backs literally up against the wall at Homeboy so that they have a view of the room at all times. It is quite common for homies to have difficulty, at first, closing their eyes during our meditation class. Homeboy longs to be a safe place and counterbalancing act of tenderness in the world. It is from this grounded heart-place that people are radically known.

And from this heart-place, we try to be a light that folks can see by. We live in "Love's confusing joy," as Rumi calls it. This kind of tenderness is deeply courageous and requires, I suppose, a bit of tenderizing on our part. A homie named Poncho just always wells up with tears at the drop of a hatful of affection. He said to me, plaintively, "I don't know why I'm so tenderoni." (Some new awful Chef Boyardee product might be called "Tenderoni.") He confided to me once: "I'm just an emotional person.

I even cried at *The Wedding Singer* with Adam Sandler." But I would remind him of this huge gift he has, the very thing that allows him to greet others with awe, honesty, and human welcome. Poncho came to know that being "tenderoni" was the scaffolding that held up his ability to be a father and in a relationship. It was the "whole language" and the particular dialect of God that sustained him.

I first met Poncho years ago on an elevator at General Hospital. He was with his lady, heading to visit her sick father. He was drunk. "I know who you are. You only help *vatos* from the projects." Poncho's gang was from way outside the projects. This was a common criticism I had to contend with in the early years. Initially, the gang outreach was only to members of those eight gangs in my parish. Later on, the effort was expanded to the sixty gangs, ten thousand gang members, in the Hollenbeck police precinct. But this was a charge often leveled at me, especially if alcohol was lubricating the speaker.

"Give him my card, if he ever gets sober," I said to his lady as I got off on my floor.

Poncho did get sober and walked through our doors at Homeboy. He accompanied me on a speaking tour once, along with one of his enemies, and we found ourselves stranded and completely lost (pre-GPS) in Burlingame, California. We were late and trying to locate this retreat house. I saw two elderly, highly coiffed ladies standing by a Cadillac. "Ask them, dawg, where's the retreat house," I said.

Poncho was not having it. "You shitting me? I ain't asking them. People in neighborhoods like this, they be having nine-one-one on speed-dial."

He'd been shot and hit three times, sending him to the hospital for fairly long bouts of recuperation. He'd been shot AT more times than he could recall. "I always walk on the side of the street that has more cars," he'd said. I dropped him off last when we returned to Los Angeles. "I wish my dad could have seen me doing good. He only saw me messing up." I had buried his father a year before.

"Well," I told him, "he's seeing you. He's watching from heaven—smiling and proud."

"Yeah, I suppose," he said, "but it's not the same." Then he perked up. "Imagine my dad and me, both of us going to work in the morning, and at the end of the day—arriving home at the same time? Imagine?" The whole trip seemed to shift his entire thinking and organize his narrative thus far. What he had conjured here was enough to propel him that much more forward and cemented some inner resolve.

His lady called and wondered why we were late. Our flight was delayed two hours. He explained, then hung up. "Hmm," he said.

"What is it?"

"She was worried about me. I don't know. This is gonna sound weird. That feels proper. I never had anyone worried about me before."

I pulled up in front of his house, and got out to hug as he left, after pulling his bag from the backseat. He hung on to me and whispered: "I feel like I known you . . . all my life." I told him I felt the same. And, of course, he needed to wait before going into his house. He had served himself up a big bowl of Tenderoni.

—◇◇◇—

Love's confusing joy. Sometimes at weddings, I clarify the vows. They don't say: "In good times, I'll be happy. In bad times, well, not so much. In sickness, I'm gonna be down, but in health, IT'S ON!!!" No. It says: "In good times and in bad; in sickness and in health . . ." What? I will be joyful. Choosing joy in all the confusion, no matter what, is transformational. The proverb is right: "Those who wish to sing, always find a song." Choosing to find a song changes any circumstance. And hope becomes the passion that thinks it is all workable and possible.

It is tenderness that helps bring the focus to delighting in the moment in front of you.

It's closing time, in the '90s, and the troops are leaving Homeboy's little storefront we called home. Folks are waving and there are choruses of "*Al rato*" and "See ya tomorrow." Everyone held as gently as they've come to expect. Topo is in the top five most imposing characters to have ever worked at Homeboy. He still looks like he's stepped off the weight pile at Folsom's B Yard. He makes it toward the front door and one of his co-workers—a rival, in fact: Giovanni—is seated in the reception area on a very worn couch. "So whatcha gonna do now, Topes?"

Topo thinks and then announces his ironclad plans to the gathered. "I'm gonna go home . . . and take me a bath." He steps to leave, and as he stands in the doorway, he swings around with a great flourish. A cape would have served this moment nicely. And with a dainty elevating of his hands, he announces: "Calgon—take me away." Before Topo actually leaves, he's gratified with the laughter and applause, everyone finding a song in delight.

At Homeboy, we don't want healing to be deferred. Now is the time. Here is the place. These are the people you can walk with. It is precisely this culture of kindness that stimulates the body and soul to heal itself. Since we are all walking wounded together, it is only tenderness that is mutually transformational. It can lead us all to awakened hearts. Calgon, take us away. For what we choose to address matters. This is why we choose healing over, say, conflict resolution, because we want to actually get underneath what's there. Nothing festers, if we do this.

I received a note from a homie, Sharky, during the pandemic. He said that some people are struck down by the virus. Others are struck down by fear. He found it all an opportunity to choose joy—a time to connect with his wife, kids, and God. He's right. No matter what, choose joy.

This time of COVID really aggravated the monkey mind; the anxious, always judging mind. Only tenderness seems to tame it. And then we are simply never invited to fear, panic, terror, or to embrace conspiracy theories. God does not invite us to check out QAnon. We are beckoned to joy. Even though we are often caught in the belief that happiness should take a particular form. Certainly, the worst things can happen, but indeed they become transformational when tender joy is chosen in the moment. In good times and in bad; in virus or in vigor.

Alex doesn't want to talk about it. His face is quite rearranged. As a preemptive, he says, "It didn't happen here, it happened on the train." Some guy just beat him down. His eyes fill with tears, and he's so humiliated. "Happens to the best of us," he says, trying to shake it off.

"That's right, son," I tell him. "You ARE the best of us." The *bodhichitta* is the "awakened and courageous heart." It is this contour of tenderness that can reach us and unhinge the casing welded around our hearts. Alex was able to keep his heart from closing down. Joy is now possible because of his bravery.

We often confuse success with joy. I heard a woman once lament with some shade of guilt that she finally had to abandon her work with refugees. She stopped because it "was too hard." Then she adds: "Sure, there were some moments of joy." I realized that she wasn't talking about joy at all. She was talking about success. Identifying progress made, goals achieved, and advancement of the work as the locus of joy is, I think, what tripped her up. It was George Carlin who asked: "If you try to fail and succeed, what have you done?" Better to reside in our own vulnerability than measure outcomes. We shouldn't confuse success with joy. They have little to do with each other.

Intention is the most powerful ability that human beings

have. We decide to be tender. We arrive at the clear intention to be tender and it catapults us out of our default mode, which is self-absorption. You find this on planes. Everyone is battling to get their carry-on into the overhead compartments. They are knocking over folks to secure the spot. No fewer than three times, the flight attendant announces that folks should "step out of the aisle" and let others pass. Three times. People aren't selfish. We aren't sinful. We aren't jerks. We are unshakably good. But sometimes we are simply self-absorbed, trapped in the small self. If you make your tender heart your highest priority, then you focus on the other. Try this on a plane. Joy ensues.

Joy has to include everything, otherwise it remains shallow and a whim of only the good times. We can't allow our joy to be conditional on how things turn out. On April 2, Louie fills out the tattoo removal form. It asks: "Why do you want to remove your tattoos?" He writes: "I just want to be able to walk around freely." An appointment gets made in our tattoo removal clinic for April 15. Two days before his appointment, the receptionist calls to remind him. She is told that he was killed three days before. This reverberated in the Homeboy family for the tragic heart wrench it represented. Joy has to include this. You find it in Louie's longing to "walk around freely." You celebrate that longing that had already freed him.

It is precisely because we so fundamentally doubt that we are worthy of love that we find it difficult to traverse the terrain of our vulnerability so that we can choose joy. This is the gentle soft spot that can reach across and connect finally with the other, to make the shift from protected heart to vulnerability. The homies discover tenderness as their weapon of choice. To be grounded in our "tenderoni" self is to know that we will endlessly struggle with our worthiness to be loved. Turns out, this is a necessary ingredient to being courageously tender with other people and is the door that opens to joy.

Oscar is calling me from his break. He has transplanted to Fresno and is working at a Wendy's. I so love this kid and am proud that he's ventured forth, even with a constancy of potholes that trip him up.

"How's it goin'?" I ask him.

"I think they're gonna fire my ass."

"Yeah? Why?"

"Cuz I always be burnin' the burgers."

"Well, stop!"

"I'M TRYIN'!!!"

There is, indeed, this gentle soft spot where we allow each other to be messy and to work with the mess. All the while, we hope homies don't settle for answers but hold out for meaning. We want to keep offering the kind of resilience that can only come from relational engagement. It is no less than a steady, harmonizing love that infiltrates the distance. It is an irresistible culture of tenderness that eliminates any creeping condescension that keeps us from being vulnerable with each other. Navigating potholes. Then we all know what it's like to try to keep the burgers from burning.

We are endlessly being created in love. So, we intensify our life in God and seek to create a contagion of tenderness. We are awake when we are more tender and kind. More tender means more sane and healthy. Folks discover, through tenderness, what makes life worth living, a flourishing in love, anchored and nurtured in relational wholeness. A homie confides to me in my office: "Before I came here, I was a nobody. Now I'm somebody." He surprises himself with his own tears. "And I don't want to be a nobody ever again." Love is the answer and tenderness is the way. Water is the love and the homie, a dry sponge. But tenderness is the contact. Water hitting sponge.

Two Enriques accompanied me to Seattle. After a talk in Renton, Washington, the two of them received a standing ovation and were resting snugly on cloud nine as we drove away from the event. One of our Enriques had to call his lady: "I just spoke . . . told my life story . . . got a standing ovation. I'm famous now in Seattle, so move up here. I mean, you're not famous, but maybe I can help you, you know, become a celebrity like me." Dry sponge, meet water.

Our joy is not meant to be an afterthought or merely occasional. "Joy is not made to be a crumb," Mary Oliver writes. It is what we choose those times when we find ourselves more loyal to our resentments than to our own unbearable beauty. We opt for this when our grievances take center stage and push aside our vulnerable delight in loving. We choose joy and it becomes our oxygen. Someone said once of Martin Luther King: "He saw us dancing before we knew we could move."

Jesus sees the "rich young man" and sees him dancing. He is caught up in the man's goodness and loves him. The young man is offered affection, fullness, and joy. The guy only hears hardship. He can't shake the imposition of following Jesus, and he walks away sad. Only joy is being given to us.

Richie, in his cell, is overwrought with anxiety and worry about facing a possible life sentence. The food arrives, and his Pakistani cellmate takes it through the slot. He asks Richie if he wants his food, and Richie says, "Nah."

After many days of this, the Pakistani yells at him, "I can't take it anymore." Richie is startled. "You have to snap out of this." He zeroes in on Richie. "Do you have the keys to that cell door? Do you know how your court date will go? No? Then stop it. You don't have your mind where your body is. Stop it. You HAVE to have your mind where your body is." And Richie did it, in an instant. And he could, quite magically, find the mystical hope and joy right here, even in the seeming hardship of it all.

Three homies, trainees, are kicking it in my office late on a Friday. One of them says: "Hey, don't we get Monday off, you

know, for Washington's Birthday?" I explain to them that LAST
Monday was Presidents Day—for both Washington and Lincoln. "But," I say to them, "I'll make a deal with you. If you guys
can come up with three true things about Washington, I'll give
you this Monday off."

Here's a sampling of their answers: "He discovered America."
"He's that fool that cut down the apple tree." "He discovered Co-
lumbia." "He discovered freedom." "He brought peace between
the Indians and the Spaniards." "He freed the slaves."

When they have exhausted all the possible answers they can
think of, I say to them, "I got three words for you: SEE YA
MONDAY." The answers we possess don't measure what matters. Having our minds where our bodies are, allowing tender
delighting in the here and now. This is what counts.

Though, oddly, some folks don't see tenderness as sanity,
but rather, think it makes us saps. A homie named Joshua said,
"When I'm talking with someone I just don't like, I remind myself, this guy's mother loves him. It softens me into a corner."
We want to get to this corner where our hearts are tender and
supple. Not saps. We pummel meat and call it "tenderizing." At
Homeboy, we don't "tenderize," but, instead, we all allow our
"tough" selves to become supple. We turn this on its head. By
allowing ourselves to receive and be reached, we all get pum-
meled and tenderized. This is how things get transformed. Our
tenacity in tenderness, then, ripens us and propels us all to live
in the luminous and infinite now. Only tenderness keeps us attentive to delight. It's not about arriving at "nice." Tenderness is
radicalized nice. It is the finishing touch in love.

"Well, it's official," Lourdes tells me. "My *ruco* has been
messing up on me. So, Ash Wednesday came. I got me them
ashes. And then . . . I gave his ass up for Lent." The clarity of
radicalized nice. Tenderness doesn't mean doormat, but it is te-
nacious and transformational. Tenderness is decisive.

Esteban texts me after having given a tour of Homeboy to a large group from out of state. We can get twenty such groups a week, from all over the world. They usually afford the tour guide a chance to tell his or her story while pointing out the sights. "My dawg," he writes. "Just wrappin' up some tours. Homeboy Industries is like a box of Lucky Charms . . . magical. We got the key and combination to any lock . . . we are the missing piece to any puzzle. We are the finishing touches to any recipe—sprinkle a little Homeboy Industries on it and it's golden. I love you, Pops." Where there is love, one can find shelter there. As my friend Mary says, "Love can hold . . . every . . . single . . . thing."

The therapeutic mysticism lived out in tenderness at Homeboy seeks to replace the very tired national narrative of meritocracy, rags to riches, folks pulling themselves up by the bootstraps (never mind, as Dr. King used to say, even if they are bootless). We seek the God of all spaciousness who delights in us rather than measuring performance. Homeboy wants to model redemptive communities that heal and triumph over shame, isolation, and the pervasive sense that we are unworthy. We want to live the Zen slogan: "Fall down fifty-three times, get up fifty-four."

Carlitos is late for work. "The cops pulled me over." I ask him why. "Cuz he said that I looked like a young Hispanic male. But damn, G, a gang of us look like young Hispanic males." True enough. He bounds into my office some days later and he is jumping out of his skin with excitement. "Pops, I just got my report card back—ALL C'S!!!!" This statement is in a holding pattern of silence. Then it lands: "Damn, G. That just gave me chills right now." Get up fifty-four.

⟡

Homeboy is a place of grace and chaos—where joy is always in the wings. The Christmas carol says it best: "Comfort and joy." Why settle for happiness when we are being offered comfort and joy? A heaping dish of Tenderoni. I pull up in front of Home-boy having returned from some errand with Leroy and Lencho. Leroy in the backseat says, "I can't believe we actually been rid-ing in G's car. It's like going to Disneyland."

Lencho elaborates. "Yeah. It's like finally getting to sit on my grandma's couch. It's covered in plastic and we were never allowed to sit on it." I'm a bit taken aback by their awe at a sim-ple car ride. We open our doors and Leroy pats me on the back. "Best Uber ever."

We talk about the Incarnation being necessary. Indeed, it was. Not because of sin—for God's sakes. But because God's love needed to become tender. There was an urgency for it to become touch and smell and action and listening; to become ten-derness in the flesh.

I wanted to get to the Oakland airport from San Francisco. If you want to know which BART train to get on, you don't need to know your destination (Oakland Airport). You need to know your train's final stop. Only trains that end in "Fremont" will get you to the airport. Our final stop, as Jesus suggests, is joy. "My joy yours, your joy complete." All roads lead to joy. Teresa of Ávila got this one right: "Just these two words God spoke changed my life: 'Enjoy Me.'" That's the Fremont train.

Jesus invites us to joy. The holiness to which we are called is to know joy in its fullness. We let ourselves be drawn to the Tender One whose face is unbridled joy. We are beckoned to this locus of joy, not a reckoning with the error of our ways, but God saying, unabashedly smiling, "Get over here."

Pedro Arrupe thought that the daily pursuit of delight should be our focus. He used words like "rejoicing" and "relish-ing." These are the things that shape our soul and lodge it in an intimacy that is real and replenishing.

Relishing can take an odd form as well. A homie, fresh out of a long stretch in prison, says to me: "Now I'm out, and I can bury my own people." He was able to rejoice in this new freedom and ability. A lifer released after thirty years sends a video to my cell phone on the Fourth of July of fireworks seen from his back porch. There are the sounds of fireworks in the distance, of course, but close at hand, you mainly hear "Ooooooh! AAAAAHHH!!!" It's the homie relishing this moment, and I replayed it several times. It made me cry each time. A homie, accompanying me on a cross-country flight, turns to me, seatbelted and ready for takeoff: "I plan on smiling all the way to Boston." Limitless relishing.

The aspiration here is to the limitless. What we discover is that there is a reservoir of love within us and this simply won't dry up. I had known Chepe for thirty years and he was in prison for these past twenty. He never once wrote me in all that time. Then he does.

His letter is both a little rusty on the news and surprising. "I hear you have cancer. Sorry to hear that. I hope you get better." Then he changes lanes. "On a lighter note, I heard you got married. Congratulations." Knowing that we have access to this source of love brings us true joy. Limitless reservoir. So, we settle into this loving luminosity that allows us to accept everything and abide and rest in it without attachment and struggle. We can relish then . . . every . . . single . . . thing.

Fearlessness will always be a contour of our ultimate joy and transformation. We don't sidestep our fear and underlying sadness, we allow acceptance of it all, and then we can connect to our pathway to joy. A scrappy twenty-year-old Black gang member named Jason confided, "I didn't have a childhood. So I'm not gonna lie. I still watch cartoons and eat cereal. Trying to relive a childhood—that I didn't have." For in the end, it's only our joy that authenticates our living, brought to you by a decided fearlessness. "One filled with joy," Mother Teresa says, "preaches without preaching." In good times and in bad. Eating cereal and watching cartoons. Smiling all the way to Boston. Turns out, joyful people are holy people.

"Sin" in its Greek origins is *hamartia*, which means to miss the mark. Because of our addiction to measuring, we think that we didn't hit a bull's-eye. We are measuring up poorly. But the mark we miss is joy. Yes, homies could not be even one bit better, but they could be more joyful. We all could. God won't love Lefty more if he stops gangbanging. But Lefty will be happier if he does. We want to fix people only because we think God wants me fixed. *Hamartia* is not about being freed from sin but is calling us to joy.

The "rich young man" walks away because he's sad, not bad (he couldn't be one bit better). Wholeness is way better than being "freed from sin."

Sleepy was kicking it in the alley where his homies always gathered. A newly arriving homie, breathless, came with a report that there were enemies at the gas station at 4th and Boyle. Sleepy was given the gun. "Go there now and take care of business." Sleepy left immediately and knew how to navigate the two alleys that could get him to the right vantage point. When he told me this story many months later, he had always been clear with himself that he would never shoot anybody. Too smart, too resilient, and though hanging by a thin thread of hope, he always seemed grateful for that thread. Sleepy opted for joy, in his way, by deciding some things beforehand.

Indeed, he saw the enemies at the gas station. He pointed the gun, straight up in the air like he was starting a race and shot. The gang members at the gas station scattered. He ran back as fast as he could to his homies, just so that he could be out of breath when he said, "I think I hit one of them."

I take two identical twin brothers, Gus and Victor, to Sacramento. When they were younger, and carousing in the projects, I was really bad at telling them apart. It's somewhat easier now.

Gus has a decided limp. He had his leg shot off and now sports a prosthetic leg. We are traveling in the early days of post-9/11. Burbank Airport and the TSA are getting the kinks out of the system. These guys have no IDs, and in those days, any photo ID worked. So, we made these Homeboy Employee ID cards. The twins look like their employer might be the Taliban.

I walk through security without a problem. Victor gets the wand treatment, since, frankly, he looks like Central Casting asked him to go to the airport and play the role of gang member. Gus, however, sets off every bell, like when you win the car on the slot machine at Vegas. I watch as the agent takes him away from the others. I also watch as his blood pressure rises and he gets increasingly agitated with this guy. "I HAVE A FAKE LEG," he yells, and well, everyone turns and looks. I try to signal that he should take things down a notch. Finally, the agent is done with him, but as he saunters away, it is clear that Gus is not done with him. "Do we LOOK like terrorists? I mean, come on—WE'RE GANG MEMBERS." Gus actually believed this would be comforting to hear. The moment comes when we do get to trade in the God who would like us to "get our act together" or to look or act differently or to be rid of our shameful past, for the God who only wants to hand us joy.

One night, nearly a quarter of a century ago, I'm walking in the projects on a warm summer evening when I spot Rafa sitting on a stoop, smoking a *frajo*. He's one of my heroes. He's a single father, raising two sons and working in a job that Homeboy located for him. The mother of his kids remains lost in some drug-using swirl. He's from a gang on the other side of the projects and now lives in his enemy's neighborhood. His rivals here don't mess with him, partly because he's clearly a "retiree" and they know they will have to contend with me if they bothered him.

While the two of us "chop it up," I notice a *bola* of homies gathered down the grassy end of this block of projects. I spot

Alex among the group and I call him over. His walk alone signals reluctance and he's leery of my impending message. Plus,
I'm talking to his enemy, so it's an uncomfortable twofer. Alex
shakes my hand. He doesn't acknowledge that Rafa lives on the
same planet. "*Oye, mijo,* I heard that your lady, who is ready to
burst, was taken to the hospital last night and you were nowhere
to be found. *Qué gacho, carnal.* You were kicking it with your
homies. Missing in action."

Alex explains, "My *suegra* was there."

I accelerate my astonishment. "*Serio?* I mean, you're not
gonna be there when your baby is born?"

There's a crack of vulnerability in his wall. "*La neta* . . . I
don't think I can hang."

I redouble my faux outrage. "*Qué, qué???*" I turn to Rafa to
bring him in as an ally. "Dawg, were you there when your two
boys were born?" Rafa nods. "Well, then, give him *kletcha*. Run
it down to him."

Rafa demurs, "Oh, I don't think he wants to hear about my
experience."

"Of course he does. That's why we're on this earth together.
To help each other."

Rafa stands and throws his cigarette away. "Well, there I was
in the *sala de espera*, waiting for my first *morrito* to be born. And
after a long-ass wait, this nurse runs in and waves at me. 'It's time!
It's time, already.' So, we run down this hall. And this nurse puts
this gown on me, and she puts *guantes* on me, and she puts a
mascara . . . across . . . my *mascara*. And we get to a door and she
opens the door, and all I see are these legs spread wide open and
a baby is coming out . . . and . . . I gotta get outta this room. I go
to the door . . . to get outta this room . . . but the nurse . . . she
pulls me back in . . . but I . . . gotta . . . get out . . . of this room."

Alex and I turn to each other, perplexed.

I ask Rafa, "Why do ya gotta get out of this room?" We wait.

"Cuz that was not my lady." Alex and I hang on to each other with the greatest of ease and magnificent laughter. Rafa remains quizzical.

Before no time at all, Rafa and Alex are both sitting on the stoop, smoking *frajos* and exploring together the joy of fatherhood to which they both feel cordially and tenderly invited.

I celebrate Mother's Day at a probation camp. Afterward, I'm shaking hands with all the guys. One says to me, "Happy Mother's Day. I mean, not for you, but, you know . . . for your wife." I tell him I'll relay his message. He later pulls me aside and says, "Can I ask you a question? How do you stay happy? I'm always sad. I don't have any happy days anymore." Staying happy. We all need to stay attentively present in the "living room," which is where the joy is. In the here and now. Otherwise, we lament only what happened yesterday (the bathroom) or are anxious only about tomorrow (the kitchen). It keeps us stuck in sadness. But the joy is happening in the living room, where some homie you don't even know is wishing you a Happy Mother's Day. And your soul can't stop singing.

Every year, Homeboy has a 5K walk/run as our fall fundraiser. Thousands participate. In the early years, we scheduled it near Halloween. Maybe fifty or so would run in a costume. Guys in giant hot dog suits or folks dressed like Mr. Peanut or big ol' tacos. A homie named Deondre pulls up alongside me as I'm walking and asks, "What you s'posed to be?"

I tell him, "An overweight, middle-aged guy exercising."

"Good costume," he counters, and walks past me. Tenderness revealed in the other's undeniable preciousness. It stands on the opposite side of the notion that finds some people a nuisance.

Irving plunks himself into a chair in my office. As he lands, he says, "Hey, G—I brought you a gift from Mexico." He is most assuredly empty-handed.

"Yeah? What?"

"A bottle of Bacardi."

"Yeah?"

"Yeah . . . But the homies drank it."

Everyone knows it's the thought that counts.

-◇‖◇-

We find our power in the tender heart. We rest there, welcoming and allowing our entire story to unfold. There is nothing we deny entrance. Our heart inclines to kindness and wants to hold it all with tenderness as a habit-forming response. Even when we want to change our address and reside in annoyance, hurt feelings, and "being right." I pick up Anthony and Hector really early so we can arrive for a talk at an airport hotel. Getting there is an ordeal. My keynote is at 9:30 and doing battle with early morning traffic "ain't nuthin' nice." We arrive at 9:00 a.m. with plenty of time to spare. The woman in charge sees me, walks toward me, and scrunches her face. "Your talk is at twelve—not nine thirty. There must be some confusion." Then she just turns and walks away. The three of us stare at her. I'm flabbergasted, dumbfounded, gobsmacked, and silent. Anthony, taking this all in, breaks the silence—"Quiet on the set." It was all I needed to find another place to rest other than annoyance. Tender silliness coaxing to joy as a decisive moment.

-◇‖◇-

Sometimes, it would be hard to understand exactly what Lenny wanted to say. The words would be disjointed and all over the place. We needed to retrace our steps sometimes before we could continue down the road of understanding him. Then we discovered that he had been so severely beaten in Mexico that he was left for dead and truly impaired. He showed the dents and mementoes of the assault that covered his head. He had been deported to Mexico and, upon his return, even ICE had compassion for this man who had been through so much and permitted him to stay. Even ICE.

Over the course of months, before our eyes, tenderness and its intentionality massaged and worked over the neural pathways of this guy. What had been disjointed began to find connection and cohesion. The tender glance constantly directed to Lenny began to make thriving possible and nearly always present. I found him alone one day in the hallway at Homeboy, leaning against the wall, with his hand to his face and weeping. When I asked him why he was crying, he pulled out his ATM card. "Cuz of this, my first bank card. I was on the train this morning, just staring at it, and I started to cry. I saw that in my car were some cholos, and I stopped, cuz you can't cry in front of cholos on a train. Then I went to Burger King, at lunch. I handed them this card, and they handed me a burger." He started to cry all over again. I didn't have the heart to tell him that the day will come when he cries over this ATM card for OTHER reasons. Yet, the whole hallway encounter with Lenny kept me in "the living room."

Lenny worked on his high school diploma and our tutors discovered that he was something of a savant in the math department. A tutor told me that he had all these Rain Man–like abilities to explain, in gang member argot, many mathematical concepts. A teacher would be going on about "finding place value" and Lenny would take over. The Homie Math Whisperer would step up and translate. "See, dawg, it's like this." And his "step-aside, let-me-handle-this" approach would issue in a roomful of gang members nodding and taking notes.

He graduated with flying colors and would identify himself in texts to me as "Lenny, the great mathematician." He walked in the other day and asked me for help with a dentist. "You know, when I got jumped in Mexico, they fucked up my grill." I told him I'd be happy to help. "I've discovered, G, that I like talking to people. I feel like words . . . have medicine in them."

Being tender is to tend to people. To land on the love that does not judge and softens us into a corner, enough to attach like mother to child. "I was born," Sufi mystic Rabia of Basra writes, "when all I once feared I could love." Tenderness finds the enduring energy of love that sustains everything.

I knew Dino as a munchkin growing up in the projects. He was always *mugroso*, in the same clothes, running the streets, and hanging out just about anywhere but his home. Years later, he described his mom this way: "She was one of those moms who just throw their kids away when stuff goes wrong." He had a series of stepfathers who never really cut it as father figures. Dino did a chunk of years in prison and kept up a regular correspondence. He was better at it than I was. When he was "short to the pad," he was ready to work. "Just think of it," he wrote me, "as an installment plan. I'll pay off in the long run."

He flourished in our community and found it to be a circle of trust, a place of regard and even high expectancy. This was all new terrain for Dino. He was surrounded with folks who just didn't seem to ever forget that they were connected to one another.

He had one of those quick wits that amazed me all the more because his growing up was so grim. Somehow, you'd think his past would be a virtual blockade to fast humor and dry banter. But it wasn't. He called once in panic mode. He DESPERATELY needed tires. "Well, what do they look like?" I ask.

"Balder than you," he says.

We were able to locate employment beyond us and he worked diligently and threw himself into truly arduous labor. This installment plan was paying off. He dropped by after work one day and was as completely *mugroso* as I remember him many years ago, running wild as a *mocoso* in the projects. "It must feel good to be a hardworkin' man?" I ask him.

"Oh, hell no. My back hurts, my leg hurts." We laughed. Then he got philosophical. "Back in my gangbanging days, I had created my own comic book character. Homeboy is my home. It gave me a place to console my change. It helped me to decide and choose to make things happen for myself. After all," he said, "only two things fall from the sky: bird shit and water."

Time passes and you don't hear from people and then you do. Dino calls me at three o'clock in the morning. My heart dives. This is not like him. He's sobbing. I always ask if homies have been drinking. It situates what he'll say to me and how much credence I should give it. Dino is as sober as ever. When there is enough subsiding in his tears, I ask him: "Why are you crying, Dino?"

"Well, you know how I got out of prison and you hired me right away?"

"Yeah."

"And you know how I worked alongside my worst enemies in the world, and they became my brothers?"

"Yeah."

"And you know how I worked on myself, finally, at Homeboy?"

"Yeah."

"And you know how grateful I am for Homeboy and this other job you guys got me and how I now have a house, my wife, and boys, and how I love my life?"

"Dino, my son for life. Why are you crying?"

"Cuz tonight—for the first time in my life—I feel this pain, for all the hurt I caused."

"Ma dawg," I tell him. "You've arrived. Congratulations— you've done the really hard work. You can choose joy now. It's right around this corner." All he had once feared, he can now love.

I suppose that in order to feel our wholeness, we need to get our fears out of the way. Come to terms with stuff. Then we can "hit the mark." Tenderness has medicine in it. Fear gets invited in without judgment, and suddenly there is nothing dry about this sponge anymore. We find ourselves saturated with the fullness that's been God's intention all along. We are soaked in love's confusing joy. Then we can hop on the Fremont train.

Chapter Nine

The Place Itself

Benjy told me about his cellie, an older *vato* who had been down for quite some time. In the morning, Benjy would greet the older gentleman and say, "Good morning. How ya doin'?"

The old guy would always say, "Sometimes you, sometimes me." It took a long time before Benjy finally asked him to explain this cryptic response. The *vato* held out a Cup Noodles. "Ya see, dawg, sometimes I have a Cup 'A Noodles and you don't. Sometimes you do. And I don't. Sometimes me. Sometimes you. Always US." James Baldwin called this "US achieving ourselves."

Martin Luther King wrote that we are "tied in a single garment of destiny." Or as a homie put it, "Here at Homeboy, we all want to be one heartbeat." I was on a panel in DC, and joining was Roy L. Austin, Jr., from the Office of Urban Affairs from the last year of the Obama administration. A question toward the end of our hour together came from some young person in the audience who asked something like, what can we do to address such vexing and complex social dilemmas in our country? Something like that. And I can't remember his answer in its fullness. But he began by saying simply: "Vicinity."

He let the word hang there. And I think he was quite right. Vicinity. Just go there. Put yourself there. Nothing gets accomplished otherwise. Single garment. One heartbeat.

When Scripture says that "God shows no partiality," it's speaking of real kinship and connection. It is a communion God longs for and the relationship itself is God. In recovery, they say, community is the opposite of addiction. Sometimes they'll say an addict alone is bad company. Indeed. Homeboy Industries announces that it is the relationship that heals, in community, and in this way Homeboy doesn't want to join some dialogue in progress but to create a brand-new dialogue. It doesn't want to argue or fight with some old model. It wants to fashion a new one. Anger, for example, at seeing the deep inequities that exist when the curtain is pulled back may initiate things. But only the relationship heals. It is invigorating to want to create a world we've never seen before. What we cannot imagine cannot come into being. Though we may be inclined initially to divide, our longing, more deeply, is for kinship and relational wholeness. Let's imagine it. At Homeboy, it's not about "saving lives" but watching lives get redefined in love. The question is not "Did we succeed with that homie?" but "Did he find community here?"

Nelson and Pedro aren't friends when they leave to travel with me to Denver but after three days, they find community in each other. At lunch one day, Nelson says, "We never realized there was fine print when we joined a gang."

Pedro adds, "AND the fine print had fine print." The time together loosens what had been forged and rigid in their competing gang worlds. One morning of the trip, Nelson takes his shower first while Pedro is asleep and on the steamy mirror, he writes, "I love you, Pedro." The steam dissipates and the message disappears. Then Pedro showers, the steam appears, and so does Nelson's message again. At breakfast they tell me about this, and the unembarrassed intimacy of it indeed creates a world they've never seen before. It's not so much about seeking the other but to find yourself in the other. Real belonging, that ends in becoming, is not about membership, it's about kinship. We're connected—not card carriers. We see each other's names in the mirror.

I took a homie named Felipe to a dermatologist. His acne was alarming, and I found a doctor who would see him for free. Afterward, we had lunch at Burger King. Felipe's English was not terrific, and though I speak Spanish, Felipe insisted on performing without the benefit of a net. His tongue was thick with accent and he was prone to the occasional mangle. I asked him, over a burger, about his lady, Lisa. "Oh, she wen' back wit' 'er ex." I expressed my sympathy. "I don' sweat it, G. You know— too much fitches in da soup." I asked for clarification. Felipe just turned up the volume. "YOU KNOW—TOO . . . MUCH . . . FITCHES . . . IN DA SOUP."

"Son," I told him, "I don't know what the HELL you're talkin' about." He relented. *"Tú sabes—hay muchos peces en el mar."*

"Ohhh," I said. "Plenty of fish in the sea . . . there are more *jainas* out there."

"Yeah," he said, "dat one."

I couldn't help myself. I shared the "too much fitches" story with the office and soon, as nearly always happens, Felipe was christened with a new nickname. Everyone called him Too Much Fitches. Actually, he loved it. He told me, before joining Homeboy, that he wanted to work there "cuz I need a belonging place." He found community in the sangha, in the delight we all shared. Later, when he got deported, the collect calls in Spanish went like this: "Will you accept a collect call from—" and Felipe would scream from Mexico: "TOO MUCH FITCHES!!" We all can live refusing mutuality and yet this only deadens us.

Our isolation insulates and then there is no incoming affection and nothing outgoing either. What keeps us awake and alive is staying interconnected with God and each other. Nicknames, collect calls, laughter, all points of connection. All reminders of the belonging place we imagine and choose to create.

As I mentioned earlier, homies always come in with huge backpacks that they will not remove, no matter how persistently you invite them. Too Much Fitches was exactly that guy. But right before your eyes, you watched the transformation from backpack to parachute. He moved from staying alive to staying in love. Indeed, in his time with us, he transformed a backpack full of sorrow and survival into a parachute of thriving wholeness. All the folks who surrounded him were part of a movement that knows that only love leads to a conjuring of kinship within reach of the actual lives we live.

The reality of everyone who walks through our doors is that they live under constant threat. They breathe in shame with every breath. We welcome them so they can first breathe easier. And second, breathe differently. A tiny fella was pleading his case to get hired. "My mom kicked me out of the house cuz I'm not bringing in enough money to the house."

"How old are you?" I asked.

"Fifteen," he said, and burst into tears. Under so much weight, homies desperately feel that their only recourse is defense and survival mode. If we let our hearts break, we discover kinship. We choose to find the tenderness under all that is harsh. In community, we conspire with God to move us toward a transcendent awe at the stress they carry and then fall backward, caught and welcomed by a tenderness in kinship.

The first McDonald's in Moscow opened in 1990. Many months of training preceded the grand opening. They were taught to "welcome" the customers. This was indeed foreign to both the workers and to the folks walking in. They were trained to convey welcome, and the Russian for this is translated as "Your arrival here is pleasing to us." There were historic lines of Russians standing in the cold to get in. It wasn't the fries or the Happy Meals. The lines were long because customers WOULD NOT LEAVE the place once they were in. They said the reason was the "welcome." Breathe easier. Breathe differently.

At Homeboy, folks are, as the poet says, "won by warmth, ripened affectionately." I got a text from a homie: "I've decided to live in love's energy—now I come to work and my heart smiles. I walk in the door at Homeboy and there it is—the aroma of kinship." Homeboy started with a vision, but then we had to build a belief system. The fundamental ethos of Homeboy is "walking with" in love's energy, not "doing for." Shirley Torres says, "The magic happens in the lobby, nearest the swinging of the door." We all walk in the door and, together, stare at our own shared ruin, and we choose to walk as kin. We find a new, spacious way of seeing. I suppose it plans for the future, but it mainly suggests that we not worry about it. Stevie always says, when he greets trainees in the morning, "Positive vibes on a Monday" (or whatever day it is). And people learn to be repurposed for positivity, ripened affectionately.

In the culture of tenderness, homies "detoxify" and discover the authority of their own voice, and their true and sacred selves. In the process, they find a love that can go anywhere it wants. Gang members are keenly aware of the limits of geography. "I can't go there," a homie might say. "You crazy? I'll get caught slippin'." What we hope homies will find in a culture of kindness is that love can be its own passport.

I stepped into the men's room at Homeboy and three homies were trying to fix the paper towel dispenser. ("How many homies does it take to fix . . .") Actually, one was working on it, the other two were giving helpful advice. One said to the worker, "Come on, dawg—even a five-year-old could fix this!"

The worker barked back, "Well, then find me a five-year-old!" The place is safe enough to seriously bump into each other. This is a movement of safety, relief, and hope that excludes no one. We bark and try to hold together something that doesn't hold together. Fortunately, not everyone in the office is crazy on the same day. But if we're not present to it, we miss it.

During the early months of the pandemic, before we settled into whatever needed settling, we all kept choosing to be each other's PPE. "Come on, Pops," a homie, Jojo, said. "You and me—we've been through pandemics before." I knew what he meant. We had been through storms and catastrophes and the darkest moments of gang violence. "I'm always gonna be there for you," he added, "through thick or thin, sharp or pointy." I felt "personally protected" by his kindness. Homies had great, liberating humor in memes they sent and texts they'd write. "NOW, can I FINALLY take a shower, or do I have to just keep washing my hands?"

Breaking points happened with some regularity during the plague as well. "I think I'm going to lose it," Lisa tells me.

I say, "No, you're not. You're going to gain it. And I don't mean gain weight from all the crap we're eating on lockdown. You're going to gain a deeper anchor in love. Watch. You will gain something beautiful during this time."

A homie, Ricky, one of my "dearly deporteds" in Tijuana, emails me. I don't hear from him very often. Before he went to prison and then got deported, he was having a hard time at home. "I lived in a house where we didn't take out the garbage, we brought it in." His alcoholic father was beyond strict. *"Aquí mando yo"*—which basically means, "This is my house, my rules." Ricky was explaining this to me: "So I had to jump through the loopholes." He was telling me once how he's clear with enemies. "First, I talk, but then, you know, if the situation . . . evaluates . . ." I knew what he meant. He added somberly: "You know what my problem is? I don't got no destination." He ended up doing time for drug sales. He writes me this morning, as we are all on house arrest during the early days of the virus. He writes simply this, in bold letters: "WE ARE YOUR MASK." Which is to say, I suppose, "We got ya; we have you surrounded; come out with your hands up; we will be your protective gear, till the wheels fall off. Sharp or pointy." I understood him. It got me through that day. I felt held and protected.

In the Spiritual Exercises, Ignatius talks about "mutual help." It means that I will only know God in entering the life of another and they in me, exquisitely mutual. God just "kicks it," hides in that exchange. We choose to be what Pope Francis calls "social poets," those anchored at the margins who imagine ways forward in this thrilling mutuality. This is how we are reminded that we are children of a vulnerable God. In the sangha, in the community of kinship, I see everyone in me and me in everyone. It takes time for folks, until, that is, they find relief and a safe haven. I suppose we still think that "when the student is ready—the teacher will appear." But at Homeboy, we want the place itself to be the teacher.

Rico, in our first storefront office, found our place safe and a space for rest. He was one of our "half of life" guys, having spent half of his life locked up. Every day I'd ask how he was doing and he'd always answer, "Things could be worser." In those days, we mainly tried to find felony-friendly employers. No one wanted to take a chance on Rico, a tall Puerto Rican gang member who towered over everyone.

Once, he was at the computer, ostensibly doing a job search, but I could see he was playing a computer card game. I asked what game it was. He said, "Solitary." I told him he had been locked up too long. There was the evening he spotted a mouse scurrying past (we were infested) and Rico screamed and leaped to the top of the desk. I rushed out of my office, thinking someone was being murdered. I tried to calm him down. "I don't like mices."

Rico told me once that "Homeboy is a place where you come broken and then you blossom. I got returned to myself. It was always there and I didn't know it." Connection matters and needs to precede any direction you might give. To the scapegoated and demonized, the hope of the mystic is to offer a radiant and attractive witness of kinship. Attraction not promotion. The hope is to dedicate ourselves to the readiness, the capacity, and the willingness to stay in relationship. No grim duty here, but a practice that rises above judgment and allows delight to take over.

As more and more lifers are released, Homeboy is where folks come. Guys who were often juveniles tried as adults and "got some action" were finally released after legislative bills (and our friend Governor Jerry Brown) loosened the hold on them. Some of these folks have been locked up for more than a quarter of a century, so they don't know, for example, to just stick your hands under a bathroom faucet and the water comes out, no need to touch anything.

Four homies are "kicking it" in my office and Juan, who spent twenty-seven years in prison, is staring at his cell phone. "Hey, G, what does LMFAO mean?"

The others laugh and I can't believe this geezer is about to supply the answer. "Laughing my fuckin' ass off."

"Really?" Juan says, "This is all new to me. I mean, I kept thinking LOL meant . . . 'Lots of Love.' Well, I found out it doesn't." All five of us find our whole beings smiling, then Juan takes us on a further ride. "Watcha—check this out. My daughter texts me that her volleyball team won their game, and I texted back 'WTF.'" Then the next day, she texts 'I passed that math test I was worried about.' And, of course, I write back, 'WTF.'

Then I see her the next day, and she says, 'Dad, do you know what WTF stands for?' and I said, 'Course I do . . . 'Why That's Fantastic.'" Juan absorbs the immediate laughter and even two homies crumbling to the floor as a sign that he is in a safe haven. Welcome home. "Your arrival here is pleasing to us."

In Luke's gospel, when James and John aren't welcomed in the Samaritan village, they ask Jesus, "Lord, do you want us to call down fire from heaven to destroy them?" Jesus rebukes his disciples, because he doesn't believe in a "Them." Jesus rejects the idea that these Samaritans don't belong to "Us." When Jesus says, "that you may be one," he is not echoing Rodney King, "Can't we just get along?" It's about belonging to each other and not just playing well together. From Katrina to COVID-19 to the movement of Black Lives Matter, the invisible is made visible. Not just poverty and systemic racism surfacing as visible, but our clinging to the illusion that we are separate. We have this human impulse to categorize, as Isabel Wilkerson maintains in her incredible book *Caste*, and that urge becomes inseparable from the artificial hierarchy and grading system that keeps us apart. The great John Lewis said, "We all live in the same house." We belong there. Always US.

Jesse comes back from lunch at the Taco Truck. "I put my *horchata* down and went to put salsa on my tacos, and this homeless guy calmly walked off with my *horchata*." Things could be worser. Jesse is unflappable and calm. "I guess," he says softly, "he needed it more than me." Then he adds quickly, "'Course, he got my cooties and *babas*." The sacred, safe haven is where everyone is seen and heard. Invisibility gets reduced. It is in this location, this "vicinity," that we arrive at the widest tolerance of ourselves and others. Every day, we inch closer to knowing that we are all one breath and one embrace. Sometimes you. Sometimes me. Tenderness reveals how precious everyone is. Cooties, *babas*, and all.

Later, Jesse would get his AA degree at East Los Angeles College and go on to UC Berkeley. He was even asked to give the valedictory address in the massive ELAC stadium. In it, he said: "None of us waste space—but we make space for each other." This is what in fact he did at a taco stand on the East Side with a homeless man. Making space for each other—excluding only exclusion itself.

Milton was sitting in front of my desk and explaining a situation, when Jim Oswald was making *señales* through my glass door. Jim is volunteer extraordinaire and he's signaling (what the homies call "hand puppets") that he only needs a few minutes of my time. I wave him in and put Milton on hold. "Hey, G, I'm wondering if you're free," Jim begins, until he glances down and sees Milton sitting there. Peals of recognition are let loose in the world, and Milton leaps to his feet. They hug each other snugly and for some time, like one of those long-lost reunions. Each keeps an arm draped over the other's shoulder as he turns to look at me, all the while pointing at the other. "I love this man, G." Jim points at Milton.

"He's the BEST." Milton points back. "This is a beautiful man right here," Milton continues, patting him on the chest, wanting to bring his point home. "In fact," he says, "if we were living in Greek times"—and I think, *Uh-oh*—"Michelangelo would make a sculpture of his ass." (Whew! Greek times? Michelangelo? Close enough.)

Anthropologist Margaret Mead observed from her travels throughout Africa, how tribes perceived a crime to be a sign of distress from the "criminal." Sometimes they'd spend two days encircling the perpetrator and only speak of his goodness. Consequently, the community around the person sought to direct healing and to alleviate this pain. Similarly, the Navajo thought that the criminal was one who acted as if he had no family. A severed belonging. Without a sense of "sin," these tribes were able to see pain and wound and thought punishment didn't make any sense. Restorative justice is also justice and not a vindication. It is about healing and alleviating pain, not about vengeance. As is often said, "We send kids to detention as punishment, not for punishment." We need to go even further than this and seek only repair and the healing of wound, and a return to a union of kin.

Ignatius never uses the word "community" but rather "union." I think he meant a kinship that may begin in "vicinity" and "community" but arrives at something quite deep and wonderfully mutual. Pope Francis writes of the same thing in *Fratelli tutti* when he speaks of "fraternity" and "social friendship." The longing in this is just to move toward our kin. It's not about getting to solutions as much as getting to each other. We connect in good times and in bad. Whatever situation we find ourselves in, it is always a vehicle to wake up and connect. "On the street," Lencho says, "my spirit darkened, but not here." This happens when every member of the sangha is constantly looking around and saying, "Who needs to be loved?" Mindful that our love is not dependent on the lovability of the other. We come to see that God IS communion and that kinship is God's only thirst. When we are together, we discover this reservoir of life whose richness is hard to see when we are apart and isolated.

There's a framed photo in my office that is among my most treasured possessions. A missionary in Guatemala named Ashley Williams works extensively with gang members in Guatemala City and principally in the prisons. The photograph features about thirty gang members, alarmingly tattooed, and even more horribly packed into a tiny cell. They are beaming like brilliant lights, each holding up a copy of my book, in Spanish, *Tattoos on the Heart*. I went and visited them once. One by one, they were escorted out of their cells, with cloth sacks over their heads to disorient them, and led into a room where I awaited them.

Guards with ski masks and rifles lined the walls. As each one's sack was removed, Ashley would whisper to the inmate in Spanish "Father Greg is here." Each one would whisper back incredulously, *"En vivo?"* (In person?).

I found out later, that although they each had a copy of my book, only one inmate could really read. So he would read out loud to the others, book held under the paltry light of a barred window that came in like a thin crack, which he would follow slowly around the cell, light hitting page, until it turned dark. To be continued tomorrow. Union moving toward the other, making the most of the light.

Several years ago, the Superior General of the Jesuits, Adolfo Nicolás, visited Homeboy Industries. I first met "Nico" in Rome, right after he was named, and had several meals with him. On our first encounter, he shook my hand and said, "Nothing stops a bullet like a job." He had been "prepped" by my good friend and his assistant, Jim Grummer. He received a tour at Homeboy, and afterward some twenty of us sat around a rectangle of tables to have lunch, catered by the Homegirl Café. We went around the room and the homies and homegirls told their stories. One by one, we were broken open to wild waves of laughter and weeping that caught us all short in the depth of authenticity and shared humanity. When we finally reached Nico's turn to speak, he was speechless. He softly wept and asked for our patience. Then he said, "This is what Eucharist is supposed to be . . . but rarely is." Union, not budging from the vicinity. We want to give ourselves to relatedness and attempt to enter into soul-honoring connection.

In the early days, during the decade of death (1988 to 1998), I suppose there were folks who wanted to transform an entire gang, rather than one gang member at a time. That never made any sense to me. People understand that a member of a white supremacist group could change, but no one would seek to transform the Ku Klux Klan into the Kiwanis club. Why would you bother? The goal is not to transform the group, but to invite individual folks into a sangha, another group. The mark of the new group, of course, is an all-inclusive, welcoming place of belonging with room for all. Richard Rohr says that all the exorcism stories in the gospel tell us that the only cure for possession is possession.

I recall at a huge gathering of Latinx young people, I brought homies to participate. After my keynote, everyone broke into small groups. Lorenzo, in the car ride home, lamented his small-group experience. "Damn, G—I mean, they talked as if gangs are ALL bad." I asked him (kindly) to name just one good thing. "They pick up litter." Seriously. He said this. Which reminded me of the local comic laureate from Pico Gardens housing projects, Felipe Esparza, who used to say, "Gangs aren't all bad—they carpool."

A homie I didn't know left this message. If you went to Central Casting in search of "menacing sounding message," they'd send you this guy's voice. It was slow, filled with gravel, and vaguely "possessed." Between each pause seemed to lurk a real live threat: "This is Stomper . . . from Fulano Gang. . . . I saw you last night . . . on the PBS channel. . . . I liked your words. . . . You use . . . big . . . vocab-u-lary words." Then, like every homie I've ever known, his voice got some fabric softener. It was like a different person took over. "You think you could help me?" Trading in one possession for another.

I took Ricky and his lady to a nice place for dinner. Ricky was one of those kids, I guess, whom I'd met in Juvenile Hall many years before. When he finally followed my business card's address to Homeboy, he tried to jog my memory. "You remember me . . . Juvenile Hall? I was little . . . you were skinny?" Once I called his house, and an old woman answered in Spanish, *"BUE-NO?"* I asked, in Spanish, if Ricky were home. *"Quién habla?"*

"*Habla Padre Gregorio.*"

"Oh, hi, G," Ricky said, discarding his grandma voice, "I thought you might be my PO. *Spensa.*"

At the restaurant, Ricky was joking about how perplexing the menu was. "It doesn't got no pictures. I'm used to seeing my food on the plastic screen and ordering the number five." Ricky has a hard time hearing something nice directed at him or if you express love or admiration. He deflects it this way: "That's a big boomerang." Back at ya. Therapeutic mysticism at Homeboy creates a spiritual vibrancy on the road to human flourishing. As the web of connection widens, a great freedom arrives for everyone. A big boomerang.

Teresa of Ávila wrote, "And only at that shrine where all are welcome, will God sing loud enough to be heard." Again, Homeboy is not so much a solution as it is a sign. And an inmate at Folsom told me, "A light does not make noise, it shines."

It was the Wednesday before our extended Christmas vacation and the last meeting of our Art Heals class run by the great Laura Miera. It's sort of arts and crafts for homies. You'd think they'd be less than interested, but it's our most popular gathering. This day, Laura has brought in prefab gingerbread walls and roofs in need of homies to make houses out of them. They'd use icing to epoxy it all together and to glue gummies to the roof and M&M's to line the walkway leading to the front door. I'm in my office cutting it up with three homies when Francisco comes in. He is the tiniest homie ever to work at Homeboy and he'd make a good jockey. He's young, with his face covered in tattoos, and I don't believe he's ever spoken more than three words to me. He barrels into my office, carrying his gingerbread house mounted on a cardboard tray. The sea of the three homies parts and Francisco places the house in the center of my desk. "I made this for you." He is all beaming light.

I'm touched. "Wow, son. Thank you, it's great."

We all stare at it, when, as if on cue, the walls fall in on themselves and the roof collapses inside. We're silent. Until one of the homies says, shaking his head, "Damn . . . Section eight housing." All five of us collapse as surely as the walls of the gingerbread house into each other's arms. This is the shrine where all are welcome.

At first, I wasn't clear what Celia was asking me to do. "A quinceañera mass for your mom, who is seventy?" It was Bertha's seventieth, and she never had a *misa* and party when she was fifteen, so her kids wanted to throw a big *pachanga* for her. Bertha raised seven children in Aliso Village all by herself. Her kids were as wild as you might expect them to be, and Bertha still held it all down heroically. So, Bertha and her daughters and sons and daughters- and sons-in-law got decked out and made up, and they walked down the aisle serenaded by mariachis. Bertha made her grand entrance in a long gown, bejeweled and split along the side. She was serene and bathing in the attention of it all. All her children wept and laughed and did a "call and response" to the folks and siblings, who got up and lavished Bertha with gratitude for saving their lives. Finally, a college-age grandson got up. He was dressed in formal attire like the other men. At first, he turned to me, seated behind him. "Thank you, Padre, for letting our dysfunctional family into your church." Big laugh. He then directed his remarks to Bertha. "We are all here . . . only because of you. You would help me with my homework when I was little. You gave me good advice. And, let's face it, I slept with you for eleven years."

The crowd went wild. One of his aunts said, looking at me, "That's right, he did."

He looked to his grandma in the front row. "So today we celebrate you." Then he turned to his aunts and uncles. "Now, let's not ruin it." Also, a mighty laugh. One didn't have to listen too intently to hear God singing loud enough to be heard.

We were waiting to take off and had been on the plane for longer than we should have been. Finally, the flight attendant spoke to us. "We are just waiting for the FO, the first officer."

A man yelled: "Well, they wouldn't wait for us." Everyone laughed. The flight attendant waited for the laughter to recede. "Unless, sir, you know how to fly this plane, there's not much we can do."

There's a beat and the man came back: "Well, I can text and drive. Does that count?" The roar of the entire plane laughing made all the waiting palatable. In an instant we floated in a union with each other that didn't just relieve anxiety but promised something larger than our self-absorption and stress.

Wallace Stevens writes: "We live in the description of the place and not in the place itself." We hold out for the place itself. That vicinity where we find ourselves essential allies to each other.

Oscar Luna hanged himself on a Saturday. With a coupling of shoelaces and belts, he held these taut over the front door and the mesh security door. He stood on the doorknob and then stepped off. Gaby, his fifteen-year-old sister, found him as she came home from a dance at 5:00 a.m. I spend the day shuttling from my many Sunday masses, to Oscar's mom's house, to the sheriff's station, to the hospital, and back again. I sit with Oscar's mom, Lupe. "What will I do without my Oscar?" she wails in Spanish. Blame abounds and eyes shift left and right, accusing everyone from the mother of Oscar's kids, to the "other woman," to Lupe herself. Grief gets compounded; pain multiplied.

How miraculously ministerial are the women from the parish with Lupe. They sit in silence. They swat flies that circle Lupe's sleeping face. They spoon *caldo* into her reluctant mouth. They caress. They say nothing. Nothing to say. I feel as useless as ever and it hasn't taken long to turn this into a failure about me.

They bring a cup of water. As they attempt to give it to a sleeping Lupe, I tell them, "Let her rest." But they correct me. She herself asked for the water and gratefully gulps it down. I feel roundly foolish at my attempt to manage the scene and, frankly, assume a place of power in controlling what happens next. The women had this, from the start.

I go with Oscar's brother, Nelson, to the house out back where Oscar killed himself. I bless the place, since I was asked to. Nelson sobs as he walks purposefully from room to room, attending to what he must. He hugs me tightly as I leave and I marvel at the purity and fullness of heart he possesses, even as it judges my divided one. Rumi writes, "You know my coins are counterfeit, but you accept them anyway." Still, the circle of trust widens and even the fraudulent are drawn in. We all can be essential allies, after all.

-◇◇-

My birthday can be kind of over-the-top (don't tell anyone that I feel this way). After cake and mariachis and well-wishers, it can consume an entire day, to say nothing of two days before and two days after. Just before we close the office that day, a tiny homie, named Elias, fifteen years old, comes into my office bearing this huge floral arrangement, plus a Mylar balloon with a mind of its own, flapping all over the place. I figure someone has dropped this off and Elias is but making the delivery. "Damn," I tell him, "who died?" as Elias situates the floral display in the center of my desk. "Where's this coming from?"

Elias steps to the left, so he can be seen unimpeded. "It's coming from my heart," he says. The flowers are from him. "I've written a speech. Can I read it to you?" Elias can barely breathe. Inhale. Exhale. "For Father Greg Boyle," he reads. "He's my friend. He's helped me like no one else has ever helped me."

Many years later, he dropped by to give me an update on his life. He got hired at one of those downtown delivery jobs, shuttling on a bike from law office to court. He was as surprised as anyone that they hired him. "My background was bad, but they liked my charisma." I mean, who wouldn't? Then he said this: "I'm the me I always wanted to be." He formed his words to find some precision. "Without Homeboy, I wouldn't have known this guy existed."

There's a long tunnel at LAX that spits returning travelers out to the curbside. Me and two homies are spent and beyond exhausted as we wordlessly make our way through the tunnel. It's quite packed and we all seem to be sharing the same mood: bad. A family group to the right of us speaks in Mandarin. A bunch of folks on our left side all speak Spanish over each other. I think the group in front of us is speaking Farsi. All of a sudden, a voice breaks in, descending from the loudspeaker: "Hi, this is Jimmy Kimmel. Welcome to LAX. We apologize for the construction, but you'll forget all about it . . . as soon as you're on the 405." The tunnel instantly transforms into an echo chamber of laughter, surprisingly sustained and suspended. All the Farsi and Mandarin and Spanish, lifted up into one language—the whole language, I suppose, that connects us where we all had forgotten we were joined.

My great friend Paul Lipscomb says that "belonging is more than inclusion." Homeboy seeks this above all: a sangha of belonging, a community of practitioners. It is this vitality of relationship and the interconnection we embrace that is so needed in the world right now.

It's the last day before our extended Christmas break. Winding down is in the air. I'm talking to a homie in my office and I hear "STORY TIME!" hollered from the reception area. I try to stay focused on the guy in front of me as I watch the swirl of homies and homegirls place chairs in a circle. Gabriel, one of our Navigators, has convened the bunch. He came to us as a trainee, with certificates in gangbanging, prison time, wild addiction, and general knucklehead-osity. The day he stepped into our place, he was greeted by Robert Juarez, who knew him and his reputation well.

"What are you doing here?" Robert asked him.

"I've come to change my life."

Robert stared at him. "No, really . . . what are you doing here?"

Gabriel practically runs the place now.

"STORY TIME!" he yells again, and thirty gang members, felons, and former drug addicts silently sit in a circle. He's purloined a copy of *Madeline and the Gypsies* from our Take a Book/ Leave a Book shelf. Someone's young daughter sits next to him while he reads loudly from the book. When he completes the page, the girl holds the book up so that this rapt audience can see the illustrations. No one speaks and their eyes simply move from Gabriel to the girl, in the kind of attention that is generally hard to gather.

Gabriel was the train conductor and every man and woman in that circle was taking a return trip to the childhood denied them. Strange as it may seem, in that circle they found their agency, and a power to resist. It was an exhibition of their cultural capital, heightened emotional resources, and creative energy not available before. No longer trapped, they find the nobility in belonging. They aren't ridding themselves of anything but bringing their authentic selves into the light. A sangha of beloved belonging, where kinship coaxes sadness to dance with it and Madeline gets to kick it with Gypsies.

It is only belonging, and not mere inclusion, that fully arouses bravery in people. You start with the broken heart and remove what encases it. You disarm what keeps you from knowing your pain. It's why we constantly drug test at Homeboy. Numbing doesn't get you to bravery. There is a freedom that comes from a sangha of belonging that liberates from comparing and competing; from labeling and the escalation of tension; from judging and the striking of the high moral distance: the drawing of tribal lines.

I'm baptizing Trusty's daughter and three of his homies come. I've known all three forever and to know them is to understand what "knucklehead" really means. You'd be hard-pressed to find three *vatos* more responsible for the whitening of my hair or for losing it entirely. They are sheepishly standing together off to one side, at some distance. After I bless the large bowl of water, I tell the gathered that I'm never quite sure if I've blessed the water enough to make it holy. So, I tell them all, I will have to test the water. "I will have to throw some of this water on these three guys over here." The giggles begin and spread. "If it sizzles on contact, we have holy water." I perform my test. The three become cooperative co-conspirators. All three melt to the floor in slow motion, with great groans like Wicked Witches of the West. Actual love is the true seeing of our oneness and our non-separateness. Belonging, not mere inclusion. Exquisite mutuality—a big boomerang.

We arrive later than I like to, but it was a Sunday, and I had an afternoon mass. Chamuco, Rob, and I arrive at Sacramento International Airport near 7:00 p.m. We have three talks the next day. We board the rental car shuttle. Rob and I face each other toward the back of the bus and Chamuco sits on the very last bench, in the middle. *Chamuco* is a playful Spanish nickname for "the Devil." He sports very large and dark devil's horns tattooed on his forehead, along with a great deal more ink. To his credit, the horns are a bit lighter, since he's receiving treatments to remove them.

I watch as the bus fills up and folks get near Chamuco, scope him out, and assiduously decide NOT to sit next to him. It's quite the dance, as folks near, then foxtrot their way somewhere else. Finally, the last two passengers have to plant their butts next to him and they are not one bit happy about it.

It's nighttime and the way to the rental car area is wooded, dark, and isolated. In an instant, all the power goes out on this electric vehicle, and we are stuck in what seems like the middle of no damn where. The driver apologizes, and we can hear the clicking of the key as she tries to restart the thing. Oddly, no one speaks. Pitch-black, utter silence, and wooded seclusion. From this silence and the back of the bus comes a lone voice. "I saw this in a movie once," Chamuco says. "It . . . does . . . not . . . end . . . well." The lights don't kick on, but our unanimous laughter does. Chamuco found some brave agency to redraw the lines. I am almost certain that half the bus voted a certain way in 2016 and the other half voted another way. But Chamuco found this gospel way, where walls and barriers dissolve into the exquisite belonging always within reach anyway.

We all live in the same house. John Lewis doesn't say, "But some live in the basement and some on the third floor." Nope. We all live in the same house. He doesn't say, "One day, we might all live in the same house." He says it straight out. We all live in the same house. Always US.

Kiko calls me as soon as he gets out and we meet for dinner at La Parrilla Restaurant on East Cesar E. Chavez Avenue. It's been eight years since I last saw him and he sports a mustache that he couldn't grow at seventeen when he was arrested. The day of his arrest, he's driving in his car and he sees one of his homies flag him down. Kiko agrees to give this guy a ride to his house but on the way, his passenger says, "*Oye,* pull over for a second." Kiko obliges and waits, then he hears four short, staccato blasts. In a heartbeat, his homie is back in the car. "Drive, dawg, drive." Kiko boils to an instant rage: "WHAT DID YA DO, MOTHERFUCKER?"

The police easily find the car, parked in Kiko's driveway. Weighted by the code of the streets, Kiko refuses to tell the detectives who his passenger was. They detain him in Juvenile Hall, which is where we met eight years prior to our dinner at La Parrilla.

He recounts how the detectives, who know Kiko isn't the shooter, retrieve him from Juvenile Hall and take him to Hollenbeck Community Police Station, where they handcuff one wrist to a table in an interrogation room. After a long spell, a woman is brought into the room and sits at the end of a very squat table. Kiko recognizes her but initially can't place her. Then he does. It is the victim's mother. He remembers her from his Little League days. Clearly, the detectives have brought her in to convince Kiko to give up his passenger from that horrific night.

When he fully remembers who she is, he rests his head on the arm not handcuffed and just sobs. The mother does the same. This continues for quite some time, Kiko tells me over dinner. It's Kiko who finally interrupts the wailing. He outstretches his free arm across the table for as long as it can reach. Still crying, he says to the mother, "I am so sorry." This ignites more crying. "What do you want me to do?"

The mother's arm reaches Kiko's and she places her hand gently on his. "I only want one thing," she says in Spanish. She can barely speak but is intent to complete this thought. "Please, carry my son in your heart every day."

Kiko looks at me over a half-eaten burrito. He's crying quite a bit. "What she said to me broke my spirit wide open." He breathes serenely. "And I've been carrying him," he says, patting his chest, "in my heart ever since."

It is our longing and natural inclination for our arms to stretch out as far as they can reach. Relational wholeness is a thing we arrive at when we move past the description of the place and hold out for the place itself. How, then, to carry each other in our hearts? One heartbeat. Single garment. We choose to be essential allies to each other and hear God's voice as loud as can be. The same house. We choose belonging. It is where we start.

Epilogue

Unmute Yourself

Leo is on his break from the bakery. He's standing in front of my desk, hairnet, mask, and apron dusted with flour. During the pandemic, I helped to have his teeth fixed. He's dropped by to thank me. "Can I take my mask off and show you my grill?"

I tell him, "Sure," and he reveals a Colgate smile, teeth aligned and white. He exaggerates the smile to put the dental work on full display. Then he says, "Not only did you pay for this smile, YOU are the reason I'm smiling." Before I can say anything, he adds, "Hey, that's good. Write it down." I do and he even re-dictates, "Not only did you pay . . ." We laugh, as the homies say, "from the stomach." I suspect he just wanted to be in my next book. Mission accomplished. Under the wire.

During this time of virtual everything, I have done more Zoom book clubs than you could shake a club at. I had one recently, a Catholic men's group who had kindly read *Tattoos on the Heart*. Every member of the group had twenty years on me. Most of our time together was spent yelling things like, "HARRY, UNMUTE YOURSELF!" as we watched Harry go on at some length to all of us and we didn't hear a word of it.

"Unmute yourself" has become the battle cry of our 2020

vision and existence. A homie out of the blue wrote me an email and asked me this: "Why would Jesus heal the man, mute from birth, then say, 'Don't say anything?'" Good question. Not saying something has proven untenable these days. We choose to prophetically unmute ourselves. What goes unexamined and unspoken can never be upended. Still, the Homeboy way is less about getting to solutions and more about getting to each other. This, of course, IS the solution.

Our 2020 vision is to fully see old wrongs in our social contract and feel newly emboldened to reverse them. Deep down, we do believe we can imagine a social contract that benefits everybody. Our old way of seeing and proceeding, our tired, say, market solutions, never deliver benefits to the margins. Safe to say, they never will. This time has supplied us with an awakened language to recognize a hidden system of social domination. Racism and white supremacy hides in systems. We need not feel defensive here. For the truth is not something we bring into the world, it brings us. This is where our 2020 vision gets tricky.

Pedro Arrupe spoke not of "peaceful co-existence" but rather "peaceful pro-existence." We look at the great "divide" in our country and we insist that everyone has something to contribute to the well-being of the other and to a nurturing kinship. Leo finding a reason to smile and posing an invitation to do the same. Unmuting is not denouncing but announcing. It is then that we find that our differences make for mutual enrichment.

I take Danny to Astro Burger for lunch. He is a week out of Camp Paige and we're celebrating. As we are standing in line, studying the illuminated plastic menu high above us, a staff member from Camp Paige arrives. It seems pretty random, and the staffer is initially reticent to see us both. But then he proceeds to become a fire hose of cautions to Danny. He goes on at some length about the litany of things Danny should avoid in order not to reoffend. I know this guy—thoroughly good person. He meant well, but it was a daunting mountain of compliance demands: content doing battle with context. Finally, he says, "Lunch is on me." We thank him. Danny and I return to reading the menu.

I tell Danny, loud enough for all, "Order the most expensive thing." Laughter from the stomach. We don't bring the truth to the world, it brings us. We want sometimes to favor advocacy over accompaniment. But it's about witness, not words. It's relational, context, an embodied advocacy. We seek a peaceful pro-existence where we all benefit and live in abundance, ordering the most expensive thing.

Ozzie always says, "for the simple fact." You can't get through a conversation without him including that phrase. He calls me once to say that he'll be late for work, and I ask him why. "I will be late, for the simple fact that I woked up late and I gotta take a shower and iron." Ozzie, when he'd be besieged by rage, would write a letter to himself. "For me," he'd say, "anger was always one letter short of danger. I don't ever want to unleash the beast." In the letter, he would lay out all the feelings of anger, mistreatment, and resentment that he held so close. Then he would mail the letter to himself. When it would arrive a few days later, he wouldn't open it. He'd simply rip it up and get on with his life "for the simple fact that I'm just trying to do the next right thing."

I once asked Ozzie how his weekend went. "Just stayed at home, eatin' Pedigree."

"The dog food?" I countered.

"Yeah, it's not bad. But I ate it for the simple fact that I paid my rent and I was left with nothing." Many Americans still think that being poor is a character defect and not an economic condition. We see that the poor suffer everything in a disproportionate way: COVID-19, low wages, lack of opportunities, the racism in our marrow. All because of the simple fact that we've forgotten that we belong to each other. "Justice," Cornell West has said, "is what love looks like in public," just like tenderness is what love feels like in private. We need to take it to the streets.

What we resist makes us frightened, hard, and inflexible, but what we embrace becomes transformed. So, we bow to all that life is and offers us and we meet on its own terms with understanding and compassion. Our prophetic unmuting isn't just about sharing God's mind and point of view but allowing ourselves to be filled with the utter fullness of God's compassionate and tender heart. I've written elsewhere that if I go to the margins "to make a difference," then it's about me. If I'm angry with righteous indignation at the dominant, oppressive system, I'm afraid that's also about me. Enlightened awakening is our heart's desire. The writer George Saunders says that kindness is the only nondelusional response to everything. Kindness is about the other and about us. It just can't be about me.

Our salvation happens squarely within the luminous union, fully relational with God and others. It's only in this kinship that God gets announced as present. It is discovering that where we are going is here and the moment of arrival is now.

Herbie was one of the four homies selected to meet Barack Obama. After a speech Obama would give at the Los Angeles Trade Technical College, we'd have our private meet-and-greet. This was during Obama's second term. Herbie was nineteen years old, with a sizable and dramatic Afro and a scruffy beard that was the definition of unkempt. I sent one of the senior homies, Louis, to take Herbie to Sears to outfit him for the presidential visit AND to talk him into shaving. While the two were in line at Sears, waiting to pay, Louis did his best to convince Herbie to shave that Brillo pad resting on his chin. Herbie was not having it. "Hell no."

Louis turned to a woman behind him, seeking backup support. "Ma'am. This guy is meeting President Barack Obama tomorrow. Don't you think he should shave?"

The lady stared at Louis and said: "I hate Obama."

Never mind. So much for your "luminous union."

I write this days after the election of 2020, and the camps, tribes, and divisions are pronounced indeed. And yet, Homeboy has taught me over these many years how it happens that one's gang allegiance melts into a common place of kinship and relational wholeness. No one needs to be reminded that there is a divide. I just heard a woman on TV complaining bitterly that "we need to look into the thousands of ballots sent here by China." Or the homie who told me the day after the election: "I just couldn't vote for Biden, cuz, you know, he's a child molester." There was a homie not wearing a mask and I asked him why he wasn't. He pointed to the sky and said, "I trust in God." I asked him why he owns a gun, then. As the homies say: "He stood quiet."

Arthur Chan points out: "Diversity is a fact. Equity is a choice. Inclusion is an action. Belonging is the outcome." But what I have hoped to propose in this book is that, at Homeboy, we begin with belonging.

Tootsie Tomanetz of Snow's BBQ said, "Nowadays, we flew too far away from each other." What has been severed gets repaired and attachment is restored to those isolated and cut off. The task at hand is not to convince folks that China, in fact, hasn't delivered ballots to our shores, but to address the fear and sadness undergirding such a belief. People don't need to be leveled but loved. Only love can tend to the severed belonging these views represent. Tenderness IS tending to the other.

Lalo lived in the projects and was a kid whom I would check in on during my regular visits to Central Juvenile Hall. A series of armed robberies was going to take him off the streets for a time. He missed his mom. He was sobbing wildly during one visit. "Tell my mom I love her." He could barely pronounce these words for all the crying. "And tell my brother"—then he dialed it way down—"that . . . I like him too." Once he could manage reflection, he said this: "I lie on my bed at night and sometimes, I just cry . . . tears just come out. I see the faces of all the people I hurted and they have frightened faces. And I think, nobody should make people's faces look like that."

We tend to what is severed and we begin with belonging. We have flown too far away from each other. Make the family circle wider. Once you're done, wider still. Then you can see the frightened faces.

A homegirl finished a lengthy conversation with me. "I wish you had come into my life sooner. That way, I wouldn't have made so many mistakes in my life. Sometimes I feel I'm gonna pay for my mistakes all my life." I tried to convince her that the whole point of mistakes is to learn from them, not to pay for them. But, in the end, the moral of the story is: How do we set about to come into each other's lives sooner?

Ernie stood in front of a gym packed with minors detained at Orange County Juvenile Hall. "You have the whole world in your hands, but you just don't know how to hold it." The same could be said for all of us. We help remind each other how the heart opens. We remind each other that we all have the same last name, so we can drop the burden of our judgments. "I love being reminded," a homie told me. That's the whole world and how to hold it.

Well over forty years ago, I remember, I am sitting in Saint Al's Church in Spokane at a Good Friday service. I am an undergrad at Gonzaga University. I'm sitting behind a mother and her very young daughter. At one point, the little girl asks the mom: "Who died?"

And the mother leans over and tells her: "Jesus."

And in a voice of complete desperation, the daughter asks: "What do we do now?" A really good question.

In the 1950s, Dorothy Day writes a friend: "The older I get, the more I meet people, the more convinced I am that we must only work on ourselves, to grow in grace. The only thing we can do about people is love them." Maybe it's old age, but I agree with her. Epilogue.

That's what we do now. Our own awakened sense of lovability within us moves us out to the other. We rest in the abundant acceptance we feel, and it propels us forward. Jesus always thought that the root cause of oppression was our lack of compassion. We receive the tender glance, then we become it. Compassionate and fluent in the whole language. We all belong to each other. We begin there. So, what do we do now? We laugh from the stomach and hold the world as tenderly as we can.

Acknowledgments

We were born for gratitude. Since that is true, we all long to stay anchored in the eternal now, where love is all there is. We choose, then, to be grateful in every moment. Every. Single. Moment. This is what I choose, at this moment, in acknowledging these people.

I want to express my deep gratitude to my agent, David McCormick. He has been steadfast and faithful all these many years. The good folks at Avid Reader Press/Simon & Schuster have all wonderfully steered this project. Alexandra Primiani, Meredith Vilarello, and Gil Cruz for enthusiastically promoting this book. Kathryn Higuchi and Carolyn Kelly for shepherding the manuscript. The folks at Simon & Schuster Audio, Elisa Shokoff, Tom Spain, and Matt Cartonis, for their gracious flexibility. Special and profound affection to my ever-gentle editor, Jofie Ferrari-Adler, whose guidance has been as kind as it has been sure.

To my five sisters and two brothers, and for the Zoom "Beer Time" during the pandemic. I DID win the sibling Lottery.

Friends in abundance never failed to carry me: the Leaps, the Priors, Matty, Consuelo, Celeste, Sergio (my spiritual guide), Sandra, Grover, John and Geri, Phil and Monica, Toto, Laura, Peter, Lauren, the Dublin crew (Jose, Hector. and Stevie), and the homies and homegirls WAY too numerous to name. I have a heart full of gratitude for Homeboy's senior staff and board, and especially for the luminous Shirley Torres and our visionary leader, Tom Vozzo.

Special thanks to Christy Juarez for keeping all my trains running on time and to Mary "Sol" Rakow for her friendship and contemplative example, and for fine-tuning this book.

As I near marking half a century as a Jesuit, I am deeply grateful to my brothers in this "least Society": Al Naucke, Jim Grummer, Mark Ciccone, Dave Mastrangelo, Jim Hayes, Mario Prietto, Frank Buckley, Scott Santarosa, and the eternally supportive Bill Cain.

Lastly, there are no adequate words left to express my heartfelt gratitude for my beloved brothers at Casa Luis Espinal. I'd shelter in place with you guys any day.

About the Author

GREGORY BOYLE is an American Jesuit priest and the founder of Homeboy Industries in Los Angeles, the largest gang-intervention, rehabilitation, and reentry program in the world. He has received the California Peace Prize and been inducted into the California Hall of Fame. In 2014, the White House named Boyle a Champion of Change. He was awarded the University of Notre Dame's 2017 Laetare Medal, the oldest honor given to American Catholics. He is the acclaimed author of *Tattoos on the Heart* and *Barking to the Choir. The Whole Language* is his third book, and he will be donating all net proceeds to Homeboy Industries. Visit the author at HomeboyIndustries.org.

"We rest in the
Merciful bath of,
self acceptance,

unjudging love

~~Important p~~

XII.

We don't change people
by arguing with them.